HERMANN J. WÜSCHER

Liberty, Equality, and Fraternity in Wordsworth, 1791–1800

UPPSALA 1980

Distributed by
ALMQVIST & WIKSELL INTERNATIONAL
STOCKHOLM, SWEDEN

Doctoral dissertation at the University of Uppsala, 1980

ISBN 91-554-1090-1

ISSN 0562-2719

Abstract

Wüscher, Hermann J., 1980. *Liberty, Equality, and Fraternity in Wordsworth, 1791–1800.* Acta Universitatis Upsaliensis. Studia Anglistica Upsaliensia, *39.* 204 pp. ISBN 91-554-1090-1. Uppsala.

Except in his retrospective *Prelude,* Wordsworth says little about his development between 1791 and 1800. By examining chronologically the early versions of Wordsworth's poetry and prose, supplemented by his letters, the present study supplies firmer evidence on this crucial time of Wordsworth's growth than can be extracted from the autobiographical *Prelude.* Linguistic, socio-cultural, and biographical methods are used to trace the development of the concepts of liberty, equality, and fraternity. Three time spans are detected: overt political commitment (1791–94), diminished interest in politics (1795–98), embedded socio-political thought (autumn 1798–1800). The continued importance of social and political ideas after 1794 is illustrated. The Preface to *Lyrical Ballads* reveals a hitherto unknown abundance of ideas of equality and brotherhood. Close attention to the vocabulary indicates that the "Prospectus to *The Recluse*" may have been written in 1802 and that Wordsworth did not use in his poetry the new-fangled social and political vocabulary of the 1790s. A correlation is discerned between Wordsworth's gradual change from revolutionary politics and the improvement of his poetic art. Reasons for Wordsworth's radical and conservative reputations are discussed. A chapter on *The Prelude* compares Wordsworth's own views on the origin and development of liberty, equality, and fraternity with what the analysis of his writings (1791–1800) has borne out. Besides the concepts under consideration, the notions of democracy, community, justice, morality, and natural law feature strongly in the discussion. It is noted that Wordsworth's social and political wisdom continues to be valid in the last decades of the twentieth century.

Hermann J. Wüscher, Department of English, Uppsala University, Box 513, S-75120 Uppsala, Sweden

© 1980 Hermann J. Wüscher

Printed in Sweden by

Almqvist & Wiksell, Uppsala, 1980

For My Children

Meiner Mutter

PREFACE

The academic freedom at Uppsala encouraged me to choose a subject for my doctoral dissertation that lies somewhat outside the scope of the Department of English. For permitting me to do this independent work I owe my first and deepest gratitude to my supervisor, Dr. Sven-Johan Spånberg, and to the head of the Department, Professor Gunnar Sorelius. Their high standards of scholarship have been a constant source of inspiration and eased considerably the burden of being the only research student at Uppsala of the English Romantic Movement. If my book is understood by the general educated reader, the merit is not entirely mine, for Dr. Spånberg and Professor Sorelius raised their warning fingers whenever my work was in danger of becoming too specialist and Wordsworthian.

Although Professor Birgit Bramsbäck became officially involved with my thesis first at its completed stage, she as well as Professor Johannes Söderlind and Dr. Ann-Mari Hedbäck showed a keen interest in my work and personal welfare throughout my time in their Department. I thank each of them most warm-heartedly for this support.

My quest for "romantic knowledge" took me across the Atlantic where the senior champion of Wordsworth's social and political thought, Professor Carl Woodring (Columbia University, New York), gave generously of his time and Wordsworthian wisdom. At the University of Cincinnati Professor Leslie Chard's sharp intellect scrutinized most of my work. At Miami University, Ohio, I consulted Professor Frank Jordan. His advice has been penetrating and abundant. I feel deeply indebted to these American scholars; in them I have found American idealism at its very best. The same devotion and brilliance I have seen repeated in Mr. Paul Walsh, who read my thesis before it was sent to the printers.

During my perky undergraduate days at Uppsala and earlier as a student at Ruskin College, Oxford, I avoided teachers who talked about dating and textual scholarship. As a research student, however, I humbly turned to Dr. Stephen Gill of Lincoln College, Oxford. He helped me to unravel textual and chronological problems that seemed insurmountable to me. As an editor of Wordsworth he was able to give me access to transcripts of Wordsworth's early poetry; he also drew my attention to the important chronological work being done by Jonathan Wordsworth. I thank him most sincerely for his help.

The meticulous and efficient co-operation of the editor of the forthcoming Cornell edition of *The Borderers*, Dr. Robert Osborn (University of Lancaster), has enabled me to update my quotations from the early text of *The Borderers* (D.C. MS. 23) at press stage. My quotations now conform exactly to the Reading Text of Dr. Osborn's edition. There may remain some slight differences in editorial conventions between the Cornell edition and my section on *The Borderers*; however, they do not affect the sense. I very much appreciate Robert Osborn's help and that of the printers and publishers Almqvist & Wiksell in squeezing in last-minute changes. Not only in this instance but throughout my years at college and university Almqvist & Wiksell have stood by me through thick and thin, giving me work whenever my funds were depleted. Since my chief hobby still is to make the printing industry more cost-efficient (and thereby benefit the world of learning), Almqvist & Wiksell and I are using in this dissertation a new setting technique that will probably go unnoticed by any reader who is not a printer.

It is a great pleasure to thank Östen Andersson, Neil Tomkinson, and Rune Trolleberg for helping me to proof-read my book under pressure of time. Special thanks are due to the staff of the University Library, Uppsala; they provided me not only with books but in a way gave me a home.

I am indebted for financial support to the following: the University of Uppsala for a research scholarship, travel grants, and a grant that very nearly covers the printing costs of my work; the Faculty of Humanities for awarding me a Törnlund Scholarship; my *nation* (Västgöta nation) for awarding me the Stalin Scholarship. A surprise donation from Dr. Werner Lansburgh (*ein Berliner*) has moved me most deeply.

Your "little, nameless, unremembered acts / Of kindness and of love" *were* noticed: Erik Åsard, Thorild Dahlquist, David Erdman, Barbara Gates, Mary Jacobus, Karl Kroeber, National Graphical Association (U.K.), Peter Martin, Mr. Trevor Osborne, and Stephen Parrish; the helpful and courteous staff of the British Library and the Bodleian; the Jonsson and Hildebrand families, the Hansens and the Jacks in Kansas; last but not least some of my friends: Bengt, Doris, Göran, Karin, Kerstin, Lena (of London), Margareta, Margit, Max, Mongi, Penny, Richard, Sonja, Vera, Uppsala's mystical foreign lecturers, and Gunnar Tideström.

Uppsala, September 1980   H. J. W.

CONTENTS

Short forms of citation 11
Editorial note 12
Introduction 13

Chapter 1. 1791–1794 25
1791–92: Descriptive Sketches 27
1793: A Letter to the Bishop of Llandaff 34
      Salisbury Plain 44
1794: Letters to Mathews 48

Chapter 2. 1795–1797 55
1795–96: Adventures on Salisbury Plain 55
      Imitation of Juvenal—Satire VIII 64
1796–97 66
      The Borderers 67
      Some work for *Lyrical Ballads* (1st edition) 81
      The Old Cumberland Beggar 83

Chapter 3. 1798–1799 89
The Ruined Cottage 91
Lyrical Ballads (1st and 2nd editions) 94
    The Last of the Flock 100
    Tintern Abbey 104
    The Brothers 117
The 1798–99 *Prelude* 120

Chapter 4. 1800 125
Hart-Leap Well 128
Michael 130
Preface to the *Lyrical Ballads* 135
Prospectus to *The Recluse* 145

Chapter 5. **The 1805 *Prelude*** 148

Origin of liberty, equality, and fraternity in Wordsworth 148
Wordsworth in France (1790, 1791–92) 158

Summary and Conclusion 174

Works cited 186

Appendix 194

Index 196

SHORT FORMS OF CITATION

Ariel	Ariel: A Review of International English Literature
ASP	Adventures on Salisbury Plain
BNYPL	Bulletin of the New York Public Library
Brett & Jones	[Wordsworth and Coleridge,] *Lyrical Ballads*, ed. R. L. Brett and A. R. Jones (1963; rpt. London, 1975)
Chard	Leslie F. Chard, *Dissenting Republican: Wordsworth's Early Life and Thought in Their Political Context* (The Hague, 1972)
CritQ	Critical Quarterly
DR	Dalhousie Review
EIC	Essays in Criticism
E.Y.	*The Letters of William and Dorothy Wordsworth: The Early Years, 1787–1805*, ed. E. de Selincourt; 2nd ed., rev. Chester L. Shaver (Oxford, 1967)
GCL I, GCL II	General Chronological List *in* Mark L. Reed, *Wordsworth: The Chronology of the Early Years, 1770–1799* (Cambridge, Mass., 1967); *Wordsworth: The Chronology of the Middle Years, 1800–1815* (Cambridge, Mass., 1975)
Harper I, Harper II	George McLean Harper, *William Wordsworth: His Life, Works, and Influence* (London, 1916), vols. I and II
HLQ	Huntington Library Quarterly
JEGP	Journal of English and Germanic Philology
JHI	Journal of the History of Ideas
MLR	Modern Language Review
Moorman I	Mary Moorman, *William Wordsworth, A Biography: The Early Years, 1770–1803* (1957; corrected rpt. Oxford, 1968)
MP	Modern Philology
N&Q	Notes and Queries
P.L.B.	Preface to *Lyrical Ballads*
PMLA	Publications of the Modern Language Association of America
1798–99 *Prelude*	[William Wordsworth,] *The Prelude, 1798–1799*, ed. Stephen Parrish (Ithaca, N.Y., 1977)
1805 *Prelude*	[William Wordsworth,] *The Prelude or Growth of a Poet's Mind*, ed. E. de Selincourt; 2nd ed., corrected by Stephen Gill (Oxford, 1970)
Prose Works I	*The Prose Works of William Wordsworth*, ed. W. J. B. Owen and Jane Worthington Smyser (Oxford, 1974), vol. I
PW I–V	*The Poetical Works of William Wordsworth*, ed. E. de Selincourt and Helen Darbishire (2nd ed. and revised issues, Oxford, 1952–59), vols. I–V
QQ	Queen's Quarterly

Reed I, Reed II   [I: *Chronology of the Early Years, 1770–1799;* II: *Chronology of the Middle Years, 1800–1815.*] *See above,* GCL
RES   Review of English Studies
SIR   Studies in Romanticism
SP   Studies in Philology
            Salisbury Plain
WC   The Wordsworth Circle

EDITORIAL NOTE

The item numbers of Reed's General Chronological Lists (GCL I:**39**, GCL II:**25**, etc.) have been included in the text, notes, and page headlines to facilitate cross-referencing and verification of the chronological sequence. As usual, years in parentheses denote the date of publication. Dates of composition are marked thus: (comp. 1797). If a poem is known by more than one title, the alternative form is included in a footnote. Untitled poems are referred to by the first line in quotation marks. In addition to the first and last pages of articles the page(s) on which an actual reference occurs is given in parentheses. For example: *EIC,* 19 (1969), 379–401 (387, 399) means that the matter quoted has been drawn from pages 387 and 399.

INTRODUCTION

The social, political, and economic ferment of the Romantic era coincided with William Wordsworth's youth and early manhood. When he made his first significant poetic attempts (*Descriptive Sketches,* comp. 1791–92), which were eventually to mature into a poetic revolution, Europe's most important political revolution was in full swing. Hazlitt says about the period: "The change in the belles-lettres was as complete, and to many persons as startling, as the change in politics, with which it went hand in hand. . . . kings and queens were dethroned from their rank and station in legitimate tragedy or epic poetry, as they were decapitated elsewhere . . ."[1] Perhaps Hazlitt exaggerates, but he is essentially right in pointing out the correlation between political and literary developments. A century after the adoption of the English Bill of Rights of 1689, which restricted the power of the monarchy and introduced free elections, the English romantic poets became keen defenders of the liberal ideal. Although most of the English reform movements in the 1790s were based more on English dissenting and libertarian traditions than on the example of the French Revolution,[2] the agitation for an extension of democracy in Britain was viewed with suspicion by the Government, and gradually the reform movements were pushed against the wall and underground: in 1795 the Seditious Meetings and Treasonable Practices Bills were introduced, the freedom of the press was curtailed in 1798, and the Combination Acts of 1799–1800 prevented the unionization of the British working class. Since at the time most writers and critics were didactic and in consequence partisan,[3] it will be rewarding to examine

---

[1] William Hazlitt, *Lectures on the English Poets* (1818; rpt. London: Oxford U.P., 1929), p. 247. For general surveys of the socio-political background of the 1790s, see, e.g., Albert Goodwin, *The Friends of Liberty: The English Democratic Movement in the Age of the French Revolution* (London: Hutchinson, 1979), and E. P. Thompson, *The Making of the English Working Class,* rev. ed. (Harmondsworth: Penguin, 1968). See also Basil Willey, *The Eighteenth-Century Background: Studies on the Idea of Nature in the Thought of the Period* (1940; rpt. Harmondsworth: Penguin, 1972).

[2] See Thompson, *Making of the English Working Class,* pp. 111 ff.

[3] Marilyn Butler, *Jane Austen and the War of Ideas* (Oxford: Clarendon Press, 1975), p. 3; Butler, pp. 29–123, gives also an excellent survey of major Jacobin and anti-Jacobin novels. For the committed poetry of the time, consult Carl Woodring, *Politics in English Romantic Poetry* (Cambridge, Mass.: Harvard U.P., 1970).

Wordsworth's work against the background of an era that saw the dawn of industrialization and bureaucracy, land enclosures and the poor laws, all events and measures that encroached on personal liberty. But it was also the period when the evils of the slave trade and slavery were being discussed and when for those disenchanted with the French Revolution the earlier, more successful American Revolution still provided some hope for an eventual amelioration of the condition of mankind.

Aims and Methods

In his recent book on Wordsworth's development from revolutionary to conservative politics Michael Friedman deplores that "Wordsworth's inner life during the period of his conversion to revolutionary politics, his despondent crisis of faith and his subsequent spiritual rebirth [1791–1800], is little recorded" and he concludes that the "critic is left with two choices. Either he must avoid investigating this crucial period in Wordsworth's life, or he must turn to *The Prelude* for help".[4] Friedman and many others (notably Ernest de Selincourt, Mary Moorman, and Leslie Chard) use *The Prelude* to draw firm conclusions about Wordsworth's life in the 1790s.[5] Since, however, *The Prelude* was written a decade and more after the events it depicts, I shall approach Wordsworth directly through the poems, letters, and prose writings he composed between 1791 and 1800. This approach, which will include an examination of the 1798–99 *Prelude,* seems more reliable to me in tracing the development of liberty, equality, and fraternity in Wordsworth. However, an entire chapter will be devoted to the 1805 *Prelude* in order to uncover what Wordsworth himself had to say on the origin and development of the concepts of the French Revolution; this final chapter of my thesis promises to be the most interesting, since it will examine Wordsworth's retrospective views on the time span that forms chapters 1–4 of the present study.

Wherever possible I shall discuss Wordsworth's writings in their order of composition; this procedure will also help us to understand better the period of Wordsworth's life which so far has been "little recorded". In arranging Wordsworth's writings as they were composed I realize that I am contravening his express wishes not to arrange his poems chronologi-

---

[4] Michael H. Friedman, *The Making of a Tory Humanist: William Wordsworth and the Idea of Community* (New York: Columbia U.P., 1979), pp. 63–64.
[5] See, e.g., Leslie F. Chard, II, *Dissenting Republican: Wordsworth's Early Life and Thought in Their Political Context* [Studies in English Literature, vol. 66] (The Hague: Mouton, 1972), pp. 18 and 144–45.

cally.[6] However, as Reed has pointed out, a chronological approach is legitimate because of Wordsworth's greatness and the consensus of major critics ever since Legouis that the poet's "development took place in a pattern definable in chronological terms . . .".[7] Furthermore, it is hoped that the attention given to dating in this thesis will result in a more accurate assessment of Wordsworth's development. A neglect of dating is as misleading as the use of the final versions of Wordsworth's poems if one wishes to illustrate his poetic evolution.[8] My study follows as closely as possible Reed's *Chronology* (vol. I: 1770–1799; vol. II: 1800–1815). This method has proved difficult and time-consuming, since as yet there is no complete chronological edition of the early versions of Wordsworth's poetry.[9] As a result I was forced to compile my own chronological edition of the earliest versions of Wordsworth's verse.

Wordsworth's minor poetry will be discussed as far as it is of evidentiary value for comprehending his development. I shall also pay close attention to Wordsworth's language in his letters and prose writings. Save for some work on "A Letter to the Bishop of Llandaff" and the Preface to the *Lyrical Ballads* (see below, chapters 1 and 4) no close studies of Wordsworth's language in his prose writings and letters have so far been made. This omission is inexcusable if we wish to enhance our understanding of the greatest romantic poet; I hope that the present analysis of his prose will be a move in the right direction. On the other hand, scholars have been diligent in closely analysing Wordsworth's verse. But as will be revealed in the following chapters, socio-cultural critics of Wordsworth have been inclined to neglect close reading; thus a whole field of social and political implications has stayed hidden. Part of my task is to remedy this: I intend to combine the socio-cultural and biographical approaches with the method of close reading. In some instances use will be made of vocabulary studies and the Wordsworth *Concordance*.

Historical events and events in Wordsworth's private life that may have contributed to his social and political thought will be juxtaposed

---

[6] See Raymond Dexter Havens, *The Mind of a Poet: A Study of Wordsworth's Thought with Particular Reference to* The Prelude (Baltimore: The Johns Hopkins Press, 1941), p. 272; consult also pp. 316–17.

[7] Mark L. Reed, *Wordsworth: The Chronology of the Early Years, 1770–1799* (Cambridge, Mass.: Harvard U.P., 1967), p. 1.

[8] For example, Alan Grob places the two-part *Prelude* (comp. 1798–99) under the same date as *Home at Grasmere* (comp. 1800–06) (*The Philosophic Mind: A Study of Wordsworth's Poetry and Thought, 1797–1805,* Columbus: Ohio State U.P., 1973, pp. 5–6).

[9] A chronological edition is being prepared by Jonathan Wordsworth. The currently published Cornell Wordsworth series is restricted to the major poems.

chronologically with his writings. Thus I shall avoid taking a reference from earlier or later periods to establish a point in the year under discussion. (Many critics take a public event from let us say 1800 to establish a point in the poetry of a few years earlier.)

Definitions

My study cannot be expected to supply or use definitions of democracy, liberty/freedom, equality, and fraternity/brotherhood that totally satisfy political theorists, and this for the following reasons: (*a*) the intricacies of these concepts are still being discussed by political scientists; (*b*) Wordsworth himself was neither a philosopher nor a professional politician; (*c*) this thesis is not a treatise in social and political theory. Instead of getting entangled in time-bound definitions that need constant revision I shall try to show how timeless and universal Wordsworth's concepts of democracy, liberty, etc. are. Thanks to this approach it will be easier to connect the meanings these concepts carried in the 1790s with the connotations they convey to the modern reader. The difficulties of the concepts under discussion are acknowledged by at least one eminent literary critic, Raymond Williams, who writes on the development of the term "democracy": "with only occasional exceptions, *democracy* . . . was until the nineteenth century a strongly unfavourable term, and it is only since the last third of the nineteenth and the first period of the twentieth century that a majority of political parties and tendencies have united in declaring their belief in it".[10]

When I use the concepts in their political meaning I intend them to be understood within the framework of the western liberal tradition (unless otherwise indicated). In its extended meaning, "democracy/democratic" signifies, for example, somebody treating people equally irrespective of class or origin. Applied to Wordsworth, I shall use such expressions as "democratic subject matter" and "linguistic democracy". Here it seems right to anticipate one of my conclusions and underline what Stallknecht says on Wordsworth's conception of democracy, namely that it is positive and idealistic, rather than positivist and sceptical.[11]

---

[10] Raymond Williams, *Keywords: A Vocabulary of Culture and Society* (London: Croom Helm, 1976), p. 83 (democracy: pp. 82–87; equality: pp. 101–02; liberty and fraternity are not covered in detail). See further Raymond Williams, *Culture and Society: 1780–1950* (1958; rpt. Harmondsworth: Penguin, 1968), especially pp. 304–06 (equality).

[11] Newton P. Stallknecht, "Wordsworth and the Quality of Man", in *The Major English Romantic Poets: A Symposium in Reappraisal*, eds. Clarence D. Thorpe, Carlos Baker, and Bennett Weaver (Carbondale: Southern Illinois U.P., 1957), p. 53.

The idea of liberty in Wordsworth is straightforward if we compare it with the semantic maze of brotherhood/fraternity. The kinds of liberty to be discussed will range from personal liberty (individualism) to political and national liberty and will include, for example, such notions as freedom of assembly, association, religion, discussion, freedom of the press, freedom of inquiry as well as "inner freedom".

The fathers of the American and French Revolutions firmly asserted that all men are created equal. The survey of equality in Wordsworth, however, will be more complex. Besides man's fundamental equality I cover political and racial equality, equality before the law, and economic equality. In some instances (especially in *The Borderers*) I shall point out the connection between equality and justice. Let us finally turn to the idea of "fraternity", that fellow feeling which safeguards equality from turning into the horror of absolute equality. Paul Hamill in a recent article substantiates the results of my own research, namely that "'fraternity' is not a key term in the English Romantic lexicon. Sympathy, communion, harmony, and brotherhood are more commonly mentioned".[12] The difficulty in Wordsworth is that there is too little in him that can be classified under "fraternity" and too much that comes under the vast semantic field of "brotherhood". "Brotherhood", by the way, is not listed as a headword in the *Encyclopædia Britannica* of 1797.[13] Nevertheless, I shall pay particular attention to words and expressions—thus including Hamill's synonyms of "fraternity"—that connote (*a*) the bond uniting all human beings ("universal brotherhood"/"brotherhood of man") and (*b*) the bond between man and man that we find in Wordsworth's ideal community. Sometimes I shall designate the latter kind "local brotherhood". This meaning of brotherhood is closely related to what Friedman calls Wordsworth's "Need for Community".[14] Although the treatment of the concept of brotherhood/frater-

---

[12] Paul Hamill, "Other People's Faces: The English Romantics and the Paradox of Fraternity", *SIR*, 17 (1978), 465–82 (467).

[13] The headword "fraternity" in the *Encyclopædia Britannica* (1797) refers to civil associations and it concentrates on religious associations; there is a brief reference only to "brotherhood, the relation or union of brothers, friends, partners, associates, &c.". The modern notions of the brotherhood of man and universal brotherhood are listed by the *OED* under "brotherhood", def. 8: "Fellowship; community of feeling uniting man and man; also *concr.* those united in such fellowship. A modern notion frequent in *brotherhood of man, universal brotherhood*, etc." The first occurrence of this meaning is dated 1784 (Cowper's *Task* III, 208). This modern meaning is not listed under the headword "fraternité" in the *Encyclopédie, ou Dictionnaire raisonné* (1757), a work that was one of the theoretical pillars of the French Revolution.

[14] Friedman, *The Making of a Tory Humanist*, pp. 1–57.

nity causes difficulties, we cannot afford to neglect it, for the "poésie de Wordsworth maintient vivants et actifs la fraternité, le respect de la valeur individuelle, le culte de l'humanité dans l'homme, le désir du bonheur pour tous, c'est à dire ce qu'il y avait d'universel et d'impérissable dans les principes de la Révolution française".[15]

Previous research

M. H. Abrams rightly says that the early Wordsworth was in "genre, subjects, and style . . . the poetical Jacobin of his generation; more radical, in this important aspect, than Shelley or even Blake",[16] and Norman Fruman (referring to Hazlitt) deplores that the "levelling social implications of Wordsworth's poetry" is "a matter still hardly ever discussed".[17] Although Wordsworth is said to have "given twelve hours thought to the conditions and prospects of society, for one to poetry",[18] relatively few studies have dealt with Wordsworth's social and political thought. George McLean Harper intersperses his biographical study *William Wordsworth, His Life, Works and Influence* (1916) with many sympathetic references to Wordsworth's political awareness. A. V. Dicey's *The Statesmanship of Wordsworth* (1917) deals with Wordsworth's views on nationalism and government. Zera S. Fink's central article on the influence of the English republicans Harrington, Algernon Sidney, and Milton, "Wordsworth and the English Republican Tradition", *JEGP* (1948), indicates a revived interest in Wordsworth as a political writer after the neglect of this aspect of Wordsworth's in the 1920s and 1930s. F. M. Todd's *Politics and the Poet* (1957) discusses Wordsworth's political development from his university days at Cambridge to his later years. This book had been preceded by Greta Hedin's *Natur och politik i Wordsworths ungdomsverk* [Nature and Politics in Wordsworth's Early Work] (1951) [in Swedish], which emphasizes Wordsworth's social commitment, but fails to pay adequate attention to Wordsworth's language. Carl Woodring's "On Liberty in the Poetry of Wordsworth" (*PMLA*, 1955) deals with the influence of Milton, Collins,

---

[15] Charles Cestre, *La Révolution française et les poètes anglais (1789–1809)* (Dijon, 1905), p. 536.

[16] M. H. Abrams, *Natural Supernaturalism: Tradition and Revolution in Romantic Literature* (London: Oxford U.P., 1971; © New York: Norton, 1971), p. 396; see also pp. 394–95.

[17] Norman Fruman, *Coleridge, the Damaged Archangel* (London: George Allen & Unwin, 1972), p. 200.

[18] Quoted in F. M. Todd, *Politics and the Poet: A Study of Wordsworth* (London: Methuen, 1957), p. 1, from [Orville] Dewey, *The Old World and the New* (1836), p. 90.

Thomson, and Dyer on Wordsworth and the images of personal and political freedom. Woodring, however, does not pay attention to the chronological development of liberty, as I do. Newton P. Stallknecht's "Wordsworth and the Quality of Man" (1957)[19] points to Wordsworth's seminal role in forming the liberal democracies of the English-speaking world, that is to say he is concerned with the effect of the poetry rather than its chronological development.

The section on Wordsworth in Carl Woodring's *Politics in English Romantic Poetry* (1970) discusses Wordsworth's republican views and his interest in ideas of liberty and equality against the background of the Romantic era. The two most recent major studies on Wordsworth's political thought are Leslie F. Chard's *Dissenting Republican: Wordsworth's Early Life and Thought in Their Political Context* (1972) which besides examining the general political background focuses on Wordsworth's connections with the movement of dissenters at the time (especially on the circle of people that centred on the radical publisher Joseph Johnson), and Michael H. Friedman's Freudian and Marxist approach in *The Making of a Tory Humanist: William Wordsworth and the Idea of Community* (1979) which attaches great importance to Wordsworth's need for community, in other words brotherhood. This Freudian–Marxist approach to Wordsworth was timely, since Wordsworth, unlike Blake, Shelley, and Byron, is neglected or disparaged by most eminent Marxist critics. An earlier sympathetic view of Wordsworth by a Marxist critic is V. G. Kiernan's "Wordsworth and the People" (1954).[20] A recent German defence of the early Wordsworth is Christoph Bode's *William Wordsworth und die Französische Revolution* (1977). Kenneth Eisold's *Loneliness and Communion* (1973; Salzburg Studies in Engl. Lit.) treats of Wordsworth's interest in equality and Rousseau's General Will. Besides these books and articles there are a few shorter or lesser known studies on Wordsworth's politics in general and his radicalism in particular.[21]

---

[19] *In* Clarence D. Thorpe, Carlos Baker, and Bennett Weaver, eds., *The Major English Romantic Poets*, pp. 52–73.
[20] *In* John Saville, ed., *Democracy and the Labour Movement: Essays in Honour of Dona Torr* (London: Lawrence & Wishart, 1954), pp. 240–70.
[21] Charles Cestre, *La Révolution française et les poètes anglais (1789–1809)* (1905); Felix Güttler, *Wordsworth's politische Entwicklung*, Diss. Breslau, 1914; W. Graham, "The Politics of the Greater Romantic Poets", *PMLA*, 36 (1921), 60–78; B. H. Lehman, "The Doctrine of Leadership in the Greater Romantic Poets", *PMLA*, 37 (1922), 639–61; H. J. C. Grierson, *Milton and Wordsworth, Poets and Prophets* (Cambridge: Cambridge U.P., 1937); A. Krüper, "Wordsworth als politischer Dichter", *Die Neueren Sprachen*, 45 (1937), 66–72; A. D. McKillop, "The Poet as a Patriot—Shakespeare to Wordsworth", in

Surveying the scholarship on Wordsworth, one is still struck by Hazlitt's essay "Mr. Wordsworth", in *The Spirit of the Age* (1825), which points out the egalitarian implications of the *Lyrical Ballads*, something overlooked by most critics in the course of the next hundred years:

[Wordsworth's poetry] is one of the innovations of the time. It partakes of, and is carried along with, the revolutionary movement of our age: the political changes of the day were the model on which he formed and conducted his poetical experiments. His Muse (it cannot be denied, and without this we cannot explain its character at all) is a levelling one. It proceeds on a principle of equality, and strives to reduce all things to the same standard. It is distinguished by a proud humility. It relies upon its own resources, and disdains external shew and relief. It takes the commonest events and objects, as a test to prove that nature is always interesting from its inherent truth and beauty, without any of the ornaments of dress or pomp of circumstances to set it off. Hence the unaccountable mixture of seeming simplicity and real abstruseness in the *Lyrical Ballads*. (p. 233)

Wordsworth, committed or unpolitical?

The misrepresentation of Wordsworth as an unpolitical poet started as early as Hazlitt's perceptive criticism. Wordsworth's best friend, S. T. Coleridge, remarked about the Wordsworth of 1795–97 that his "conversation extended to almost all subjects, except physics and politics; with the latter [Wordsworth] never troubled himself".[22] In *Biographia Literaria* Coleridge points to the "close connection of poetic genius with the love of liberty and of genuine reformation",[23] and he instances Pindar, Chaucer, Dante, and Milton but omits Wordsworth. Another reason why Wordsworth's social and political radicalism has often been played down is that he is judged by his later conservatism. Furthermore, many readers and critics are only acquainted with the revised texts of Wordsworth's early poetry; however, these final versions (which form the basis of most editions and anthologies) tone down Wordsworth's radical-

---

The Rice Institute Pamphlets (Houston, Tex.) xxix, No. 4 (1942), 309–36; Z. S. Fink, "'Dion' and Wordsworth's Political Thought", *SP*, 50 (1953), 510–14; Allan Rodway, "Radical Romantic Poets: Wordsworth", in *The Romantic Conflict* (London: Chatto & Windus, 1963), pp. 139–58; E. San Juan, Jr., "Wordsworth's Political Commitment", *DR*, 45 (1965), 299–306; J. P. Ward, "Wordsworth and the Sociological Idea", *CritQ*, 16 (1974), 331–55; Barbara T. Gates, "Wordsworth's Lessons from the Past", *WC*, 7 (1976), 133–41.

[22] Quoted in Havens, *The Mind of a Poet*, p. 550.

[23] S. T. Coleridge, *Biographia Literaria*, ed. J. Shawcross (Oxford: Clarendon Press, 1907 [1st ed. 1817]), ch. X, p. 140.

ism.[24] Thus to get a more accurate picture of Wordsworth's thought during the 1790s I have chosen the earliest available texts for my study. Thanks to the current publication of the early manuscripts by Cornell University the young Wordsworth will appear in a more trustworthy light to a wider audience.

Some criticism of Wordsworth has been and is more characterized by political prejudice than literary appreciation.[25] Statements to the effect that "Coleridge and Wordsworth . . . had much to say about Liberty in the abstract, and were ever ready to direct the attention of Englishmen away from political abuses at home to affairs outside the British Isles",[26] do not apply to the early Wordsworth and have been refuted by the work of Woodring, Chard, and others.

In 1950 Lionel Trilling deplored the lack of academic and popular interest in Wordsworth.[27] Things are very different now: Wordsworth has benefited from the end of the anti-Romantic era. But even nowadays, among the major Romantics, Shelley and Byron are better known than Wordsworth in mainland Europe and Scandinavia: Matthew Arnold's complaint in 1888 that Wordsworth "is not recognized at all abroad"[28] can be modified today into a regret that he is not sufficiently recognized. Although the political implications of Wordsworth's writings have been acknowledged by some scholars, it will take quite some time to completely remedy the neglect of history and politics by the New Criticism, which had also influenced Wordsworth scholarship. Another reason why Wordsworth—and especially his social criticism—has been neglected is, it seems to me, that many critics have failed to notice Wordsworth's concern with reality; this explains why Wordsworth is

---

[24] Jonathan Wordsworth observes that commonly "poets are known by the best versions of their works: Wordsworth is almost exclusively known by the worst" (*The Music of Humanity,* New York: Harper, 1969, p. [xiii]).

[25] For example, although Wordsworth experienced economic hardship during most of the time up to 1803, Christopher Caudwell insinuates that the "division of labor involved in industrialism has made it possible for sufficient surplus produce to exist to maintain a poet in austere idleness in Cumberland [etc.]". ("The Bourgeois Illusion and English Romantic Poetry", in *Romanticism: Points of View,* eds. Robert F. Gleckner and Gerald E. Enscoe (Englewood Cliffs, N.J.: Prentice-Hall, 1962), p. 124, from Christopher Caudwell, *Illusion and Reality* [1936].)

[26] Walter Graham, "The Politics of the Greater Romantic Poets", *PMLA,* 36 (1921), 60–78 (65).

[27] Lionel Trilling, "Wordsworth and the Iron Time", *Kenyon Review,* 12 (1950), 477–97.

[28] Matthew Arnold, *Essays in Criticism,* second series (1888; rpt. London: Macmillan, 1900), p. 132.

reproached for "bourgeois illusion".[29] Our excessive relativism too may be responsible for our disliking a poet who claims that nearly all of his poems "aim to direct the attention to some moral sentiment, or to some general principle . . ."[30] Pottle gives yet a further reason why Wordsworth had lost ground: "Wordsworth's poetry was consciously opposed to the Metaphysical mode. Wit he avoided on principle as being petty and cold-hearted . . . [He] scorns all the density, the obliquity and indirection treasured by the moderns."[31] The metaphysical mode stands in stark contrast with the democratic linguistic theory of Wordsworth's poetry. From my discussion of the Preface to the *Lyrical Ballads* we will see how the ideas of brotherhood and equality are embedded in his theoretic prose as well.

In tracing the theme of brotherhood in Wordsworth I hope to disperse, at least in part, the impression created by Coleridge of a Wordsworth who was unmoved by the subjects of his poetry, who was a "spectator *ab extra*", "feeling *for*, but never *with*", his characters.[32] A more recent critic, David Ferry, perpetuates Coleridge's criticism: "Wordsworth is not a great lover of man but almost a great despiser of him."[33]

I do not seek to make Wordsworth into a social and political reformer, for, except in such early writings as "A Letter to the Bishop of Llandaff" (comp. 1793), he is concerned with individual man's moral reform, in contrast with most politicians who concentrate on the reform of institutions. Wordsworth's "language of men" and humble subject matter, however, and his ideas on liberty, equality, and fraternity subvert the hierarchical order of the Augustans and thus prepare the ground for political change. In no way does his art blur social reality. Ernst Fischer

---

[29] See, e.g., Caudwell, "Bourgeois Illusion", in Robert F. Gleckner and Gerald E. Enscoe, eds., *Romanticism,* p. 125.

[30] Letter to Lady Beaumont, 21 May 1807. *The Letters of William and Dorothy Wordsworth*. II. *The Middle Years 1806–1811,* ed. Ernest de Selincourt, rev. Mary Moorman, 2nd ed. (Oxford: Clarendon Press, 1969), p. 148. See also Dorothy Wordsworth to Sara Hutchinson on 14 June [1802] (*E.Y.,* p. 367). See further Matthew Arnold's essay "Wordsworth" on the connection between Wordsworth's art and morality (in *Essays in Criticism*); David Perkins, *Wordsworth and the Poetry of Sincerity* (Cambridge, Mass.: The Belknap Press of Harvard U.P., 1964), p. 1; and J. A. W. Heffernan, *Wordsworth's Theory of Poetry: The Transforming Imagination* (Ithaca, N.Y.: Cornell U.P., 1969), pp. 227–28.

[31] Frederick A. Pottle, "Wordsworth in the Present Day" [1972], in *Romanticism: Vistas, Instances, Continuities,* eds. David Thorburn and Geoffrey Hartman (Ithaca, N.Y.: Cornell U.P., 1973), p. 117.

[32] Quoted in Stephen Parrish, *The Art of the* Lyrical Ballads (Cambridge, Mass.: Harvard U.P., 1973), p. 238.

[33] David Ferry, *The Limits of Mortality: An Essay on Wordsworth's Major Poems* (Middleton, Conn.: Wesleyan U.P., 1959), p. 52 (see also ibid., pp. 51, 110, and 143).

correctly observes that critical Realism has sprung from romantic revolt, from a mixture of aristocratic and plebeian denial of *Bürgerlichkeit*; the "romantische Protest gegen die bürgerliche Gesellschaft wurde mehr und mehr zur Kritik an ihr . . . Romantik und Realismus sind keineswegs einander ausschließende Gegensätze, sondern im kritischen Realismus ist Romantik ein aufgehobenes Moment".[34] Although Fischer does not here refer to Wordsworth, this general statement on the link between Romanticism and critical Realism could partly be applied to Wordsworth who, after all, was out to purge and "rectify" the feelings of the middle classes.[35] Even if Wordsworth did not directly intervene in the political machinery of his day, he, exactly as the other romantic bards, "sought to influence legislation, policy, and current events".[36]

The great influence of Wordsworth on philosophers and statesmen from his day to ours confirms the views of critics such as Matthew Arnold, T. S. Eliot, F. R. Leavis, M. H. Abrams, Richard Hoggart, and Raymond Williams that the literary imagination has indeed a special effect on society:[37] John Stuart Mill and A. N. Whitehead were deeply indebted to Wordsworth, and Woodrow Wilson and Viscount Grey revered him; a more recent approbation of Wordsworth by a philosopher is Mary Warnock's *Imagination*.[38] Carl Woodring goes so far as to say that Wordsworth's influence on the "people who speak or read English has been sufficient to sway art and affairs universally".[39]

In *Descriptive Sketches* (comp. 1791–92) and "A Letter to the Bishop of Llandaff" (comp. 1793) Wordsworth incited people to revolutionary action, like most artists of our time who side with revolutions that promise a chance of political liberation. Wordsworth changed gradually from an advocacy of a more or less abstract notion of universal brother-

---

[34] Ernst Fischer, *Zeitgeist und Literatur: Gebundenheit und Freiheit der Kunst* (Wien: Europa Verlag, 1964), p. 72. For the concept of "reason" in English romantic poetry, see Harold Bloom, "To Reason with a Later Reason: Romanticism and the Rational", *Midway*, 11, No. 1 (1970), 97–112.

[35] See, e.g., Wordsworth's defence of "The Idiot Boy" in his letter to John Wilson (*E.Y.*, pp. 352–58).

[36] Carl Woodring, *Politics in English Romantic Poetry* (Cambridge, Mass.: Harvard U.P., 1970), p. 47.

[37] Malcolm Bradbury, "Literature and Sociology", *Essays and Studies*, N.S., 23 (1970), 87–100 (89). See also M. H. Abrams, *The Mirror and the Lamp: Romantic Theory and the Critical Tradition* (1953; reissued Oxford: Oxford U.P., 1971), pp. 326 ff.

[38] G. M. Harper, "The Crisis in Wordsworth's Life and Art", *QQ*, 40 (1933), 1–13 (2); Anna J. Mill, "John Stuart Mill's Visit to Wordsworth, 1831", *MLR*, 44 (1949), 341–50; Abrams, *The Mirror and the Lamp*, p. 333; Newton P. Stallknecht, "Wordsworth and the Quality of Man", pp. 64–65; Mary Warnock, *Imagination* (London: Faber, 1976).

[39] Carl Woodring, *Wordsworth* (Cambridge, Mass.: Harvard U.P., 1968), p. 211. For a similar view, see Stallknecht, "Wordsworth and the Quality of Man", p. 52.

hood to the call for an immediately felt brotherly bond between individual and individual and the championship of inner liberty. In tracing his development we ought not to forget to ask ourselves which of his attitudes are of continuing relevance to the human condition, for the concepts of liberty, equality, and fraternity belong indeed to the perennial issues of mankind.

CHAPTER 1

1791–1794

The concept of individual liberty appears in one of Wordsworth's earliest poems, "Lines Written as a School Exercise at Hawkshead" (GCL I:5; *PW* I, pp. 259–61). In this laudatory verse on the second centenary of Hawkshead School the fifteen-year-old William praises the spirit of truth and free scientific inquiry dominant at Hawkshead. His school rejects those "rigid precepts" that "trained the boy / Dead to the sense of every finer joy" (7–8). The disapproval of "rigid precepts" implies the acceptance of an important idea in Romanticism, the fulfilment of the individual. Another piece of Wordsworth's juvenilia, his translation "From the Greek" (GCL I:7; *PW* I, pp. 299–300), reveals his interest in political liberty. The story of Harmodius and Aristogiton,[1] who the "tyrant's bosom gored / Gave to triumph Freedom's cause, / Gave to Athens equal laws" (27–29), probably is the first instance of the theme of political liberty in Wordsworth's opus if we agree with Reed's dating.[2] The next poem with a slight socio-political tone is "The Vale of Esthwaite" (GCL I:13; *PW* I, pp. 270–83).[3] Although on the whole Gothic and sentimental, it contains the first reference to Wordsworth's democratic subject matter: common man and ordinary human activity (13–24). Pity, poverty, and charity are also touched on, though treated in the unrealistic mode of the poetic convention of the period (139–52). Wordsworth's first published poem is also conventional; it is a sentimental tribute to Helen Maria Williams (GCL I:16, *PW* I, p. 269)[4] whose humanitarian verse captivated him. A few years later Helen Maria

---

[1] "Harmodius and Aristogiton (d. 514 B.C.), the *tyrannoktonoi*, or 'tyrannicides', . . . according to popular, but erroneous, legend freed Athens from the Peisistratid tyrants" (*Encyclopædia Britannica: Micropædia* (1974 ed.)). Cf. 1805 *Prelude* X.165 ff. and below, p. 166.
[2] "Probably composed between 1786 and 1791 inclusive, very likely close to 1786 . . ." (GCL I:7).
[3] "Bulk of composition probably spring–summer 1787" (GCL I:13).
[4] Its full title is "Sonnet on Seeing Miss Helen Maria Williams Weep at a Tale of Distress". Published in the *European Magazine* for Mar. 1797.

Williams's humanitarianism, like Wordsworth's, was to be transformed into political sympathy for the French revolutionaries.[5]

Except for possibly a few lines written as early as mid-1787—and included in "Lines Left upon a Seat in a Yew-Tree" (GCL I:20; below, pp. 79–81) in 1797—young William wrote nothing else of socio-political interest until his work on *An Evening Walk* (GCL I:28; *PW* I, pp. 4–38 [1793 version]) between 1788 and 1789. This poem contains 446 lines, and except for an interspersed passage in the Gothic manner (179–90), the poem conveys a note of harmony up to about line 238. Man's activities are peacefully integrated into the natural surroundings:

> The peasant from yon cliff of fearful edge
> Shot, down the headlong pathway darts his sledge;
> Bright beams the lonely mountain horse illume,
> Feeding 'mid purple heath, "green rings", and broom;
> . . .
> From lonesome chapel at the mountain's feet,
> Three humble bells their rustic chime repeat;
> Sounds from the water-side the hammer'd boat;
> And blasted quarry thunders heard remote.
> (111–14, 121–24)

The sense of peace reaches its climax in the portrayal of the swans: "Safe from your door ye hear at breezy morn, / The hound, the horse's tread, and mellow horn; / At peace inverted your lithe necks ye lave" (233–35). The safety of the young swans is contrasted with the risk of death that the offspring of human beings experience: "Ye ne'er, like hapless human wanderers, throw / Your young on winter's winding sheet of snow" (239–40). After the ideal of an uninjured natural and social order we are confronted with the lot of the mother,

> Who faint, and beat by summer's breathless ray,
> Hath dragg'd her babes along this weary way;
> While arrowy fire extorting feverish groans,
> Shot stinging through her stark o'er-labour'd bones.
> (243–46)

Lines 239–56, more or less in the middle of the poem, are also thematically central to Wordsworth's social protest; it is noteworthy that these lines contain comparatively little "poetic diction" of which elsewhere

---

[5] See also "Wordsworth and Helen Maria Williams", in F. M. Todd, *Politics and the Poet* (London: Methuen, 1957), pp. 217–28 (Appendix). Most of this appendix was first published as an article in *MLR,* 43 (1948), 456–64.

there are many instances in the poem. Wordsworth was aware of the social misery caused by war and its aftermath, in particular the American Revolution, before he experienced the French Revolution. The homeless, destitute widow "bids her soldier come her woes to share, / Asleep on Bunker's charnel hill afar"[6] (253-54); her forsaken state is a disquietening reminder that the brotherhood of man is non-existent for her.

At approximately the same time as Wordsworth composed *An Evening Walk* he made a translation, "In Part from Moschus—Lament for Bion" (GCL I:29; *PW* I, pp. 286-87). In the first eight lines of this little piece we encounter the same democratic sentiment that characterizes many of Wordsworth's later original compositions (e.g., "The Oak and the Broom", GCL II:18, below). The seemingly weak, "the lowliest children of the spring, / Violets and meekest snowdrops", are resilient and revive after apparent death, whereas the seemingly strong, "we, the great, the mighty and the wise", perish for ever.

1791-92

Descriptive Sketches

According to Chard "Wordsworth's political development really began in January, 1791, when he left Cambridge and went to London, thus for the first time coming in touch actively with the political controversies of the day".[7] This is first reflected in *Descriptive Sketches* (*PW* I, pp. 42-90 [1793 version]), most of which Wordsworth probably wrote between 6 December 1791 and early December 1792 (GCL I:39), roughly the period of his second visit to France. Wordsworth disembarked at Dieppe on 27 November 1791 and arrived in Paris on 30 November (Reed I, p. 125), where he found revolutionary France determined to withstand any foreign threat to invade her. Liberty is a key concept in the declaration of 29 November 1791, which the Assembly demanded that Louis XVI send to the foreign powers gathering their armies on the frontier: "if the princes of Germany continue to favour preparations

---

[6] This refers to the Battle of Bunker Hill of 17 June 1775, one of the earliest engagements of the American Revolution.

[7] Leslie F. Chard, p. 42. For a detailed account of the social and political scene of 1791-94 that is of relevance to Wordsworth's socio-political development, see Chard's chapters I-V.

made against the French, the French will carry into their midst, not fire and sword, but liberty! Let them calculate what result may follow the awakening of nations."[8] Wordsworth's letter to his brother Richard on 19 December [1791] from Orleans brings out his lack of sympathy with the persons of wealth and power and implies his agreement with the principles of the French Revolution:

> the King has been [ ] national assembly and that [ ] are going to attack the emigran[ts]. We are all perfectly quiet here and likely to continue so; I find almost all the people of any opulen[ce are] aristocrats and all the others democrates. I had imagined that there were some people of wealth and circumstance favorers of the revolution, but here there is not one to be found. (*E.Y.*, p. 70; square brackets in *E.Y.*)

The phrasing of the letter evinces Wordsworth's caution: he couples opulence with the aristocrats but restricts his assertion by "almost", and although he observes that "people of wealth and circumstance" do not favour the revolution, the "here there is not one to be found" may well apply to Orleans only. In the letter the word democrat is used in the sense of "one of the republicans of the French Revolution of 1790 (opposed to *aristocrat*)" (*OED*, def. 1). (For the unfavourable connotation of "democracy" in the 1790s, see above, Introduction.)

If we compare *Descriptive Sketches* with Wordsworth's first long poem, *An Evening Walk* (comp. 1788–89), the direct impact on Wordsworth's political thought of his visit to France in 1790 and particularly the longer one-year stay between 1791 and 1792 is revealed, as well as the influence of his "actual study of Rousseau and French pamphleteers" (Harper I, p. 12).[9] The couplet-poetry of *An Evening Walk* and *Descriptive Sketches* is in the sentimental conventional strain of the period[10] but undoubtedly better than the verse of some contemporary

---

[8] Quoted by George McLean Harper, *William Wordsworth: His Life, Works, and Influence* (London: John Murray, 1916), vol. I, p. 137. On the prospects for a successful issue of the Revolution in Nov. 1791 and its approval by many Englishmen, see Harper I, p. 135.

[9] For the influence of these visits to France on Wordsworth's social and political thought, see also below, pp. 159–73. Todd, in *Politics and the Poet*, p. 42, is far too limited when he ascribes Wordsworth's progress solely to Beaupuy: "it was Beaupuy who kept the zeal awake, who made Wordsworth believe that political ideas were important, even paramount . . . It was Beaupuy who was responsible for Wordsworth's progress from the conventional social sympathies of 'An Evening Walk' to the political ardour of the 'Descriptive Sketches' and the *Letter to the Bishop of Llandaff*".

[10] Mary Jacobus has dealt with this aspect of the early Wordsworth in her *Tradition and Experiment in Wordsworth's* Lyrical Ballads *(1798)* (Oxford: Clarendon Press, 1976), pp. 133–58.

poets, for example that of the philanthropic radical poet Thelwall,[11] touching here on the topical theme of the brotherhood of man:

> That thus, as with all I alternately blend,
> The *mind* may expand and the *heart* may amend;
> Till, embracing Mankind in one girdle of Love,
> In Nature's kind lesson I daily improve,
> And (no haughty distinctions to fetter my soul)
> As the brother of all, learn to feel for the whole.[12]

The main difference between *Descriptive Sketches* and *An Evening Walk*—in fact all his pre-1792 poetry—lies in the direct references to current political theory in the second half of *Descriptive Sketches*. In the first part political ideals are at best implied. There is for instance the private little world of the wanderer who "calls the passing poor" to share his spare meal (*PW* I, p. 44, l. 32), and there is the idyllic local brotherhood of a small community, implicit in "With bashful fear no cottage children steal / From him [the wanderer], a brother at the cottage meal, / His humble looks no shy restraint impart, / Around him plays at will the virgin heart" (37–40). Wordsworth does not, however, allow us to forget the wider world, lands where personal and political liberty are non-existent, where ". . . Slavery, forcing the sunk mind to dwell / On joys that might disgrace the captive's cell, / Her shameless timbrel shakes along thy marge, / And winds between thine isles the vocal barge" (158–61). Slavery was a hotly debated issue in the 1790s.[13] The struggle against tyranny and for national liberty is advocated in a reference to Tell, the legendary Swiss patriot who symbolizes the fight for political and individual freedom,[14] and in a reference to the Battle of Marathon in which the Athenians repelled the Persian invaders: "But lo! the boatman, over-aw'd, before / The pictur'd fane of Tell suspends his

---

[11] On the impact of Jacobinical writers in 1791 in furthering liberty, see Crane Brinton, *The Political Ideas of the English Romanticists* (London: Oxford U.P., 1926), p. 41 [reissued by the Univ. of Michigan Press in 1966].

[12] Quoted by Brinton in *The Political Ideas of the English Romanticists*, p. 27, from J. Thelwall, *The Peripatetic* (1793), vol. ii, p. 228. The italics are in Brinton.

[13] "Wordsworth shared the attitude of virtually all the radicals in supporting the many humanitarian reform plans then current, chief among them being Wilberforce's abolition bill" (Chard, p. 60). For a detailed calendar of events relating to slavery and the slave trade in 1791–1805, see David Brion Davis, *The Problem of Slavery in the Age of Revolution, 1770–1823* (Ithaca, N.Y.: Cornell U.P., 1975), pp. 28–31.

Dorothy Wordsworth too shares Wordsworth's abhorrence with slavery as seen in a letter to Jane Pollard of May 1792: "I hope you were an *immediate* abolitionist and are angry with the House of Commons for continuing the traffic in human flesh so long as till [17]96 but you will also rejoice that so *much* has been done. . . ." (*E.Y.*, p. 75.)

[14] Friedrich Schiller took up this theme in his drama *Wilhelm Tell* (1804).

oar; / Confused the Marathonian tale appears, / While burn in his full eyes the glorious tears" (348–51).

The second half of the poem begins with explicit political philosophy:

520   Once Man entirely free, alone and wild,
            Was bless'd as free—for he was Nature's child.
            He, all superior but his God disdain'd,
            Walk'd none restraining, and by none restrain'd,
            Confess'd no law but what his reason taught,
525   Did all he wish'd, and wish'd but what he ought.
            As Man in his primæval dower array'd
            The image of his glorious sire display'd,
            Ev'n so, by vestal Nature guarded, here
            The traces of primæval Man appear.
530   The native dignity no forms debase,
            The eye sublime, and surly lion-grace.
            The slave of none, of beasts alone the lord,
            He marches with his flute, his book, and sword,
            Well taught by that to feel his rights, prepar'd
535   With this "the blessings he enjoys to guard".
                                       (520–35)

The passage has been a great favourite with critics in dealing with the socio-political elements in Wordsworth's work ever since Harper I (p. 196) in 1916 pointed out that lines 520–25 "might have been written by the hand of Pope recalled to life for the purpose of condensing into maxims the philosophy of Rousseau".[15]

In these lines Wordsworth deals first and foremost with the concept of personal liberty of primeval man, who "alone and wild", could afford to enjoy his natural rights. The notion of that virtually absolute liberty is reinforced by qualifying "free" with "entirely" (520) and by repeating "free" in the line following (521); the sacred nature of liberty is underlined by ranking together "bless'd" and "free" (521). There were no social classes and ranks. Man acknowledged only God as his superior: equality between man and man was a reality (522). "None restraining" and "none restrain'd" reiterate (with the same use of repetition) the

---

[15] Although Chard says that "it would be foolhardy to attempt to say where Wordsworth was influenced by Rousseau as a consequence of his reading, and where he was merely sharing Rousseau with his age as a whole" (p. 91), he comments on this key passage, "Rousseau's concept of man in the state of nature appears without modification in *Descriptive Sketches*. Here Wordsworth manifests all the idealistic enthusiasm of a new convert to political radicalism." (p. 93).

For one of the few sympathetic Marxist interpretations of Wordsworth, see V. G. Kiernan, "Wordsworth and the People", in *Democracy and the Labour Movement: Essays in Honour of Dona Torr*, ed. John Saville (London: Lawrence & Wishart, 1954), pp. 241–42. Kiernan concentrates on the concept of liberty in *Descriptive Sketches*.

notion of liberty in the preceding lines. With the picture of the "absolute" liberty of our distant forefathers we are reminded by contrast of the kind of liberty existing in the more sophisticated society of the 1790s. "Absolute" liberty has become the liberty defined by the "law", upheld by society's customs, power, and authority. "Confess'd no law but what his reason taught" (524) reflects the enlightened faith in reason as the means of recapturing some of the "absolute" liberty of primeval man. "Free", "alone", "wild" make up the very simple vocabulary Wordsworth uses to depict the ideal state of liberty (520).[16] The state of liberty is reflected in man's bearing and appearance. The "eye sublime" portrays his grandeur and high moral stature; "lion-grace" connotes the pride and strength fostered by liberty, but a strength that through "grace" is prevented from turning into wild ferocity (531). This free man, "slave of none" (532), develops better than others his artistic, intellectual, and martial qualities as symbolized by "flute", "book", and "sword" (533). Wordsworth is very much aware of the concept of natural rights. There is a parallel between this early "revolutionary" poem in which the notion of man feeling his rights (534) is treated and the much later "Rob Roy's Grave" (GCL II:139: comp. 1805–06) that has Rob Roy utter his philosophy of natural rights: " '. . . we lose / 'Distinctions that are plain and few: / 'These find I graven on my heart: / *'That tells me what to do*".[17]

Now that the heroic stature of the Swiss has been built up, Wordsworth leaves individual liberty behind and, in the next verse paragraph (536–49), concentrates on national liberty and the struggle of the Swiss to retain their national independence. Since individual man has been shown to develop his martial qualities to the full as a free human being, the defeat of an army of between fifteen and twenty thousand by three hundred and thirty men[18] does not come across as an exaggeration: ". . . Oppression shriek'd, and flew. / Oft as those sainted Rocks before him spread, / An unknown power connects him with the dead" (541–43).

[16] Moorman I, pp. 198–99, and Paul Sheats in *The Making of Wordsworth's Poetry, 1785–1798* (Cambridge, Mass.: Harvard U.P., 1973), pp. 64–65, deal with Swiss virtue and Swiss liberty and both comment on Wordsworth's chief literary source of the poem, Ramond de Carbonnière's translation of Coxe's *Travels—Lettres de M. William Coxe à M. W. Melmoth* . . . [I have taken the title from *PW* I, p. 325], whence Wordsworth, according to Professor Beatty, took his " 'thesis that Switzerland is the representative of primeval man, who is free, independent, hospitable—at least so far as the herdsmen and hunters are concerned' . . . 'a belief' which in Ramond was a 'flaming conviction which fires others with an unquenchable zeal for the betterment of mankind . . .' " (*PW* I, p. 325).

[17] *Poems in Two Volumes, 1807*, ed. Helen Darbishire, 2nd ed. (Oxford: Clarendon Press, 1952), p. 179.

[18] See Wordsworth's footnote (*PW* I, p. 74).

These lines convey a sense of history—"holy is the air" (545)—and create a mood of defiance against any possible foreign oppressor; both of these attitudes are relevant to the situation of the young vulnerable French State.

Wordsworth's concern with liberty is also discernible in religious tolerance. He treats the Roman Catholicism of the pilgrims to the shrine of Einsiedeln very sympathetically: "Oh give not me that eye of hard disdain / That views undimm'd Einsiedlen's wretched fane" (654–55). Wordsworth disparages the "hard disdain" of the eye of religious intolerance and makes his little contribution to Catholic Emancipation which William Pitt was to advocate in 1800.

Lines 702–39 resume the theme of political liberty. The political enslavement of Savoy (706) produces poverty:[19] "poor babes that, hurrying from the door, / With pale-blue hands, and eyes that fix'd implore, / Dead muttering lips, and hair of hungry white, / Besiege the traveller whom they half affright" (709–12). The vocabulary is overdone; "hair of hungry white" is Gothic and sensational, and yet, despite their shortcomings, the lines make plain Wordsworth's rage over this kind of destitution. Wordsworth was more politically aware than those of his contemporaries who thought that the lavish mode of life of the rich provided employment and subsistence for the lower orders.[20] He connects loss of liberty and all its attendant miseries with monarchy and aristocracy (Harper I, p. 98; Chard, p. 85):[21]

> In the wide range of many a weary round,
> Still have my pilgrim feet unfailing found,
> As despot courts their blaze of gems display,
> Ev'n by the secret cottage far away
> The lily of domestic joy decay[.]
>
> (719–23)

The white purity implied in the figure of "lily of domestic joy" is blighted by the luxury of the despot courts. The image of the decayed lily prepares us for lines 726 ff. where political liberty effects a positive change in Nature herself: "more luscious" is the woodbine, and "weedless" the garden.

The secret cottage becomes infected by the political corruption of the

---

[19] These lines were written before France annexed Savoy on 27 Nov. 1792. See also Harper I, pp. 196–97.

[20] Harper I, p. 197.

[21] In Oct. 1792 Dorothy Wordsworth differed considerably from her brother William over monarchy. She was pro-monarchy and labelled "Liberty and Equality" "the newfangled Doctrine" (*E.Y.*, p. 83).

court, whereas "... Freedom's farthest hamlets blessings share, / Found still beneath her smile, and only there" (724-25); the final position of "and only there" lends weight to the correlation between "freedom" and "blessings", and "only" makes the restriction to that state definitive. The following lines (726-39) contain an accumulation of comparatives that stress the superior quality of life in a state of political liberty. These twelve comparatives in fourteen lines are unique in the early poetry of Wordsworth.

It is usually Nature that engenders thoughts of liberty in Wordsworth and hence Nature brings about political change indirectly. As seen above and as can be seen in lines 756-73, the situation is reversed in *Descriptive Sketches*; where liberty reigns, flora and fauna improve: "—Yet, hast thou found that Freedom spreads her pow'r / Beyond the cottage hearth, the cottage door: / All nature smiles..." (756-58). The choice of the lowly "cottage hearth" and "cottage door" to introduce this important passage on the impact of political liberty on the environment underlines Wordsworth's democratic spirit: Wordsworth pays his first respect to what are the "grassroots" in the terminology of today.

"—Tho' Liberty shall soon, indignant..." (774), have to go to war, new virtues will spring from the "innocuous flames" (782). Wordsworth, carried away by revolutionary fervour, describes the flames of war as harmless. From the ashes of the old order the principles of the revolution will thrive and Nature will become again as she was in her prime; justice and truth will be reborn, consumption will be eradicated.[22]

All the latter part of *Descriptive Sketches* is a eulogy of liberty; the final lines (792-809) assume the form of a fervent prayer for the victory of liberty.[23] The fire and sword (803) of the war of liberty[24] will eradicate from the earth the evils of conquest, avarice, pride, famine, oppression, machination, persecution, ambition, and discord. Wordsworth prays that monarchy, "every sceptred child of clay, / Who cries, presumptuous, 'here their tides shall stay', / Swept in their anger from th' affrighted shore, / With all his creatures sink—to rise no more" (806-09).[25] The political tone of *Descriptive Sketches* is optimistic and

---

[22] See also Harper I, pp. 197-98.

[23] de Selincourt remarks that "it is worth noting that this apostrophe to Freedom survives all revisions up to 1836..." (*PW* I, p. 328). Moorman I, p. 199, makes the same observation.

[24] "On November 18 [1792] the Convention passed a motion declaring that the French Republic desired the liberty of all other nations and would assist them to gain it..." (Harper I, p. 179).

[25] Louis XVI was actually executed on 21 Jan. 1793.

progressive, if by "progressive" we mean the championship of liberty, equality, and fraternity.

During the last few weeks of composition the Revolution began to show its dark side: in November 1792 the extremist Jacobins wrested the power from the moderate Girondins. However, Wordsworth's passionate love for humanity and concern for the amelioration of society made him, in his poetry, stick to his initial belief in the ideals of the French Revolution.[26] In a letter to William Mathews of 19 May [1792] Wordsworth strikes another note; there he singles out England as a haven of political liberty and fair employment: "You have the happiness of being born in a free country, where every road is open, where talents and industry are more liberally rewarded than amongst any other nation of the Universe...." (*E.Y.*, p. 77.)

In contrast to Wordsworth's idealization of the freedom-loving Swiss in his poetry, an early letter of his (September 1790; *E.Y.*, p. 36) depicts them unfavourably, in particular Swiss inn-keepers. Thus we detect two voices in Wordsworth, the private voice of his letters and the public voice of his poetry. In 1792, and when *Descriptive Sketches* was brought out by the radical publisher Joseph Johnson in 1793, the poet-reformer addressing a wider audience felt he could not desert the high principles of the Revolution. For the young Wordsworth not only the fate of France was at stake but also the fate of the human race. For him the French Revolution was the cause of mankind, as is shown by "A Letter to the Bishop of Llandaff".

1793

A Letter to the Bishop of Llandaff

Mary Wollstonecraft's *Vindication of the Rights of Woman* and the second part of Paine's *Rights of Man* were published in 1792. In "A Letter to the Bishop of Llandaff"[27] (GCL I:42), written in spring or

---

[26] See also Moorman I, p. 221.

[27] W. J. B. Owen and Jane Worthington Smyser give a full summary of literary and philosophical influences on the "Letter", referring also to contemporary social and political events (*Prose Works* I, pp. 19–25, 50–66; their Commentary to ll. 656–57 (ibid., p. 64) contains a select bibliography illustrating the reform movement of 1792–93). See also Woodring, *Wordsworth*, p. 135, and Chard, pp. 58 and 116–17. On repressive measures (against egalitarians and republicans) by the Government in 1793, see Harper I, pp. 233–34; and Philip Anthony Brown, *The French Revolution in English History* (1918; rpt. London: Frank Cass, 1965), pp. 82–99. For instance, saying in a public place such as a coffee-house: "'I am for equality.... Why, no kings!'" could cost you eighteen months imprisonment

summer 1793,[28] we are given Wordsworth's interpretation of the rights of man,[29] coupled with his attack on monarchy and nobility. The unpublished "Letter" answers Bishop Watson's protest[30] against the execution of Louis XVI on 21 January 1793; it is a piece of direct political theory on the concepts of liberty, equality, and, to some extent, democracy. The concept of brotherhood on the other hand is embedded in the "Letter" and needs to be extracted.

Throughout the "Letter" Wordsworth uses the notion of brotherhood to contrast man's common brotherhood with monarchy's separation from that fraternal bond: the king's isolation is an "unnatural situation, which requires more than human talents and human virtues, and at the same time precludes him from attaining even a moderate knowledge of common life and from feeling a particular share in the interests of mankind...."[31] (*Prose Works* I, p. 33, ll. 81–85.) Bishop Watson too is treated as though he were separate from the rest of mankind. In the typical language of a revolutionary Wordsworth reproaches the bishop: how, in a "period big with the fate of the human race", dare he be sorry for the "personal sufferings of the late royal martyr" (I.32.52–54). Wordsworth, in attacking the bishop's admiration for English legal proceedings, implies that injustice is inherent in the English legal system, since its judges have isolated themselves from the greater part of the brotherhood of man; they are too remote from ordinary men whose "sorrows should be familiar to you, of which if you are ignorant how can you redress them?" (I.47.612–13). The importance of brotherhood is

---

(E. P. Thompson, *The Making of the English Working Class*, rev. ed., Harmondsworth: Penguin, 1968, p. 124 [Thompson's ellipsis]). Ben Ross Schneider, Jr., *Wordsworth's Cambridge Education* (Cambridge: Cambridge U.P., 1957), pp. 206–11, points out the risks of publishing the "Letter" and gives an account of the political suppression at Cambridge University in 1793.

On pamphlets from 1793 intended to show the lower classes the connection between economic and political evils, see James T. Boulton, *The Language of Politics in the Age of Wilkes and Burke* (London: Routledge & Kegan Paul, 1963; Toronto: Univ. of Toronto Press, 1963), pp. 86–87.

[28] Reed: "Probably composed June 1793 or shortly after." However, Owen and Smyser (*Prose Works* I, p. 20) believe that the "Letter" "was most probably composed in February or March [1793] . . .".

[29] Lines 401–02 (*Prose Works* I, p. 42) of the "Letter" prove Wordsworth's reading of the *Droits de l'homme et du citoyen* (Aug. 1789). This and subsequent page and line references to the "Letter" are to W. J. B. Owen and Jane Worthington Smyser, eds., *The Prose Works of William Wordsworth* (Oxford: Oxford U.P., 1974), vol. I, pp. 31–49.

[30] The protest was written on 25 Jan. 1793 and published a few days later as an Appendix to a sermon he had preached in 1785. For a bibliography of the bishop's pamphlet, see *Prose Works* I, p. 50.

[31] On Thomas Paine's influence here, see Owen and Smyser's Commentary (81–85), *Prose Works* I, p. 53.

built up throughout the "Letter" by the frequent use of words and word combinations suggesting universal brotherhood: mankind, human race, bulk of mankind, race of men, mass of mankind, heart of man. The repetition of these expressions (e.g. I.32.52, 33.80, 33.85, 33.88–89, 34.118, 36.192–93, 36.199, 36.210, 37.252, 43.477, 47.612, 48.649) makes the existence of a brotherhood of man that shares the "common feelings of humanity" (I.40.334) and the "eternal nature of man" (I.41.388) appear inevitable.

In some instances the "Letter" is more like an inflammatory speech, better when heard than read. Wordsworth uses the typical hyperbole of the political orator in disparaging the character of Louis XVI:

a man of philosophy and humanity [Bishop Grégoire] as distinguished as your Lordship [Bishop of Llandaff], declared at the opening of the national convention, and twenty-five millions of men were convinced of the truth of the assertion, that there was not a citizen on the tenth of august who, if he could have dragged before the eyes of Louis [XVI] the corse of one of his murdered brothers, might not have exclaimed to him, Tyran, voilà ton ouvrage. . . . (I.32.63–68.)

Needless to say, it is the height of political rhetoric to state categorically that twenty-five million people were convinced of Louis's guilt. This overstatement would undoubtedly have had the same effect on a political platform as Grégoire's image of a murdered brother dragged before the eyes of Louis. Wordsworth's adaptation of Grégoire's speech of 15 November 1792 in the National Convention (*Prose Works* I, p. 52) is very effective. It touches the deeply rooted emotions that man feels for his kindred; the picture of spilled blood is evoked. Retaining the original French at the end of the sentence, where it carries most weight, brings out the authenticity of the situation: Louis XVI, who in the "Letter" is representative of all monarchs, has gravely wronged twenty-five million people, representative of "the whole human race" (I.33.88–90).[32]

The righteous cause of the human brotherhood is pitted against the sectional interest of a small minority, namely the monarchy and nobility. Wordsworth implies that in a revolution the end justifies the means and that the spirit of brotherhood which demands compassion for everyone has to be suspended: it is "evidently dangerous where traitors are to be punished . . ." (I.34.112). Whenever Wordsworth wishes to single out the privileged or rich, he uses a vocabulary suggesting that they are apart

---

[32] Compare this with Wordsworth's private voice in his letter to William Mathews on 19 May [1792] (*E.Y.*, p. 78) where he concedes that "there are in France some [?millions] . . ." who hope for a counterrevolution. (Square brackets in *E.Y.*)

from the rest of humanity. We can see this when we compare the "race of men" (I.34.118) with lines 138-40: "While you reflect on the vast diminution which *some* men's fortunes must have undergone, your sorrow for *these individuals* will be diminished . . ." [my italics]. In addition to implying a minority, "these individuals" has a caustic tone.

Wordsworth lashes out against any kind of artificial distinction that separates man from man. He concludes that "titles . . . stars, ribbands, and garters, and other badges of fictitious superiority" (I.44.480-81) are "separations among mankind" and therefore "absurd, impolitic, and immoral" (I.44.485). In dealing with hereditary nobility, i.e. a whole group of people, Wordsworth uses the singular form of pronouns. This stylistic device of particularization is used to drive a wedge between mankind in general and the representative individual under attack: "we bind ourselves to address *him* and *his* posterity with humiliating circumlocutions, calling *him* most noble, most honourable, most high, most august, serene, excellent, eminent and so forth . . ." (I.44.496-98; my italics). Another significant use of the singular to decry hereditary nobility appears at I.45.523-25: "a man's past services are no sufficient security for his future character: he who today merits the civic wreath may tomorrow deserve the Tarpeian rock. . . ." The use of the singular seems significant, since in the "Letter" Wordsworth never particularizes when referring to the brotherhood of man.

Making wage assessments responsible for the economic misery of workmen,[33] Wordsworth contrasts the "few" who "afford so much" with the "multitude of our brothers" who "exist in even helpless indigence" (I.43.456-58). The emotive "brothers" engenders a sense of wage earners belonging together. Wordsworth is sensitive to gross economic inequality, indeed any kind of inequality that produces injustice. And he is aware that only the movement of the unenfranchised majority towards political liberty and equality could bring about a change for the better in legislation. Thus Wordsworth's definitions of liberty and equality[34] in the "Letter" become of primary importance. Perhaps Wordsworth's keen political insight and discussion of various forms of democratic government make Harper say that the "Letter" deserves to be ranked

---

[33] Wordsworth's attack on wage assessments indicates how far to the left he stood at the time. On wage assessments, see *Prose Works* I, p. 61.

[34] Kenneth Eisold, *Loneliness and Communion: A Study of Wordsworth's Thought and Experience,* Salzburg Studies in English Literature. Romantic Reassessment, No. 13 (Salzburg: Universität Salzburg, 1973), pp. 10-15, discusses the concept of equality and Rousseau's General Will in the "Letter".

with the writings of Burke, Paine, and Mackintosh, as one of the most philosophical treatises occasioned in England by the Revolutionary movement. It goes as far below the surface of human nature as Burke's "Reflections", and is only less eloquent than that great work. "The Age of Reason" is scarcely more pungent and audacious, and Mackintosh's "Vindiciæ Gallicæ" is far less vigorous. . . . (Harper I, p. 217.)

Harper's ranking of Wordsworth's "Letter" with the works of outstanding political philosophers is a great honour for Wordsworth. However, it must be conceded that most of the political ideas in the "Letter" are derivative. What makes it remarkable nevertheless is Wordsworth's skilful use of the various political theories current in his time.

Before dealing with Wordsworth's political philosophy a brief glance at his handling of the technique of political propaganda will highlight his versatility in that field. His insinuations against Bishop Watson illustrate the point. The bishop, in his Appendix, hopes to show the fallacy of equality and liberty as understood by the thought of the French Revolution. However, Wordsworth in his reply to the bishop manages to convey the impression that Watson's interpretations of liberty and equality are irrelevant, since, in pointing out the absence of impartiality and sagacious inquiry in the bishop (I.32.40–41), Wordsworth implies that Watson has acted immorally and superficially. A few lines farther down Wordsworth condones the execution of Louis XVI and reprimands the bishop: "If you had attended to the history of the French revolution as *minutely* as its importance demands, so far from stopping to bewail his death, you would rather have regretted that the blind fondness of his people had placed a human being in that *monstrous* situation which rendered him unaccountable before a human tribunal. . . ."[35] (I.32.58–62; my italics.) The bishop has not paid enough ("minutely") attention to the historic facts of the Revolution. Furthermore, Wordsworth subtly insinuates that Watson has no knowledge of man's nature (I.33.99–100); in consequence his political theories are against Nature and therefore the bishop is not equipped to understand natural rights, the theoretical framework of the Revolution of 1688 and of the American and French Revolutions as implied in the American Declaration of Independence (1776) and expressed in the French Declaration of the Rights of

---

[35] Chard, p. 89, points to the similarity between Milton's defence of regicide in the *Tenure of Kings and Magistrates* and Wordsworth's approval of the execution of Louis. Boulton, *The Language of Politics*, p. 87, supplies a contemporary justification couched in moral terms to rise against a royal oppressor of liberty: ". . . the thrones of true kings by the PEOPLE are made, / And when kings become tyrants—submission is sin." (From Thomas Spence, *Pigs' Meat* (1793–95), I, 181; small capitals in Boulton.)

Man and of the Citizen (1789): *Les hommes naissent et demeurent libres et égaux en droits*. Wordsworth transforms the Bishop of Llandaff, who formerly propagated equality, and was therefore called the "levelling prelate, bishop of the dissenters . . ." (I.31.32), into a political ass, one of the "advocates of error" (I.35.174-75), who cannot grasp the rationally demonstrable natural rights of the seventeenth and eighteenth centuries and who is apparently "ignorant of the overwhelming corruption of the present day" (I.46.588-99). Thus in addition to being separate from the rest of the human brotherhood the bishop offers interpretations of liberty and equality unworthy of serious consideration when contrasted with the reasoned socio-political ideas of the methodical "politician" Wordsworth.

For Wordsworth liberty and equality are inherent in the nature of man. Referring to the confiscation of Church property, he says that the "assembly were true to *justice* and . . . *enforced their right:* they took from the clergy a considerable portion of their wealth, and applied it to the alleviation of the national misery. . . ." (I.34.132-36; my italics.) Linking "justice" to "enforced their right" evinces Wordsworth's approval of the measures: redistribution of excessive wealth, i.e. a move towards greater economic equality, is nothing but a fulfilment of the natural law that allocates every man enough property for survival. Democratic rule by the "people", either through representatives or through referendums, is based on the "original power" (I.37.233) and "original authority" (I.38.268) of the people, "original" implying that any other kind of authority and power is superimposed on or tolerated by the originally independent popular authority and power. Bearing this in mind, Wordsworth's demands for more liberty and equality for the people gain greater weight, for reforming the laws to that effect would restore to some extent the people's natural, i.e. universally true, rights; his objection to monarchy, based on the same universal principle of "the eternal nature of man" (I.41.388), gains greater force as well. It is significant that Wordsworth underscores the universal nature of man by "eternal" in an instance that is most central to the argument of the "Letter", his attack on monarchy. The concept of universality implies that only a fool or a person with malicious intentions would argue against it. Finally, the way Wordsworth regards natural rights indicates that he sides with the progressives of his time against the traditionalists such as Burke (I.48.629-35 illustrate Wordsworth's rage over Burke).

In the second paragraph of the "Letter" Wordsworth announces his determination "not [to] preclude [himself] from any truths" in the cause which he has undertaken to defend. His search for truth compels him to acknowledge political reality, for instance, "that a time of revolution is not the season of *true* Liberty. . . ." (I.33.100–01; my italics.) Liberty is too often obliged to borrow the very arms of despotism to overthrow him, and in order to reign in peace must establish herself by violence. She deplores such stern *necessity*, but the safety of the people, her supreme law, is her consolation. This *apparent* contradiction between the principles of liberty and the march of revolutions, this spirit of jealousy, of severity, of disquietude, of vexation, *indispensable* from a state of war between the oppressors and oppressed, must of *necessity* confuse the ideas of morality and contract the benign exertion of the best affections of the human heart. Political virtues are developed at the expence of moral ones; and the sweet emotions of compassion, evidently dangerous where traitors are to be punished, are too often altogether smothered. But is this a sufficient reason to reprobate a convulsion from which is to spring a fairer order of things? It is the province of *education* to rectify the erroneous notions which a habit of oppression, and even of resistance, may have created, and to soften this ferocity of character proceeding from a *necessary* suspension of the mild and social virtues; it belongs to her to create a race of men who, *truly free*, will look upon their fathers as only enfranchised. (I.33–34.102–19; my italics.)

The "necessity" to guarantee the safety of the people, i.e. fulfilment of one of man's basic needs, freedom from fear, obliges liberty to establish her rule by force (103–04). Political indoctrination is practised in lines 105–10: the contradiction between the ideals of liberty and the violent Revolution is only seeming. Since this "apparent contradiction" is "indispensable" in a state of war, the freedom fighters, "of necessity", are relieved from the burden of moral responsibility. The absence of liberty is blamed for the erroneous ideas among the people (115–16). However, education will bring forth a new breed of "truly free" men; but prior to this, men will have to suffer through "a necessary suspension" of brotherly love (116–18). The concept of "necessity" is used three times in the above excerpt: Wordsworth concedes the unpleasant realities of a revolution. Later on he perceives that initially the people are likely to misuse their newly gained political liberty (I.38.270), and necessity is implied once more: "a people could not but at first make an abuse of that liberty which a legitimate republic supposes. The animal just released from its stall will exhaust the overflow of its spirits in a round of wanton vagaries, but it will soon return to itself and enjoy its freedom in moderate and regular delight." (I.38.275–80.) The image of the animal let loose is strong. However, Wordsworth is certain that the long-term political objective, a democracy characterized by moderation and regularity (280), will be achieved.

The preceding has shown that Wordsworth advocates popular political liberty, although he is aware of its defects. On the first page of the

"Letter" he lashes out against "slavery civil and religious" (I.31.30); lines 181–83 couch the absence of liberty in yet stronger terms: "Slavery is a bitter and a poisonous draught" but a nation has the right to "dash the cup to the ground when she pleases". For Wordsworth inequality between men is due to upbringing and habit: "we are taught from infancy that we were born in a state of inferiority to our oppressors . . ." (I.36.190–91). He counters Bishop Watson's attack on the republican form of government as a tyranny of equals[36] effectively by implying that a democracy provides the means of getting rid of governments if the majority of the electorate are not convinced of the government's goodwill: "as soon as [the] tyranny [of equals] becomes odious, the principal step is made towards its destruction. . . ." (I.36.197–99. See also I.40.348–50.) Despite the danger of "imprisonment and the pillory" (209) Wordsworth feels a moral obligation to speak out in defence of republican democracy: "a republic *legitimately* constructed contains *less* of an oppressive principle than any other form of government." (I.36.213–14; my italics. See also I.39.324–26.) The sentence attests Wordsworth's political shrewdness. "Legitimately" illustrates that he has thought about the principle of legitimacy in government. He concludes correctly that most people obey voluntarily if they believe in the legality of government authority and, furthermore, that less coercion is necessary, since a democratic government ultimately derives its authority from the consent of the electorate. The following excerpt is a goldmine of illustrations for Wordsworth's ideas on universal suffrage, representative democracy, direct democracy by referendum, and the influence of Rousseau, Paine, and Harrington on the "Letter":[37]

As the magnitude of almost all states prevents the possibility of their enjoying a pure democracy, philosophers, from a wish, as far as is in their power, to make the governors and the governed one, will turn their thoughts to the system of universal representation, and will annex an equal importance to the suffrage of every individual. Jealous of giving up no more of the authority of the people than is necessary, they will be solicitous of finding out some method by which the office of their delegates may be confined as much as is practicable to the

---

[36] Bishop Watson's text: "I think a republic the most oppressive to the bulk of the people: they are deceived in it with the show of liberty; but they live in it under the most odious of all tyrannies, the tyranny of their equals. . . ." (Alexander B. Grosart, ed., *The Prose Works of William Wordsworth*, London: Edward Moxon, 1876, vol. I, p. 25.)

[37] See Commentary to ll. 219–24 and 226–29 (*Prose Works*, pp. 56–57) for the influence of Rousseau, and especially Paine's *Rights of Man*. For Harrington's impact, see Zera S. Fink, "Wordsworth and the English Republican Tradition", *JEGP*, 47 (1948), 107–26 (112–13), and Chard, pp. 90–91.

proposing and deliberating upon laws, rather than to enacting them; reserving to the people the power of finally inscribing them in the national code. (I.37.219–29.)

Subsequently Wordsworth instances the example of the young American democracy to refute the notion "that the people are not the proper judges of their own welfare. . . ." (I.37.249–50.) His trust is in the people (1805 *Prelude* X.577, below, p. 172) and their capacity to discern their own "true interests" (253). Economic inequality shall be no reason to prevent somebody from becoming a people's representative. On the contrary, Wordsworth disparages the rich: "a people will not *immorally* hold out wealth as a criterion of integrity . . ." (I.38.282–83; my italics). He differs from Locke in not demanding a property qualification for holders of political office.[38] Wordsworth's ideal representative is the literate ordinary citizen, "the herdsman with the staff in one hand and the book in the other. . . ." (I.39.302–03. See also *Descriptive Sketches*, l. 533, GCL I:39.) Here Wordsworth's democratic sentiment is focused on the political emancipation of the common man, paralleled later (as in the *Lyrical Ballads*) by the poetic emancipation of the common man as a subject worthy of serious poetic treatment.

Liberty and democracy are implied in the discussion of Rousseau's General Will (I.39.320–24). The theory of the General Will supplies Wordsworth with the ammunition to attack the system of monarchical government: "Pure and universal representation, by which alone liberty can be secured, cannot . . . exist together with monarchy. It seems madness to expect a manifestation of the *general* will, at the same time that we allow to a *particular* will that weight, which it must obtain in all governments, that can . . . be called monarchical. . . ." (I.41.389–94; Wordsworth's italics.)[39] In an earlier passage (I.35.151–66) Wordsworth bases his praise of political liberty on Bishop Watson's assertion that man is only subject to that law which is expressed by the General Will. Wordsworth approves of Watson's previous support of the French, who destroyed "arbitrary power" in order to erect a "temple to liberty" (156), and rages against the bishop's now reproaching "a people for having imagined happiness and liberty more likely to flourish in the *open field* of a republic than under the *shade* of monarchy" (159–61; my italics). The contrast between "open field" and "shade" effectively

---

[38] For the parallel with *Droits de l'homme,* see Commentary to ll. 281–86 (*Prose Works* I, p. 58).

[39] I.46.567 ff. answer Bishop Watson's distortion of the General Will and demand universal suffrage (see also Owen and Smyser's Commentary to ll. 570–73). On Wordsworth's modification of Rousseau's General Will, see Chard, p. 93.

invokes the forces of light and darkness. (In other instances, e.g. I.39.295–96, Wordsworth refers to the "plain and open manner" of democratic government.) As earlier, here in connection with liberty, Wordsworth repeats his hyperbole of the twenty-five million Frenchmen and says that "they could have no security for their liberties under *any modification* of monarchical power. They have in consequence *unanimously* chosen a republic. You cannot but observe that they have only exercised that right in which by your own confession liberty essentially resides." (163–66; my italics.) This excerpt makes Wordsworth a political propagandist of the less agreeable kind, for the vote was far from universal: only five million Frenchmen were enfranchised, and of these only one million voted in the election of 1792 (*Prose Works* I, p. 55).[40] His strong opposition to monarchy does not permit "any modification" of that form of government, and one year later he still adheres to the same uncompromising attitude in his private correspondence (below, letter to Mathews of [8] June [1794]). For Wordsworth liberty and philosophy are "the eyes of the human race" (I.48.649). This strong metaphor links and strengthens his defence of "liberty and equality" (638–39 and 658; see also lines 402–03).

However, political equality for Wordsworth is not absolute. He acknowledges an "inevitable inequality" (408) as inherent in the nature of government which authorizes some people to command, but he enjoins "not to give greater force to such authority than is *essential* to its *due* execution" (410–11; my italics). This, and the suggestion of a rotation in office, witness to Wordsworth's political wisdom: "the person in whom authority has been lodged should occasionally descend to the level of private citizen . . ." (417–18; see also I.37.240–43). In accepting the economic inequality, "which always will attend superior talents and industry . . ." (427–28), Wordsworth does not deviate from the thought of the French Revolution whose primary aim was to establish political equality and abolish privileges enjoyed by the aristocracy. Seen against this background, Wordsworth's defence of "a more equal distribution" of Church property (122), his strongly worded attack on the higher clergy whose wealth he regards as "the rewards of their vices and their crimes" (145–46), and his advocacy of the redistribution of riches "to preserve from famine some thousands of curés . . . pining in villages unobserved by courts" (149–50) throw into focus his political radicalism.

In the "Letter" Wordsworth anticipates much of what was to be

---

[40] For Wordsworth's private opinion on the true state of affairs, see *E.Y.*, p. 70, and this chapter, n. 32.

written throughout the nineteenth and twentieth centuries about social and political reforms. He sees the "oppressive principle" in excessive wealth (435–36). These very words are still being used by some Socialists and Communists when pointing out the correlation between economic and political power in defending their "true" against western "formal" democracy. The "verbosity of unintelligible statutes" (618–19) hampers the citizens' equality before the law as it did in Wordsworth's day. In "A Letter to the Bishop of Llandaff" Wordsworth is radical all along: from a reform of the letter of the law to his condoning of regicide. In the latter respect he is more radical than Thomas Paine, who opposed the execution of Louis XVI. Owen and Smyser's Commentary to the "Letter" and some of my ensuing pages show that any evidence in England of sympathy with France after the beginning of hostilities in February 1793 was regarded as sedition. Seen against this background, Wordsworth emerges as a political extremist in the "Letter".

The only poem of socio-political significance between the composition of "A Letter to the Bishop of Llandaff" and the *Salisbury Plain* poems is the little piece "How Sweet to Walk along the Woody Steep"[41] (GCL I:43: "probably written between perhaps late June, more likely early July and late July or early August 1793"). This poem contrasts the beautiful peacefulness of a summer sunset at the seashore with the noisy interruption of that scene by the sunset cannon of the Navy, "at the sound [of which] / The star of life appears to set in blood, / And ocean shudders in offended mood, / Deepening with moral gloom his angry flood" (*PW* I, p. 308). These lines depict the gloomy ponderings of a young man who does not agree with the war his country is waging. For him his country's policy has turned the "star of life" (the sun) into the star of death. As will be seen, the sombre tone of "How Sweet to Walk" is also the predominant tone in *Salisbury Plain* (MS. 1).

Salisbury Plain

William Godwin's *An Enquiry Concerning Political Justice*[42] had been in print for over five months when Wordsworth, probably in late July

---

[41] de Selincourt (*PW* I, p. 307) entitles "At the Isle of Wight. 1793". In his Notes (ibid., p. 374) he calls the poem a "fragment", which is misleading for the following reasons: (1) the poem is not fragmentary in content; (2) it is not fragmentary in form, since it closes with three lines rhyming identically, not two; (3) it is not fragmentary in presentation in the MS [personal communication from Stephen Gill].

[42] For a summary of Godwin's philosophical system, see Chard, pp. 190ff. A possible influence of Godwin on Wordsworth has been debated since Hazlitt in his *Spirit of the Age*

1793, began to compose the major part of *Salisbury Plain* (MS. 1).[43] According to Reed (GCL I:45) the bulk of the composition was completed by 17 September. The difference between on the one hand the politically inflammatory "Letter to the Bishop of Llandaff" (written in the spring or summer of 1793) and the direct political statements of the second part of *Descriptive Sketches* (completed in the winter of 1792) and on the other hand *Salisbury Plain,* which does not propound any specific socio-political theories, is striking. This lack, however, does not make it less effective as a socio-political statement; on the contrary, the poem makes us understand the miserable social conditions of the England of the early 1790s.[44] It conveys an impression of reality similar to that conveyed by the prose account of Arthur Young's *Travels in France* (1792–94) which is concerned with the social and political conditions during the *ancien régime*.[45] The basis of both works is their authors' direct personal, deeply felt experience of and insight into the contemporary situation.

Wordsworth breaks with a generally accepted convention of the period, that of portraying the condition of prelapsarian man as a state of bliss. He reverses the tradition of primeval man's existence in a golden age, in the very opening of the poem: "Hard is the life when naked and unhouzed . . . [the] hungry savage . . . lifts his head in fear" (*Salisbury Plain Poems,* p. 21, st. 1).[46] To compare the afflicted man of the 1790s

---

(1825) regarded Wordsworth as a thorough Godwinian (see Ernest Bernbaum, James V. Logan, and Ford T. Swetnam, "Wordsworth", in *The English Romantic Poets: A Review of Research and Criticism,* ed. Frank Jordan, 3rd ed., New York: MLA, 1972, p. 97).

[43] For the social and political climate during the writing of *Salisbury Plain,* see this chapter, n. 27.

[44] "Wordsworth conceived in 'Salisbury Plain' a blistering attack on warring England, complementing his 'Letter to the Bishop of Llandaff'. . . . the focus of the poem's action is the meeting of two destitute travellers and the narration of the story of the Female Vagrant, but the poem's real energy is centered on the opening and closing [ll. 541–48] declamations in which Wordsworth examines and denounces feature after feature of contemporary life. Always the point of attack is the same. Wordsworth sees two nations, the privileged and protected and the victims. Both are in conflict so that the whole nation is threatened. The only hope is complete renewal." (Stephen Gill, "'Adventures on Salisbury Plain' and Wordsworth's Poetry of Protest 1795–97", *SIR*, 11 (1972), 48–65 (50).)

For further comments on Wordsworth's social protest and a comparison of *Salisbury Plain* with the "Old Cumberland Beggar", see Stephen Gill, "Wordsworth's Breeches Pocket: Attitudes to the Didactic Poet", *EIC,* 19 (1969), 385–401 (387, 399).

[45] Boulton, *The Language of Politics,* p. 177. However, it is noteworthy that Arthur Young adopted an anti-French attitude in a later pamphlet, *The Example of France, a Warning to Britain* (1793) (Boulton, p. 94).

[46] This and all subsequent references are to Stephen Gill, ed., *The Salisbury Plain Poems of William Wordsworth,* The Cornell Wordsworth (Ithaca, N.Y.: Cornell U.P., and Hassocks, Sussex: Harvester Press, 1975).

with the non-idealized prehistoric man is far more persuasive than to follow the usual poetic practice of idealizing him.[47] Although two basic needs—food and shelter—are not guaranteed in the life of Wordsworth's primeval man, he belongs to a community of

> ... men who *all* of his hard lot partake,
> Repose in the *same* fear, to the *same* toil awake[.]
> (st. 2; my italics)

However hard the lot of prehistoric man, "all" implies that all men share equally the adversities and hardships of existence; the state of equality is general. The reiteration of "same" in connection with "fear" and "toil" leaves no doubt that the burden is indeed the very same for all.

This universal equality, indicative of social justice, is contrasted with the inequality in contemporary society which is torn between rich and poor. The difference between the two groups is sharp:

> Of *those* who on the *couch* of Affluence rest
> By laughing Fortune's sparkling cup elate,
> While *we* of comfort reft, by pain depressed,
> No other pillow know than Penury's *iron breast*[.]
> (st. 3; my italics)

The construction "those who" particularizes and thereby singles out the rich; it also distances them, making them seem remote, lofty, and by extension indifferent. The contrast between the two groups is emphasized by "While" (as contrasting conjunction) and the opposing pairs of "those" ↔ "we" (the latter generalizes broadly) and "couch of Affluence" ↔ "Penury's iron breast". The pronoun "we" elicits a response of sympathetic identification with the poor, and the hard image of "Penury's iron breast" finally leaves no doubt as to the state of inequality and lack of brotherhood.

Whilst a few can enjoy refinement and luxury, the multitude is "Beset with foes more fierce than e'er assail" the savage of prehistoric times without any shelter "in winter's keenest gale" (st. 4). Stanzas 1–4 also suggest that the inequality of modern times has deprived man of his original state of human dignity.

Stanzas 1–4 deal with society in general. After this introduction our attention is focused on the fate of individuals in stanzas 5–44: first on the wanderer and then on both him and the female vagrant. This man and woman are representative for the mass of the poor. Wordsworth puts the technique of individualization to good use: as the poem progresses, our

---

[47] See also the contrast between sts. 48 and 49.

sympathy for the two increases. Wordsworth in *Salisbury Plain* is still employing Gothic phraseology. Its function, however, is not to produce goose flesh in the reader but to engender genuine pity, and this is relevant, for this kind of pity is most likely to lead to acts of reform. The comfort of brotherhood is absent in the stanzas dealing with the lonely wanderer on the plain: thirst, hunger, and exposure are his companions. The dark vocabulary depicting a desolate landscape underlines the dire state of the traveller. In stanza 16 he finds his first relief: "A human voice! and soon his terrors fled". Two strangers have met and we feel the comforting impact of brotherhood in the ensuing stanzas. Fellow feeling is also the undertone when the female vagrant tells the story of her life (sts. 26 ff.), illustrating thereby the many kinds of injustice in society: economic inequality in expelling a smallholder from his land (st. 29),[48] homelessness, and all the miseries that result from war. The scathing attack on the disruption of brotherhood in war—

> Better before proud Fortune's sumptuous car
> Obvious our dying bodies to obtrude,
> Than *dog-like* wading at the heels of War
> Protract a cursed existence with the *brood*
> That *lap,* their very nourishment, their *brother's blood.*
> (st. 35; my italics)

—evokes by contrast the existence of an opposite state of affairs, peace, in which brotherhood would find a more fertile soil. The disgust felt for the unnatural state of war is emphasized by the vocabulary. There can be no human brotherhood where men have given up their humane qualities: they become dehumanized. The vocabulary advances from "dog-like" (i.e. in the manner of animals) via "brood" as a contemptuous term for men, but here implying animals, to "lap" that connotes the greedy drinking of animals to, finally, lap "brother's blood", which is the peak of dehumanization.

As in stanza 35 so also in other parts of the poem (e.g. st. 43: "homeless near a thousand homes I stood, / And near a thousand tables pined and wanted food";[49] st. 49: "For want how many men and

---

[48] For "a story of local oppression, known to WW, in which an old couple are tyrannized because they will not sell a field to a local landowner", see Z. S. Fink, *The Early Wordsworthian Milieu* (Oxford, 1958), pp. 88–89 and 134–35 (quoted in Gill, *Salisbury Plain Poems,* p. 29). See also sections "Enclosure of Open Fields" and "Enclosure of Commons", in Kenneth MacLean, *Agrarian Age: A Background for Wordsworth* (1950; rpt. Archon Books, 1970), pp. 12–26. Yale Studies in English, vol. 115.

[49] On the effects of the loss of human ties, see also Jacobus, *Tradition and Experiment,* pp. 149–50.

children die?") the lack of brotherhood implies its contrary, a state of affairs where brotherhood is intact. The poet leaves no doubt about his solidarity with the lower ranks of society, for it is the "lowly cot" that extends the hand of hospitality. Stanzas 50, 57, 58, and 61 witness to Wordsworth's political insight: he refers to the colonization policies of the European powers, implying that they ought to redirect their efforts to rid themselves of their own domestic problems (st. 50); you cannot rule by force, and, further, long-term stability depends on the rules worked out by the "labours of the sage" (st. 57)[50]; stanza 58 reiterates the same theme, and moreover, where freedom of inquiry is abolished, "justice" becomes a mockery and the "law" has to punish those very crimes that were engendered by it. Stanzas 57 and 58 imply a government that enjoys the consent of the majority of people, consequently aiding indirectly the idea of political freedom.

1794

Letters to Mathews

Revisions on *An Evening Walk* and *Descriptive Sketches,* some work on *Salisbury Plain,* and the composition of "Inscription for a Seat by the Pathway Side Ascending to Windy Brow" (GCL I:46) are the small harvest of poetic creation that Reed can establish beyond any doubt for 1794.[51] The little, thoughtful "Inscription" poem appealing to our feelings of brotherhood for the aged and sick was probably composed a few days or weeks before Wordsworth wrote a letter on 23 May [1794] to William Mathews on the subject of their joint plan to bring out a monthly magazine (*E.Y.,* p. 118). This and the subsequent letters to William Mathews throw light on Wordsworth's socio-political thought in 1794.[52]

The May 1794 letter witnesses to how sensitive to political issues

---

[50] Line 5 (st. 57): Note that as early as 1793–94 Wordsworth adapts a whole line from a very famous sonnet of Milton ("On the Lord Gen. Fairfax at the Siege of Colchester", l. 10) (Gill, *Salisbury Plain Poems,* p. 37). Thereby Wordsworth invokes the greatest English poet who has dealt with the theme of liberty. See also de Selincourt (*PW* I, p. 341) who notes that the concluding stanzas of *Salisbury Plain* are "far more inspired by Milton's great political utterances in prose and verse than by Godwin".

[51] There is no evidence for Chard's assertion that the spring of 1794 was a fruitful creative period (Chard, p. 171).

[52] V. G. Kiernan, "Wordsworth and the People", in *Democracy and the Labour Movement: Essays in Honour of Dona Torr,* ed. John Saville (London: Lawrence & Wishart, 1954), p. 242, supplies a Marxist's interpretation of the May and June letters and regards Wordsworth's political views in 1794 as "very radical indeed". On the letters to Mathews, in particular the June 1794 letter, see Chard, pp. 179ff.

Wordsworth is; although only twenty-four years of age, he has no illusions about the difficulties of editing a monthly with another person. He realizes that major political differences would be detrimental to their common venture and consequently declares his political opinions and proposed editorial policy from the outset: "I solemnly affirm that in no writings of mine will I ever admit of any sentiment which can have the least tendency to induce my readers to suppose that the doctrines which are now enforced by banishment, imprisonment, &c, &c, are other than pregnant with every species of misery. You know perhaps already that I am of that odious class of men called democrats, and of that class I shall for ever continue. . . ." (*E.Y.*, p. 119.)

As he had done a little earlier in stanza 58 of *Salisbury Plain*, Wordsworth here too supports the right to dissent from the official "doctrines which are now enforced by banishment, imprisonment". Political liberty had become more endangered since the time when the bulk of *Salisbury Plain* was written.[53] The Habeas Corpus Act was suspended on 16 May 1794; the mail of reformers could be tampered with.[54] And if E. P. Thompson is right in assuming that Wordsworth was disinclined to express his radical political opinions in letters,[55] the fact that he called himself a "democrat" in 1794 means that he belonged to the "Reds" of his time. Some of Wordsworth's relatives must have had cause to worry about the young radical in their midst, for Dorothy Wordsworth finds it necessary to reassure Richard Wordsworth on their brother William's "caution about expressing his political opinions. He is very cautious and seems well aware of the dangers of a contrary conduct" (letter of 28 May [1794]; *E.Y.*, p. 121). I think Dorothy Wordsworth was wrong in her assumption. In 1794 Wordsworth's relationship with her was probably not so close that he would share his radical political beliefs with her; and if he were to have burdened her woman's world with the radical politics of a man's world, Dorothy's words would be a good defence of her

---

[53] Thomas Hardy, originator and secretary of the London Corresponding Society, had been arrested for treasonable practices on 12 May 1794, and a few days later John Horne Tooke and John Thelwall, members of the Society, had been committed to the Tower on charges of high treason (*E.Y.*, p. 119n.).

[54] John Thelwall, a Jacobin, enjoined a correspondent in Mar. 1794, "Seal your letters first with a wafer, & then some good wax over it". "Get good wax! get *good* wax! When rogues & robbers are in authority every man ought to keep a good lock upon his door." Quoted by E. P. Thompson, "Disenchantment or Default? A Lay Sermon", in *Power and Consciousness*, eds. C. C. O'Brien and W. D. Vanech (London and New York: © New York University, 1969), p. 155. Italics in Thompson. On Thelwall, see also below, pp. 67 and 78–79.

[55] Thompson, "Disenchantment or Default?", pp. 154–55.

brother's views against more conservative opinions. Richard Wordsworth's view is probably more trustworthy; as a lawyer he thought it was essential for Wordsworth to be "cautious in writing or expressing [his] political opinions" (Richard to William Wordsworth on 23 May 1794, *E.Y.*, p. 121, note). William's independent spirit did not heed the warnings of his more experienced brother. In a long letter of [8] June [1794] to Mathews,[56] Wordsworth spells out his political opinions. He begins with an attack on the forces that hamper political and other kinds of equality:

I disapprove of monarchical and aristocratical governments, however modified. Hereditary distinctions and privileged orders of every species . . . must necessarily counteract the progress of human improvement: hence it follows that I am not amongst the admirers of the British constitution. . . . (*E.Y.*, pp. 123–24.)

He is uncompromising in his opposition to any form of government, "however modified", whose members hold office by virtue of their birth. His demand for equality is absolute and does not allow any hereditary distinctions and privileged orders in his concept of government, for "*every* species" [my italics] of their kind "necessarily" hampers human improvement.

Although radical in the context of 1794, the tone of this letter is not nearly so inflammatory as the scathing indictment of the monarchy and aristocracy a year earlier in "A Letter to the Bishop of Llandaff". Even bearing in mind that his reply to Bishop Watson's Appendix was intended for publication and is therefore an expression of Wordsworth's public voice, it is worth noting that now, in this letter to Mathews, Wordsworth condemns severely what he had practised in "A Letter to the Bishop of Llandaff", namely "all inflammatory addresses to the passions of men, even when [they are] intended to direct those passions to a good purpose" (*E.Y.*, p. 125). This letter is free from political rhetoric; it is an accurate and detailed transmission of Wordsworth's political thought. The careful phrasing in the following instance witnesses to Wordsworth's growing political awareness; although he opposes the British Constitution and those political organizations that inhibit the general implementation of liberty, equality, fraternity, and democracy, his politi-

---

[56] This letter is more radical in tone than his May letter and may be Wordsworth's reaction against the conservative panic and repression of radicals in May 1794. Harper I, p. 318, for example, instances the persecution of Thelwall in the same month. See also n. 53, above. On the repression of radicalism in 1793–94, see further Carl B. Cone, *The English Jacobins: Reformers in Late 18th Century England* (New York: Charles Scribner's, 1968), pp. 150–51, and above, Introduction, n. 1.

cal insight makes him remark cautiously: "The destruction of those institutions which I condemn appears to me to be hastening on too rapidly. I recoil from the bare idea of a revolution . . ." (*E.Y.*, p. 124). Wordsworth favours an orderly dissolution of the established political institutions; he disapproves of the process "hastening on too rapidly"; hastening implies a want of deliberation that entails the impossibility of reflection.[57] This is very different from the vein of *Descriptive Sketches* (comp. 1791–92), where liberty is born "from th' innocuous flames" of war (*PW* I, p. 88, l. 782), and from "A Letter to the Bishop of Llandaff", where liberty, "in order to reign in peace must establish herself by violence . . ." (*Prose Works* I, p. 33). The revolutionist of 1792–93 is, in 1794, gradually turning into a political evolutionist. He shrinks from the idea of a revolution; the revolution is a "dreadful event" and ought to be discouraged by those who have the "welfare of mankind" at heart (*E.Y.*, p. 124).

It may be a coincidence that Wordsworth in the comparatively long "Letter to the Bishop of Llandaff" does not once use the combination "welfare of mankind" (from the discussion of the "Letter" we have seen that "bulk of mankind" and "mass of mankind" are his favourite expressions there); if so, it is a significant coincidence, since "welfare of mankind" occurs three times in the June letter to Mathews. The quantitative "bulk" and "mass" of the human brotherhood appears to have given way to the quality of happiness and well-being implied in joining "welfare" to mankind. This notion of "welfare of mankind" is incompatible with revolutionary enthusiasm; Wordsworth's genuine feelings of brotherhood favour "a gradual and constant reform" and only when that fails does a "revolution" become "desirable" (June letter, *E.Y.*, p. 124). Most critics overlook that Wordsworth does concede a revolution as a last resort.[58]

We discern Wordsworth's wish to advance general socio-political rules, i.e. those that are "applicable to all times and to all places".[59] For him these "general principles" safeguard political liberty from the danger of despotism and "if a revolution must afflict us, they alone can mitigate its horrors and establish freedom with tranquillity". Most conducive to the well-being of the body politic are "those doctrines which

---

[57] For Wordsworth's notion of "wise passiveness", see ch. 3, n. 30.
[58] It is therefore wrong to say that "in the middle of his supposedly radical period, Wordsworth displayed his natural timidity or conservatism" (Charles W. Roberts, "Wordsworth, *The Philanthropist*, and *Political Justice*", *SP*, 31 (1934), 84–91 (91)).
[59] For Wordsworth's concern with generality, see passages referred to in my Index.

long and severe meditation[60] has taught them [good men] are essential to the welfare of mankind" (*E.Y.*, pp. 124-25). Wordsworth realizes that the freedom of the press is the basis of all other liberties in a modern society:

Freedom of inquiry is *all* that I wish for; let *nothing* be deemed *too sacred* for investigation; rather than restrain the liberty of the press I would suffer the most atrocious doctrines to be recommended: let the field be *open* and *unencumbered,* and truth must be victorious. (*E.Y.*, p. 125; my italics.)

The tone of the passage is modern: the human rights embodied in liberty, equality, fraternity cannot be furthered or defended without the freedom of intellectual inquiry in all spheres of life. The italicized words in the excerpt bring out some of the stylistic means Wordsworth employs to convey the idea of liberty about which he feels so deeply. He suggests to Mathews that their monthly should cover the biographies of those who have exerted themselves in the cause of liberty, namely Turgot, Milton, Sidney, Machiavelli, and Beccaria,[61] and a few lines further down he hopes to find supporters for the intended periodical "amongst the dispassionate advocates of liberty and discussion . . ." (*E.Y.*, p. 126). The qualifying "dispassionate" is an example of Wordsworth's keen political insight, for the freedom of inquiry implied by the phrase will lead to real progress only when the discussion is conducted dispassionately. His qualification suggests that purely revolutionary fervour or solely the will to liberty are not sufficient. Undoubtedly the events of the French Revolution and the political climate in Britain make him stress the importance of calm and impartiality implied by "dispassionate".

The title Wordsworth suggested for the journal, "The Philanthropist, a monthly Miscellany", speaks for what he felt and wanted to do. The dictionary definition of "philanthropist", "one who from love of his fellow-men exerts himself for their well-being" (*OED*), is to some extent true of the Wordsworth of 1794, for in his case the notion of brotherhood extends beyond the British Isles: he sympathizes with the spirit of national liberty in Poland and wants to allocate space in the "Philanthropist" for an "accurate account of the Polish revolution" (*E.Y.*, p. 128). In an earlier letter to Mathews (17 February [1794]) he was likewise concerned with political liberty abroad, namely in Portugal (*E.Y.*, p. 113).

---

[60] Wordsworth's demands for "severe meditation" in the field of social and political legislation are paralleled by what he demands of the poet in the Preface to the *Lyrical Ballads:* "habits of meditation", "emotion recollected in tranquillity", the capacity to think "long and deeply".

[61] For their works, see *E.Y.*, pp. 125-26, n. 3.

"The Philanthropist" did not materialize. Wordsworth's next letter to William Mathews (7 November 1794) affirms Wordsworth's sense of brotherhood in practice: most of his time was spent nursing his friend Calvert. He was longing to go to London, and now that he could not propagate his social and political ideas in a publication of his own, he was determined to fight for political reform on an "opposition paper, for really I cannot in *conscience* and in principle, abet in the *smallest degree* the measures pursued by the present ministry. They are already so deeply advanced in iniquity that like Macbeth they cannot retreat" (*E.Y.*, p. 135; my italics). The phrasing of these sentences reveals how deeply concerned he is with the desperateness of the situation (underlined by the allusion to Macbeth) and how much he wishes to align himself with the forces of the opposition. However, this seems to be the first instance in which Wordsworth does not condemn those who have gone over to the Government's side: "I am far from reprobating those whose sentiments on this point differ from my own; I know that many good men were persuaded of the expediency of the present war . . ." (*E.Y.*, p. 135). Here Wordsworth shows that he has become tolerant, and by implication he now writes as though he were a democrat in the western twentieth-century meaning of the word, namely embracing pluralism. He hopes that his cousin Myers "continues a patriot[62] of unabated energy" (*E.Y.*, p. 135), i.e. a republican who believes in the brotherhood of man. The tone of this letter is subdued; politically the letter is comparatively moderate. The accumulated atrocities in France and especially the very recent French campaign of conquest against the Netherlands in October 1794 probably dampened Wordsworth's sympathy with the French Republic.

In his letter of [24 December 1794] to Mathews, Wordsworth rejoices over the release of the political prisoners Hardy, Tooke, and Thelwall. But he has become sceptical about the motives of Tooke. Tooke does not come up to the high moral standards that Wordsworth demands of his champions of liberty. Wordsworth's political shrewdness is developing: he distinguishes between the political activist "swayed by personal considerations" (*E.Y.*, p. 137) and his counterpart who is an altruistic instrument of public good. In the June letter (*E.Y.*, pp. 123–24) Wordsworth had belittled the British Constitution. On Christmas Eve 1794,

---

[62] For the meaning "republican" of the word "patriot" in the 1790s, see Carl Woodring, *Politics in the Poetry of Coleridge* (Madison: Univ. of Wisconsin Press, 1961), p. 88. The *OED* instances under "patriot" a sarcastic quotation from the *Anti-Jacobin* of 1798 which illustrates the international connotation: "A steady patriot of the world alone, The friend of every country—but his own."

referring to the acquittal of Hardy, Tooke, and Thelwall, he concedes that this same constitution "contains parts upon which too high a value cannot be set", implying that it safeguards even the civil liberties of men who propagate doctrines unpalatable to the privileged: "To every class of men occupied in the correction of abuses it must be an animating reflection that their exertions, so long as they are temperate will be countenanced and protected by the good sense of the country." (*E.Y.*, p. 137.)

In this chapter we have noted the idea of liberty and its correlation with equality and fraternity in Wordsworth's earliest poems. We have found direct references to political theory—especially political and national liberty—in the second part of *Descriptive Sketches* (comp. 1791–92). The radicalism in the poetry in *Descriptive Sketches* corresponds to the subversive ideas in the prose of "A Letter to the Bishop of Llandaff" (comp. 1793) where we have seen Wordsworth emerging as a more extreme revolutionary than Thomas Paine himself. The letters to Mathews (comp. 1794) have revealed Wordsworth's gradual move from radicalism (summer 1794) to less revolutionary points of view in the winter of 1794. The political moderation that Wordsworth had shown in an early letter to Mathews (19 May [1792]) was very much the exception.

My examination of the early text of *Salisbury Plain* (MS. 1) has shown that as early as 1793, roughly contemporaneous with "A Letter to the Bishop of Llandaff", Wordsworth's political ideas were expressed implicitly. In 1793–94 the prose is overtly radical, whereas in the poetry the political theory is implicit. We must thus distinguish between Wordsworth the overtly political propagandist and the poet whose political commitment is indirect. Hence although the letters to Mathews come chronologically after *Salisbury Plain*, the link with most of the next chapter is the politically indirect *Salisbury Plain*. Between 1791 and 1794 Wordsworth's emphasis is, except in *Salisbury Plain,* first on liberty, second on equality, and to a minor extent on brotherhood. As will be seen, this order is reversed in 1795–97.

CHAPTER 2

1795–1797

1795–96

Adventures on Salisbury Plain

In the autumn of 1795 Wordsworth revised *Salisbury Plain* (MS. 1) extensively. This resulted in MS. 2, *Adventures on Salisbury Plain* (identical with GCL I:45c),[1] which according to Wordsworth "may be looked on almost as another work . . .".[2] A comparison between its socio-political commitment and that of *Salisbury Plain* brings out a significant difference: in *Adventures on Salisbury Plain* Wordsworth is no longer overtly concerned with international issues. This difference is worth pointing out, since Gill (above, ch. 1, n. 44) and others concentrate so much on the indictment of the condition of England in *Salisbury Plain*—admittedly the most important aspect of the poem—but in doing so they overlook Wordsworth's implied appeal for universal freedom and an end to slavery ("The nations, though at home in bonds . . .", *SP*, st. 50) and universal political liberty and international peace ("Say, rulers of the nations, from the sword / Can ought but murder, pain, and tears proceed?", *SP*, st. 57). This mission to save the whole human race—so characteristic of the thought of the French Revolution—is absent in *Adventures on Salisbury Plain*. Had Wordsworth been one of the writers in 1795 who reflected closely the radical ideas of the period, his radicalism would perhaps have been as transparent and direct as that in this topical piece by J. Samson on the golden age of liberty and equality supposedly realized in the United States:

---

[1] This title is used in Gill, *Salisbury Plain Poems*. My quotations from *Adventures on Salisbury Plain* are drawn from this edition. I base my chronological arrangement on the evidence of Stephen Gill: "the 1795 poem is now lost to us, there is no doubt that substantially, if not in every detail, it has survived in the poem in MS. 2 . . ." (*Salisbury Plain Poems*, p. 12). The composition of the poem between the autumn of 1795 and spring 1796 seems the likeliest. This date differs from Reed's who classifies the work between April 1799–June 1800 (GCL I:45c).
 I shall not deal with passages in *Adventures on Salisbury Plain* (except st. 34) that are similar or identical with portions of *Salisbury Plain*.

[2] William Wordsworth to the Revd. Francis Wrangham, 20 Nov. [1795], *E.Y.*, p. 159.

> There social order first began
> And man was reverenc'd as man.
> All were obedient, all were free,
> And GOD's own law—equality—
> Dispensed its blessings with a lib'ral hand,
> And banished vile oppression from the land.[3]

In January 1795 French troops overran Holland, in April there were bread riots in Paris. In June Luxembourg capitulated to the French, in July Spain made peace with France, and in October Poland lost its national liberty, suffering its third partition by Prussia, Austria, and Russia. These examples may illustrate that there would have been plenty of current international material to depict; but perhaps these very events contributed to make Wordsworth despair of radical political solutions.

Literature had become a vehicle to advocate socio-political ideas. One of Wordsworth's contemporaries, for instance, fears the impact of the novelists Mrs. Charlotte Smith and Mrs. Inchbald on young female readers whose "heads turn wild with impossible adventures, *and now and then are tainted with democracy*".[4] Coleridge's radical socio-political outlook in 1795 was more public than Wordsworth's: he delivered a series of political lectures and published some of them, for example, *The Plot Discovered* and *Conciones ad Populum*.[5] Coleridge's anti-war and anti-Pitt attitude is pronounced in these lectures.[6] In 1795 Joseph Fawcett, a radical and pacifist preacher, published *The Art of War*, which

---

[3] Quoted by Brinton, *The Political Ideas of the English Romanticists*, p. 26, from J. Samson, *Oppression, or the Abuse of Power* . . . (1795); small capitals in Brinton. The reality was different; in 1793 the U.S. had passed a law compelling the return of fugitive slaves to their owners.

[4] Quoted by Brinton, *The Political Ideas of the English Romanticists*, p. 42, from T. Mathias, *Pursuits of Literature* (1794–97). The italics are in Brinton. On the novels of protest and egalitarianism of the period 1794–96 in general, see Brinton's discussion (ibid., pp. 33–36) on the works of T. Holcroft (*The Adventures of Hugh Trevor*, 1794; *Letter to Windham*, 1795), R. Bage (*Hermsprong, or Man as he is not*, 1796), and Mrs. Elizabeth Inchbald (*Nature and Art*, 1796). For more recent work on the Jacobin novel, see Marilyn Butler, *Jane Austen and the War of Ideas* (Oxford: Clarendon Press, 1975), especially pp. 29–87.

[5] Wordsworth may have seen Coleridge for the first time in the autumn of 1795, but "only a little" (Reed I, p. 173). The earliest direct correspondence between Wordsworth and Coleridge took place between Mar. and May 1796 (Reed I, p. 179). For the lectures, see [S. T. Coleridge,] *Lectures 1795 on Politics and Religion*, eds. Lewis Patton and Peter Mann, The Collected Works of Samuel Taylor Coleridge, vol. I (London: Routledge & Kegan Paul, and Princeton, N.J.: Princeton U.P., 1971).

[6] On Coleridge's admiration for the English Republicans and for the dissenters, see Chard, pp. 223–24, which includes a useful footnote on studies dealing with Coleridge's political thought; on his political thought in 1798 and later, consult also *Essays on His Times* (I and III), ed. David V. Erdman, The Collected Works of Samuel Taylor Coleridge (London: Routledge & Kegan Paul, and Princeton, N.J.: Princeton U.P., 1978).

possibly influenced Wordsworth.[7] In 1798 Fawcett commented that his anti-war poem "was neither a simple attempt to amuse the fancy nor to soothe the heart, but an indignant endeavour to tear away the splendid disguise which it has been the business of poets in all nations and ages to throw over the most odious and deformed of all the practices by which the annals of what is called civilized society have been disgraced" (quoted by Harper I, p. 262). This remark could equally well apply to *Adventures on Salisbury Plain*.

As will be shown in the following pages, *Adventures on Salisbury Plain* is the first poem in which Wordsworth appeals more to brotherhood than equality and liberty. Wordsworth's love of man begins to focus on the life of the human individual as seen against the background of an era of wars and social injustice. The first stanza introduces a recurrent motif of the poem: naked unrelieved poverty. The opening lines evoke the question of what is wrong with a society in which an old man, a former soldier, handicapped by disease, his "feet half bare; / Propp'd on a trembling staff . . ." should, despite the pain he experiences, try to cross Salisbury Plain alone, an enterprise demanding a good physique even in a young man. Stanza 2 intensifies the dire state of the old man. Here as well as in stanza 1—and often elsewhere in the poem—the diction is not accusatory, but the vocabulary of factual description points over and over again to the misery caused by the rich and powerful. The natural brotherhood between individuals, here expressed by the younger wanderer's friendly spontaneity, "Come, I am strong and stout, come lean on me" (st. 2), becomes one of Wordsworth's most important themes as the poem progresses. The inn on the wanderers' way has no "board inscribed the needy to allure, / The grapes hung glittering at the gilded door" (st. 4). Hospitality is not extended to those who have fought the wars of the "haves". The truly needy are the young sailor and old soldier who cannot afford to travel in a carriage. The situation of the impoverished ex-servicemen as such is indictment enough; the alliteration in the key line, "grapes, glittering, gilded", impresses on us the contrast between the state of the poor and the luxury of the affluent. Wordsworth does not use a single denouncing word in this stanza, and yet he fully succeeds in bringing the injustice of the state of England to our hearts. The impact of the sailor's brotherly

---

[7] Wordsworth listened to some of Joseph Fawcett's sermons in the winter of 1792–93 (Reed I, p. 138). Harper I, pp. 262–63, deals with the egalitarian (i.e. Godwinian) element in Fawcett. For the influence of *The Art of War* on *Adventures on Salisbury Plain*, see this chapter, n. 15.

act—securing the old man a lift—is noticeable in both the old, who "trembled with delight", and the young, "self-satisfied" (st. 5). The mutual brotherly acts of the common people (including the postboy) have restored hope. The brotherhood that ought to be between all groups of society exists at least among the lower orders.

The life history of the sailor (sts. 9 ff.) is also a part of English social history. After two hard years away from his wife his longing for sexual union with her is strong. Wordsworth's portrayal of a downright healthy sexuality ("enflamed with long desire", etc.) is effective, and remarkable, since he does not often deal with sex in his poetry. The sailor's dreams of love and family life are thwarted by another evil of the times: the sailor is pressed into the Navy.[8] For him and many able-bodied lower-class men personal liberty was an abstract concept only. After years in the war he dreams a second time of domestic bliss. He claims his bounty for the "work of carnage", the "bloody prize of victory" (Wordsworth's strong disapproval of that denial of brotherhood, war, comes across in linking bounty with "bloody") but is cheated of this pay:

> He urged his claim; the slaves of Office spurn'd
> The unfriended claimant; at their door he stood
> In vain . . .
>
> (st. 11)

To label those who contemptuously rejected the sailor's claim as "slaves" of office underlines the injustice; one could imagine "spurning" between equals or between master and slave. The image, however, of a "slave" spurning a serviceman's claims is outrageous but appropriate, since the officials have surrendered to a despotic system their independent right to do good. Recourse to the law would have been unsuccessful. By "unfriended claimant" Wordsworth implies that his rightful claim would have had a chance of success if the sailor had had influential friends. In the letter to William Mathews of December 1794, in connection with the release of Hardy, Tooke, and Thelwall (above, ch. 1), Wordsworth expressed more hope for equality before the law. Then he believed that under British justice "neither the violence, nor the art, of power can crush even an *unfriended individual,* though engaged in the propagation of doctrines confessedly unpalatable to privilege . . ." (*E.Y.,* p. 137; my italics). In *Adventures on Salisbury Plain,* on the other

---

[8] For the lawless recruiting methods of the period, see S. Maccoby, *English Radicalism 1786–1832: From Paine to Cobbett* (London: George Allen & Unwin, 1955), p. 84.

hand, Wordsworth denounces the inequality in the administration of justice. The sailor's prospect of richly rewarding his family for years of deprivation and frustration is spoiled. He cannot fulfil the most basic needs of his family: he bears to "those he loved nor warmth nor food" (st. 11). The diction of these central lines is simple and direct, "He met a traveller, robb'd him, shed his blood" (st. 11). No gory details—as otherwise in the convention of the period—surround the murder. The accumulation of injustices has driven the sailor to commit unpremeditated murder;[9] he is one of a "numerous class of mankind . . . held down in a state of abject penury" who "are continually prompted by disappointment and distress to commit violence upon their more fortunate neighbours".[10]

However mitigating the circumstances of the sailor's accidental killing, murder is the most serious sin against brotherhood, and in a majority of cases the effect on the human mind is catastrophic.[11] Murder rends the bond of brotherhood that unites all men, and the violator of that bond becomes isolated. This mental isolation and subsequent torment is brought out in stanzas 12–21; the dark vocabulary depicting an unpopulated and bleak landscape reflects the state of the sailor-murderer's mind. Nothing evokes the notion of human brotherhood, "No swinging sign creak'd from its cottage elm / . . . / No gypsey cowr'd o'er fire of furze or broom; / No labourer watch'd his red kiln glaring bright, / Nor taper glimmer'd dim from sick man's room" (st. 20). Although the sailor-murderer is on the run and although his mind is estranged, he is glad "at length to find a place / That bore of *human* hands the chearing

---

[9] Mary Moorman thinks that Wordsworth created in the character of the sailor "as perfect an example as he could of Godwin's theory that a man's good dispositions may, under the pressure of external circumstances, lead him into crime. . . ." (Moorman I, p. 262; see pp. 262–63 for other instances of Godwin's impact and for the personal acquaintance between Wordsworth and Godwin.) Both Stephen Gill, " 'Adventures on Salisbury Plain' and Wordsworth's Poetry of Protest 1795–97", *SIR*, 11 (1972), 48–65 (56–57), and Sheats, *The Making of Wordsworth's Poetry*, p. 109, reach similar conclusions. They back up their argument with Godwin's *Caleb Williams* (1794) and Gill adds Coleridge's *Conciones ad Populum* (1795). Chard on the other hand thinks that Godwin epitomized the liberal thought of the time and doubts the direct influence of Godwin's *Political Justice* on Wordsworth (Chard, pp. 189–90, 202–05). Thompson, "Disenchantment or Default?", pp. 150–51, feels that too much attention has been paid to the impact of Godwinism and not enough to Wordsworth's actual lived historical experience.

[10] William Godwin, *An Enquiry Concerning Political Justice* (1793), vol. I, p. 9. On similar lines, see also Holcroft's *The Adventures of Hugh Trevor* (1794), quoted in Brinton, *The Political Ideas of the English Romanticists*, p. 36.

[11] Jacobus, *Tradition and Experiment*, p. 155, comments on the "remarkable insight into the psychology of guilt . . ." of *Adventures on Salisbury Plain* and discusses Wordsworth's source for the sailor-murderer.

trace" (st. 22; my italics). The sailor-murderer's mental torment could have led to his withdrawing into himself, but the feelings for brotherhood implied by his happiness at discovering traces of human activity are stronger than the tormenting forces which pull him away from mankind. The essential goodness of the sailor-murderer is gradually built up by showing his spontaneous warm-hearted acts towards his fellow-men and introducing people's comments on his good character. He renders assistance to the old soldier (sts. 2 and 5); he is gentle (st. 29) and attentive (st. 63) towards the female vagrant; he rages against child battering (sts. 69 ff.); and he indicts especially inhumanity and propagates brotherhood (st. 74). One comment by the sailor-murderer's wife may suffice to illustrate the way Wordsworth brings out the good nature of the sailor: "he was kind and good; / Never on earth was milder creature seen; / He'd not have robb'd the raven of its food" (st. 85).

The gradual heightening of the sailor-murderer's good qualities throws into sharp focus the injustices committed against him. The impression is created that he of all people ought to have fared better. Wordsworth uses the same method to emphasize the integrity of the female vagrant's father (st. 31). Although he is honest and a "good and pious man", he is expelled from his little plot of land by the tyranny of a landlord. When the old father fights for the little economic freedom inherent in his old hereditary nook, he encounters the same inequality in the law as the sailor-murderer (sts. 34–36).

The socio-political circumstances of contemporary economic oppression are dealt with in greater detail in *Adventures on Salisbury Plain* than in the equivalent stanza 29 of *Salisbury Plain*. The circumstances of the old father's active resistance against eviction and of the landlord's manipulation of the law are new in the expanded version. There is as well poetic improvement between the earlier and later poem in handling the note of social protest. A juxtaposition of the opening of stanza 29 (*Şalisbury Plain*) with the beginning of stanza 34 (*Adventures on Salisbury Plain*) will illustrate the point:

> "The suns of eighteen summers danced along
> Joyous as in the pleasant morn of May.
> At last by cruel chance and *wilful wrong*
> My father's substance fell into decay.
> *Oppression trampled* on his tresses grey
>
>   (*SP*; my italics)

> "The suns of twenty summers danced along,—
> Ah! little marked, how fast they rolled away:

300   Then rose a mansion proud *our* woods among,
        And cottage after cottage owned its sway,
        No joy to see a neighbouring house . . .
                                    the master took[.]
                                    (*ASP*; my italics)

The excerpt from *Adventures on Salisbury Plain* contains no accusatory vocabulary. The social injustice is made plain by contrasting "summers danced along" with "rose a mansion proud", suggesting the sudden springing up of an alien object in "*our* woods". "Mansion" evokes the power and influence of a lord or large landowner that cannot be gainsaid. The phrasing is matter of fact; this enables us to ponder the injustice of the situation instead of indulging our feelings in a revolutionary vocabulary. Only the inversions in lines 300 and 303 mar the poetic quality.

Stanza 50 depicting the horrors of war is also new. As elsewhere, the vivid description of the chaos of war implies its opposite, a state of brotherhood. Wordsworth is particularly concerned with the very innocent victims of war: ". . . Murder, by the ghastly gleam, and Rape / Seized their joint prey, the mother and the child!" The monstrous situation is underlined by adding definite articles to the collocation "mother and child" that usually stands without them. The story of the female vagrant illustrates the miseries of war and social injustice. The female vagrant does not find food and shelter among the members of civilized society, some of whom are responsible for war and the resulting social misery. Those whom established justice regards with suspicion, the wild gipsies, "saw me weep, my fate enquired, / And gave me food, and rest, more welcome, more desired" (st. 56); they practised the law of brotherhood, as it ought to be practised in any healthy society or community. The speed and matter-of-factness of the lines suggest with what little fuss help was rendered immediately. The fact that Wordsworth chooses gipsies to perform kindly acts proves once more his democratic sentiment and, in a modern interpretation, his advocacy of racial equality. Amongst the group of gipsies "all belonged to all, and each was chief" (st. 57). This entails a state of economic and political equality. (Cf. the general equality in *SP*, st. 2.)

The inn for the rich had not extended its hospitality to the sailor and old man (st. 4). This can be contrasted with the welcoming atmosphere of the rustic inn, where "lustily the master carved the bread, / Kindly the housewife press'd, and they in comfort fed" (st. 76).[12] The female

---

[12] Seen in its historical context, the generosity is particularly impressive. See, e.g., Thompson, *The Making of the English Working Class*, pp. 70–73, on the bread riots of 1795. See also "The Baker's Cart" below, GCL I:55.

vagrant and sailor-murderer find "Comfort by prouder mansions unbestow'd". The line is typical of the early Wordsworth. It links the practice of brotherhood with simple, unassuming people who extend a homely welcome to the victims of war and social oppression. Although charity is the duty of all and was practised by all classes, Wordsworth keeps upper-class benevolence out of *Adventures on Salisbury Plain*. In 1795-96 his heroes are mostly drawn from the lower strata of society, where oppression creates social cohesion among the oppressed.[13] This is not always the case, but in a sound society under duress mutual brotherhood develops, and Wordsworth endeavours to show how some of the poor help each other to relieve the misery inflicted on them by the ruling class. When the innkeeper's wife hears of the poor sick woman outside her house, her immediate reaction is to thank God for her own comparatively adequate situation and to help the woman: "I have a house that I can call my own; / Nor shall she perish there [in the road], untended and alone!" (st. 80). The poor wretch shall not be "alone". During her last hours she shall have the human warmth and rest of which the harsh poor laws have deprived her. According to these laws she is entitled to relief only in her own parish and in consequence—irrespective of her illness—she is "carried back from stage to stage" (st. 82).[14] Wordsworth attacks this kind of legislation, since it is in conflict with the spirit of brotherhood. Brotherhood had become a legal abstraction, whereas Wordsworth emphasizes actions based on feeling.

The sailor-murderer confesses to his dying wife. His sensitivity, sincerity, resignation, and relief are brought out in stanzas 86-88 and 91. He gives himself up to the law that is supposed to uphold the brotherhood between all men, but as the poem has shown, the powerful and influential direct it against human dignity. Miscarriage of justice (not the law as

---

[13] The political repression is mirrored by the introduction of "the treasonable practices bill" in 1795 which "extended the crime of treason to spoken and written words not followed by any overt act, and created a new crime by subjecting to heavy penalties any one convicted of inciting others to hatred of the sovereign or the established government . . . the seditious meetings bill [also 1795] forbade all political meetings of which notice had not previously been given by resident householders, and empowered any two justices to dissolve a legally constituted meeting at their discretion by using the riot act. Both these measures were grievous encroachments on liberty" (William Hunt, *The History of England,* London: Longman, 1930, vol. X, p. 379).

[14] For the terrible consequences of this law, see an instance in John Langhorne's *Country Justice* (1774-77), quoted by Roger Sharrock, "Wordsworth and John Langhorne's 'The Country Justice'", *N&Q*, N.S., 1 (July 1954), 302-04. In the same place Sharrock discusses the influence of *The Country Justice* on Wordsworth. For a comparison between *Adventures on Salisbury Plain* and *The Country Justice*, see also Jacobus, *Tradition and Experiment,* pp. 144-46.

such) is partly responsible for the sailor's crime, and now that law which for him has meant injustice deals the stroke that ends for ever his mental torment. Justice has been "violated" (st. 91); this is strong language but appropriate in a poem where justice and the law never coincide. Mary Moorman says that *Adventures on Salisbury Plain* "is the bitterest, most unsparing indictment of social injustice that [Wordsworth] ever wrote . . ." (Moorman I, p. 295).

Throughout the poem Wordsworth is interested in demonstrating what links even a man like the sailor to humankind.[15] Wordsworth indicts the ignorant crowd who exclude the sailor from the human brotherhood without reflecting on the causes of his crime (st. 92). Wordsworth does not simplify. Having depicted the best qualities and mutual self-help of the lower classes, he now shows their prejudice in this final stanza:

> . . . dissolute men, unthinking and untaught,
> Planted their festive booths beneath his face;
> And to that spot, which idle thousands sought,
> Women and children were by fathers brought[.]

As he later wants to purge the middle classes of their disgust for idiot children (cf. "The Idiot Boy", below, GCL I:67) he now feels it necessary to combat lower-class prejudice. In *Adventures on Salisbury Plain* the reformation of "unthinking and untaught" men into thinking and taught men is for Wordsworth as important as the transformation of inequality before the law into equality. Although *Adventures on Salisbury Plain* is bitter and unsparing in its social criticism, its political tone is not in the least revolutionary. It does not propound any wholesale political solutions. In the *Descriptive Sketches* of 1792 Wordsworth thought that progress could be achieved by the fire and sword of the war of liberty. Now he concentrates on the terrible consequences of war and how the lack of liberty, equality, and brotherhood destroys individuals and that cornerstone of society, the family. *Adventures on Salisbury Plain,* unlike the terror-invoking tradition of the period, evokes the pity which perhaps makes a moral regeneration of the whole body politic possible. The final stanza shows the blindness of untaught men, but the literacy of the smallholder and his daughter,

---

[15] For an incisive comparison between Joseph Fawcett's *Art of War* (1795) and *Adventures on Salisbury Plain* that brings out the element of brotherhood in Wordsworth's poem, see Stephen Gill, "'Adventures on Salisbury Plain' and Wordsworth's Poetry of Protest 1795–97", *SIR*, 11 (1972), 48–65 (62). In the same article (pp. 62–65) Gill deals with the similarities between *Caleb Williams* (1794) and *Adventures on Salisbury Plain* with particular attention to the importance of the bond between man and man "independent of all sanctions of law, authority and the state . . ." (p. 62).

> I read, and loved the books in which I read;
> For books in every neighbouring house I sought,
> And nothing to my mind a sweeter pleasure brought
>
> (st. 31)

proves that the labouring classes can equip themselves with the necessary tools to understand society, for literacy is the key to their participation in the governing of a more just society.

Imitation of Juvenal—Satire VIII

With the "Imitation of Juvenal—Satire VIII" (GCL I:47)[16] Wordsworth reverts to socio-political directness, and his verse suffers accordingly; Carl Woodring labels it a "jejune" imitation.[17] The composition of the "Imitation" coincides probably with the first direct correspondence between Wordsworth and Coleridge (Reed I, p. 179). The latter's radical political and literary journal, *The Watchman,* was published for the first time on 1 March 1796. It was issued in open defiance of the Seditious Meetings Bill and the Treasonable Practices Bill (1795)[18] and "its confessed object was to secure their repeal . . ." (Moorman I, p. 291). Now Wordsworth is under the direct and indirect influence of two revolutionary poets, Coleridge and Southey (he had met Southey in August 1795 and was given a copy of the latter's *Joan of Arc* in January 1796). No wonder their radicalism reinforces his rage over the political situation. Censorship did not catch up with Coleridge's *Watchman*; it finished in May 1796 for lack of subscribers. However, John Thelwall's *Tribune* was suppressed in April 1796 (Harper I, p. 319). For Wordsworth the restriction of the freedom of the press and erosion of civil liberties are not surprising in a state where the Kings' "freaks are worse than any sick man's dream" (2);[19] "freaks" suggests that monarchical heads of government change their minds for no reason. Wordsworth contrasts the past with the present and concludes that present times are worse, for "no Tyrant ere design'd / Malice so subtle, vengeance so refin'd" (3-4), "tyrant" implying absence of liberty. He then continues his attack on social and political evils by singling out members of the nobility. His utter detestation of Lord Lonsdale, known for tyrannizing his dependants and tenants and withholding the inheritance of the Wordsworth

---

[16] The work on the "Imitation of Juvenal" extended from 1795 to 1797. For full details of composition, see Reed I, pp. 340–41.

[17] Woodring, *Politics in English Romantic Poetry,* p. 90.

[18] See this chapter, n. 13.

[19] Line references are to *PW* I, pp. 302–06.

children, is quite forceful: "Must honour still to Lonsdale's tail be bound? / Then execration is an empty sound" (13–14). His indictment of Thurlow, a staunch defender of the slave trade, shows Wordsworth as champion of the equality and brotherhood of all men (21). Chard, p. 210, points out that the reference to the Uhlans (42) implies England's compact with the nations responsible for Poland's loss of national liberty. Wordsworth's deep concern with inequality before the law is expressed in some of the better lines of the poem:

> But ye who make our manners laws and sense
> *Self-judged* can with such discipline dispense,
> And at your will what in a groom were base
> Shall stick new splendour on his gartered grace.
> (53–56; my italics)

He censures those who act as judges in their own cases and by implication points at what is paramount in a democratic state, the separation of powers between legislature, executive, and judiciary.

Lines 59–66 take up the attack on liberty by an army of paid government informers.[20] Wordsworth sees through the kind of pseudo-equality game that was played by the King (and still is by more modern dictators) to boost the popularity of the monarch: "His Grace's watermen in open race / Are called to try their prowess with his Grace" (87–88). The scorn for sham equality is followed by a relentless denunciation of the system of hereditary monarchy (100–10); by implication Wordsworth advocates democracy: "Were Kings a free born work—a people's choice, / Would More or Henry boast the general voice?" (101–02). Lines 147–48[21] also take up the theme of popular democracy: "Plebeian hands the [ ][22] mace have wrenched / From sovereigns deep in pedigree intrenched", a concept lent additional revolutionary support by "wrenched" denoting violent means. The anti-war attitude is discernible throughout the poem. In the midst of the war against France the poet praises the local sense of brotherhood that had united the "*six simple burghers*" of Calais to save their city (137–46).[23] The revolutionary optimist of 1792–93 and political evolutionist of late 1794 (December letter to Mathews) has become an extremely bitter satirist in the "Imitation of Juvenal—Satire VIII".

---

[20] For an analysis of ll. 59–66, see Gill, "'Adventures on Salisbury Plain' and Wordsworth's Poetry of Protest 1795–97", *SIR*, 11 (1972), 48–65 (52).
[21] According to de Selincourt ll. 137–46 correspond to Juv. 254–58, and 147–62 to Juv. 259–75 (*PW* I, pp. 373–74).
[22] de Selincourt's square brackets.
[23] See above, n. 21.

1796-97

Wordsworth's extant letters of 1796 and 1797 do not throw much light on his socio-political thought during that period except for a letter to Francis Wrangham of [February 1797] (*E.Y.*, p. 172), in which he quotes most of the "Imitation of Juvenal". However, "The Convict" (GCL I:49: "perhaps written early 1796, more probably between 21 Mar. and early Oct. 1796") evinces Wordsworth's continued anti-monarchical stand and the influence of Godwin. Its outspoken republican strain is reminiscent of "A Letter to the Bishop of Llandaff", and in its indictment of prison conditions it sides with the few radical humanitarians of the period.[24] Wordsworth sees the basic goodness of the criminal, and he asserts somewhat naively that the convict's remorse is genuine:

> His bones are consumed, and his life-blood is dried,
>   With wishes the past to undo;
> And his crime, through the pains that o'erwhelm him descried,
>   Still blackens and grows on his view.
>   (Brett & Jones, p. 111)

Wordsworth censures the public violence of the monarch who, returning from the "dark synod, or blood-reeking field", is rewarded in chambers where "All soothers of sense their soft virtue shall yield, / And quietness pillow his head"; by contrast he implies the private violence of the criminal whose reward is the punishment in the "comfortless vault of disease" (Brett & Jones, p. 112). A prison visitor addresses the criminal as "poor victim" and comes "as a brother [his] sorrows to share" thus making a direct reference to the brotherhood between all men (ibid., p. 112). In May 1796 S. T. Coleridge considered Wordsworth "the best poet of the age".[25] This appraisal can hardly be based on "The Convict" which, in its overt didacticism, is more in line with the ephemeral newspaper verse of minor contemporary poets.[26] In comparison with *Adventures on Salisbury Plain* it is poetic regression.

---

[24] Wordsworth emerges as a progressive if we consider that the humanitarian tradition had become "warped beyond recognition" and that the "abuses which Howard [in his *State of the Prisons* (1777-80)] had exposed in the prisons in the 1770s and 1780s crept back in the 1790s and 1800s". (Thompson, *The Making of the English Working Class*, p. 61.) F. W. Bateson, *Wordsworth: A Re-interpretation*, 2nd ed. (1956; rpt. London: Longman, 1971), p. 103, thinks that the poem was influenced by a possible visit to the convict prison at Portland.

[25] *Collected Letters of Samuel Taylor Coleridge*, ed. Griggs (Oxford: Clarendon Press, 1956), vol. I, p. 215.

[26] For an example of this kind of verse, see Edward Allen Whitney, "Humanitarianism and Romanticism", *HLQ*, 2 (1938-39), 159-78 (170).

The *Edinburgh Review* was to complain bitterly of the leniency the "new school of poetry" showed towards criminals: These poets express for "all sorts of vice and profliga-

The Borderers

The composition of "The Convict" overlaps with that of *The Borderers* (GCL I:52);[27] however, the play contains no direct statements of humanitarian and political optimism.[28] Its writing coincides with the harassment by the Government of John Thelwall, who, nevertheless, continued lecturing on social and political questions and whose demand for social equality in his *Rights of Nature* (1796) transcends the request for purely political equality and for a little more economic justice in the 1790s.[29] Mrs. Inchbald as well, in her *Nature and Art* (1796), showed no

cy in the lower orders of society . . . virtuous horror, and . . . tender compassion. While the existence of these offences overpowers them with grief and confusion, they never permit themselves to feel the smallest indignation or dislike towards the offenders. The present vicious constitution of society alone is responsible for all these enormities: the poor sinners are but the helpless victims or instruments of its disorders, and could not possibly have avoided the errors into which they have been betrayed. Though they can bear with crimes, therefore, they cannot reconcile themselves to punishments; and have an unconquerable antipathy to prisons, gibbets, and houses of correction, as engines of oppression, and instruments of atrocious injustice. While the plea of moral necessity is thus artfully brought forward to convert all the excesses of the poor into innocent misfortunes, no sort of indulgence is shown to the offences of the powerful and rich. Their oppressions, and seductions, and debaucheries, are the theme of many an angry verse; and the indignation and abhorrence of the reader is relentlessly conjured up against those perturbators of society, and scourges of mankind." (Review of R. Southey's *Thalaba, Edinburgh Review* (Oct. 1802), No. 1, p. 71.)

[27] My quotations are from the Reading Text of the Cornell Wordsworth edition of *The Borderers* (Ithaca, N.Y.: Cornell U.P., in press), edited by Robert Osborn. Robert Osborn's text is based on the 1799 fair-copy readings of DC MS. 23. Dove Cottage "MS. 23" (new number) corresponds to the old number "MS. Verse 15"/"MS. 15" (used throughout this thesis) and represents the play as it probably stood in 1796–97.

[28] For a general interpretation of *The Borderers*, see Chard, pp. 211–19, who also supplies references to the most important scholarship on *The Borderers* (see especially footnotes to p. 212). In addition to these references the following are valuable: Woodring, *Politics in English Romantic Poetry*, pp. 90–93, on the connection with politics; Stephen Parrish, *The Art of the Lyrical Ballads* (Cambridge, Mass.: Harvard U.P., 1973), p. 71, on the source, which is apparently Schiller's *Die Räuber* (but cf. Moorman I, p. 302: "The story is entirely Wordsworth's invention . . ."); Geoffrey H. Hartman, "Wordsworth, *The Borderers*, and 'Intellectual Murder'", *JEGP*, 62 (1963), 761–68, and Hartman's *Wordsworth's Poetry, 1787–1814*, 2nd ed. (1964; New Haven and London: Yale U.P., 1971), pp. 125–35, which throw light on the modernity of the play's intellectual hero. *Note:* Most of the criticism on the play refers to the published version of 1842.

[29] "'I affirm that *every* man, and *every* woman, and *every* child, ought to obtain something more, in the general distribution of the fruits of labour, than food, and rags, and a wretched hammock with a poor rug to cover it; and that, without working twelve or fourteen hours a day . . . from six to sixty.—They have a claim, a sacred and inviolable claim . . . to some comfort and enjoyment . . . to some tolerable leisure for such discussions, and some means of or such information as may lead to an understanding of their *rights* . . .'" (Quoted in Thompson, *The Making of the English Working Class*, p. 175.) On Thelwall's radicalism in the 1790s (ibid., pp. 172–76) and his relationship with S. T. Coleridge and Wordsworth (ibid., pp. 180–81), also pp. 78–79 below. See further Thompson, "Disenchantment or Default?", pp. 158–59.

lessening of faith in the natural goodness of man.[30] Wordsworth met William Godwin, on whose Preface to the second edition of *Political Justice* he had commented disparagingly in March [1796] (*E.Y.*, p. 170), several times in June 1796 before he started work on *The Borderers* later in the year. Godwin's anarchistic philosophy which involves the dissolution of the institutions of society, however, is as much rejected by *The Borderers* as is the belief in the amelioration of mankind by changing the institutions of society, as advocated by Thelwall and implied by Mrs. Inchbald. What, then, is the social and political significance of that Gothic drama, set in the thirteenth century, whose "Border . . . is Wordsworth's Paris, Blois, and Orleans of 1791-1792", according to Carl Woodring, and in which Roger Sharrock sees "the impact of the most significant political and social thought" of Wordsworth's time "embodied in a concrete situation . . ."?[31]

"Justice" and words related to it are frequently used in *The Borderers*, but in the majority of cases the terms stand for outrageous injustice.[32] The plot of *The Borderers* is simple:[33] The distorter of justice, Rivers (an Iago-like character), tricks the kindly Mortimer, leader of a band of benevolent brigands, into causing the death of the blind old Baron Herbert. Mortimer, who loves Herbert's daughter, Matilda, is led to believe that her father has sold her into prostitution. Rivers's repeated insinuations that the public law does not exist for both him and Mortimer are the chief reason leading eventually to a monstrous crime against an innocent old man:

> Happy are we
> Who live in these disputed tracts that own
> No law but what each man makes for himself.
> Here justice has indeed a field of triumph!
> (II.1.51-54)[34]

In creating his private law, Rivers repudiates the collective wisdom of the body politic as expressed in the public law: mock justice is trium-

[30] Brinton, *The Political Ideas of the English Romanticists*, pp. 33-34.

[31] Woodring, *Politics in English Romantic Poetry*, p. 92; Roger Sharrock, "*The Borderers:* Wordsworth on the Moral Frontier", *Durham Univ. Jnl.*, 56, N.S. 25 (1964), 170-83 (171).

[32] Lane Cooper's *Concordance* lists "justice" eleven times in *The Borderers* (1842), seven times in *The Prelude* (1850), and five times in *The Excursion* (1814). In MS, 15 of *The Borderers* "justice" appears fifteen times.

[33] Those acquainted with the 1842 text may note the following name-changes: Mortimer → Marmaduke, Rivers → Oswald, Matilda → Idonea.

[34] References are to acts and scenes. The line numbering has been adopted from the final galley proofs of the forthcoming Cornell edition. (The reasons for not adopting the correct system of numbering scenes in roman lower case and for omitting some line numbers are indicated in my Preface.)

phant. We recall that the predominant eighteenth-century ideas of law favoured natural law. Based on deduction and the nature of man, it was held to be universal. In not adhering to a system that rests on the conviction of that fundamental equality, Rivers denies, by implication, the basic equality among men. Seen against this historical background, Rivers emerges as a particularly modern hero, who, instead of reasoning impartially, rationalizes his acts of private justice.

> You have taught mankind to seek the measure of justice
> By diving for it into their *own* bosoms.
> To day you have thrown off a *tyranny*
> That lives but by the torpid acquiescence
> Of our *emasculated* souls, *the tyranny*
> *Of moralists and saints and lawgivers.*
> You have obeyed the only law that wisdom
> Can ever recognize: the immediate law
> Flashed from the light of circumstances
> Upon an independent intellect.[35]
>
> (III.5.24–33; my italics)

The excerpt witnesses to Wordsworth's keen insight into the innermost recesses of an anarchist intellect. We discern intellectual conceitedness and a reversal of general truths in nearly every line. Private justice is made to be something highly commendable, for, after all, it is certainly moral to throw off any kind of "tyranny". Further, tyranny elicits a longing for liberty. Lastly, only an effeminate soul harbours tyranny. Thus Rivers appeals to three different responses in Mortimer to drive home his defamation of "moralists and saints and lawgivers": he kindles Mortimer's sense of justice, instils the moral obligation to shake off "tyranny", and plays on his masculine pride ("emasculated souls"). Another instance of the inversion of morality occurs at IV.2.188–91:

> ... we are fellow-labourers—to enlarge
> The intellectual empire of mankind.
> 'Tis *slavery*—all is *slavery,* we receive
> Laws, and we ask not whence those laws have come.
>
> [my italics]

The critical rejection or acceptance of custom or law is what is distinctive of morality.[36] Rivers uses this critical tool for his own ends. He is not concerned with the spirit and letter of the law but insinuates that the

---

[35] Repeated in 1805 *Prelude* X.828–29: "One guide, the light of circumstances, flash'd / Upon an independent intellect."

[36] S. I. Benn and R. S. Peters, *Social Principles and the Democratic State* (London: George Allen & Unwin, 1959), p. 26.

law is derived from a person or persons who seek to safeguard their own interests. Rivers implies that the law is "slavery"; he needs to rid himself of its constraints to feel his intellectual self-consciousness. We, however, know that where there is no law, there is no freedom. Here and elsewhere in *The Borderers* Wordsworth argues negatively for justice, liberty, equality, and brotherhood chiefly through the dramatic means of letting Rivers reject these concepts.

Poetically *The Borderers* is uneven, and it is too static to be performed on stage.[37] However, its intellectual concern with the nature of good and evil, the scepticism it conveys in its description of a good man's gullibility,[38] and the warning finger it raises against placing one's hope of curing the world in actions that concentrate primarily on the surface of things make the play relevant for twentieth-century man:

> [*Mortimer:*] . . . we look
> But at the surfaces of things, we hear
> Of towns in flames, fields ravaged, young and old
> Driven out in flocks to want and nakedness,
> Then grasp our swords and *rush* upon a cure
> That flatters us, because it asks *not thought*.
> The deeper malady is better hid—
> The world is poisoned at the heart.
> (II.3.337–44; my italics)

Wordsworth's voice is subdued here in comparison with most of his earlier verse (1791–94): he now suggests inner reform before sociopolitical reform. If little concerned with particular current public events in *Adventures on Salisbury Plain* a year earlier, in *The Borderers* he is even less concerned with day-to-day political issues. Recalling Wordsworth's interest in and aptitude for politics in "A Letter to the Bishop of Llandaff", it now becomes doubtful to what extent he still is a prospective political leader, for the period was troublesome enough to invite an overt political commitment. In 1796–97 the French continued their military success: in May 1796 Sardinia ceded Savoy and Nice to France. Spain declared war on Britain in October 1796, and in December France refused further peace negotiations with Britain. Throughout 1797 there were fears of French invasion. In Britain, internal politics had led to the disarray of the radicals. The naval mutinies at Spithead (April 1797) and at the Nore (May to June 1797) probably fall as well within the period of

---

[37] It was publicly performed for the first time at Grasmere in 1970.
[38] Sheats's penetrating analysis of *The Borderers* implies that man's best qualities are vulnerable to perversion (Sheats, *The Making of Wordsworth's Poetry*, p. 128).

composition of *The Borderers*.³⁹ These historical facts and especially Wordsworth's earlier experience of the French Revolution and the separation from his French daughter and her mother were bound to have contributed to the sombre tone of *The Borderers*, although in it he does not mention these particular private and public events.

Trying to tackle the mystery of evil in such a comprehensive manner as in *The Borderers* distinguishes Wordsworth from the major writers of the Enlightenment who underestimated the strength of evil. As will be seen in the following pages, Wordsworth believed that the absence of brotherhood and equality in human affairs engenders evil. Thus it will be revealing to trace in *The Borderers* ideas and words that express or imply anti-brotherhood and anti-egalitarianism (i.e. implicit anti-democratic notions).

The first lines of II.1 could have been uttered by Iago and evoke also the "impaired" Satan of *Paradise Lost:*

> [*Rivers:*] They chose him for their chief!—I had a gnawing
> More of contempt than hatred! . . .

Rivers cannot accept the democratic decision of his fellow brigands. His words are spoken in soliloquy and thus throw light on his true character. The impact of these foreboding lines is reinforced by their position at the start of a new act. Rivers's anti-democratic and anti-egalitarian sentiment is also brought out by his contempt for common people later in the same scene: "a tribe of vulgar wretches" and "The eye / Of vulgar men knows not the majesty / With which the mind can clothe the shapes of things" (II.1.97, 98–100). One of the gang, Lennox, comments: "Natures such as his [Rivers's] / Spin motives out of their own bowels . . . / . . . / . . . Power is life to him, / And breath and being; where he cannot govern / He will destroy . . ." (III.4.6–13). This is an apt comment on the dictatorial Rivers, who cannot subordinate himself to the internal rules that govern the band of borderers. Rivers has nothing but contempt for egalitarian and democratic principles which reign "in this universe, / Where the least things controul the greatest, where / The faintest breath that breathes can move a world" (III.5.83–85).

Before Herbert enters the scene in II.1, Rivers describes to Mortimer the route they are going to take: "A few leagues hence we shall have open field, / And tread on ground as *free as the first earth* / Which nature

---

³⁹ The "greatest revolutionary portents for England were the naval mutinies at Spithead and the Nore in April and May 1797. There is no doubt that appal[l]ing conditions of food, pay and discipline precipitated the mutinies, but there is also some evidence of direct Jacobin instigation. . . ." (Thompson, *The Making of the English Working Class*, p. 183.)

gave to man. . . ." (II.1.111–13; my italics.) Eventually Mortimer causes Herbert's death (through exposure and hunger) on that very ground. The physical freedom foreshadows the ensuing "freedom" from moral constraint. The italicized words recall the liberty, the natural rights, of prehistoric man—and the right to life (a principle not shared by Rivers) was one of those rights; thus the freedom of prelapsarian man alluded to here becomes a mockery. Later on, one of the gang, Lacy, in order to vindicate private law and private justice, makes a false parallel between man's soul and the biological process of the free growth of oaks:

> We will have ample justice.
> Who are we, friends? Do we not live on ground
> Where souls are self-defended, *free* to grow
> Like mountain Oaks, rocked by the stormy wind?
> Mark the almighty *wisdom* which decreed
> This monstrous crime should be laid open—*here*,[40]
> Where *Reason* has an eye that she can use
> And men alone are umpires. . . .
> (II.3.418–25; my italics)

Rivers's fallacious belief—or, better, his sly pretence to believe—in human self-sufficiency and the supremacy of reason, disseminated through the play, is reinforced here by a minor character expressing the same thoughts. In the play's final act "almighty wisdom" and "Reason" will be perverted into the folly and unreason of the lynch law that "dispatches" the instigator of crime himself, Rivers. At the back of Wordsworth's mind may have been the kind of "Reason" that was supposed to liberate first France and then the nations of the world: ironically, ten days before France commemorated the triumph of reason in the "Fête of Reason", the moderate Girondins had been executed (31 October 1793)!

Lacy does not manipulate language on purpose, whereas Rivers delights in doing so throughout the play. Denying someone the basic equality due to him as a human being or depriving him of important liberties produces injustice. This Rivers does, and he does more; he excludes Herbert from humanity:

> Shall it be law to stab the petty robber
> Who aims at one poor life, and shall *this* monster—
> (II.3.200–01; italics original)

If you stab a robber—who is human after all—nothing should restrain you from killing a "monster". The parallels that Rivers draws between

---

[40] In this line italics original.

the animal kingdom and Herbert become a devilish device of dehumanization, since, not being regarded as human, man is deprived of that minimum of protection and consideration that the concept of brotherhood has helped to establish in human relationships. Referring to Herbert, Rivers uses "what", a pronoun normally applied to things and animals:

> . . . Murder! what, of whom?
> Of whom—or *what?* we kill a toad, a newt,
> A rat—I do believe if they who first
> Baptised the deed had called it murder, we
> Had quaked to think of it. . . .
> (II.3.230–34; my italics)

The disconnected syntax and the stress on objects reinforce the sense of the unnatural. Later the perversion of language becomes nightmarish when Mortimer—a character representing all men of goodwill—at the end of III.2 (line 107) speaks of Herbert as "That mole, that weazle, that old water rat". This line is very important; it exerts an incantatory force on Mortimer's mind. Now Mortimer need have no qualms in doing away with old Herbert. The twisting of language is a significant contributory cause eventually leading to the old baron's death (III.3); the misuse of language[41] as a tool of dehumanization under Hitler, Stalin, and their present imitators may speak for itself and underline the significance of Wordsworth's insight into the psychology of crime against mankind. Another example occurs in III.5.99–104: "If a viper / Crawl from beneath our feet, we do not ask / A licence to destroy him", etc.

In many instances dehumanization is expressed in terms of a distorted or denied brotherhood:

> [*Rivers:*] . . . A gentle dose [of poison]!
> That will compose him [Herbert] to a child-like sleep:
> There is no justice when we do not feel
> For *man as man.*
> (II.3.170–73; my italics)

Rivers suggests that poisoning an old man can be implicitly linked to "justice". Brotherhood ("man as man") is likewise mocked by associating it with a proposed crime. A few lines farther down (i.e., lines 181–183) Rivers refers to Herbert as "the *property* of him who best / Can feel" [italics mine] the old man's so-called crimes. ". . . I [Rivers] have resigned a privilege [to kill] / It now becomes my duty to resume it."

---

[41] See, e.g., Arnold Wesker's pamphlet *Words as Definitions of Experience* (London: Writers and Readers Publishing Co-operative, 1976).

Designating Herbert as "property" transforms him into a soulless thing or animal. Rivers puts on his Romance kidgloves of "resign", "privilege", and "resume" to disguise his perverted thoughts. A straightforward Anglo-Saxon-derived vocabulary, such as "I have given up my right (to kill)", would probably have made Mortimer suspicious. Here, however, the refined language fits the situation and Rivers's deceitful character: it is an example of the early Wordsworth's linguistic sensitivity.

What little dramatic action there is in *The Borderers* takes place in III.3. Throughout the scene Mortimer and Herbert are by themselves. Shortly before abandoning Herbert to his fatal ordeal, Mortimer talks to himself as though Herbert were non-existent:

> And he was still a *brother* in my love—
> These tears—I did not think that aught was left in me
> Of what I have been.—Yes, I thank thee, heaven:
> *One happy*[42] thought has passed across my mind—
> It may not be—*I am cut off from man,*
> *No more shall I be man, no more shall I*
> *Have human feelings!* . . .
>   (III.3.66–72; my italics)

The bond of brotherhood between two solitary human beings is intact in the first four lines of the excerpt. In this state it is absolutely impossible to commit the atrocious act. To perpetrate the crime it becomes necessary to cut that brotherly bond, and the consequence of this immoral act will result in the loss of a healthy mental state. Wordsworth has dealt similarly with the impact of murder on the human mind in *Adventures on Salisbury Plain*. In *The Borderers* the mental torture as a result of the crime against brotherhood is yet more pronounced. Mortimer becomes crazed, whereas the sailor-murderer of *Adventures on Salisbury Plain* had found some kind of peace in the end; however, his deed had not been premeditated. At the moment of desertion Mortimer relinquishes his individual responsibility towards a fellow human being entirely (III.3, line 153). He deludes himself that, since God is everywhere, Herbert could be saved by divine intervention. Moreover, Mortimer acts as though he were a tool of God: ". . . I have led thee hither / To save thy spirit from perdition—" (III.3.137–38). Over and over again Wordsworth seems to suggest that a good man cannot kill an innocent man unless man first renounces his primary affections and deeply rooted feelings of brotherhood.

---

[42] In this line italics original.

Once more Wilberforce's bill for the abolition of the slave trade had been defeated in the House of Commons in 1796—this time by four votes, which was an improvement over 1795 when the bill had been rejected by a wide margin;[43] indeed, the concept of the universal brotherhood of man[44] was slowly evolving in the eighteenth century. In a way the old Baron Herbert stands for those who believe in universal brotherhood; his command was "to bless *all* mankind" (V.3.61; my italics). On the other hand, we find an extreme example of the negation of any kind of brotherhood—in its universal and restricted sense—in Rivers, who according to Lennox "did despise alike / Mohammedon and Christian—" (III.4.19–20). The era of the Crusades had united the Christians. Contrary to the usual reaction in times of a "just war" Rivers hates his own group as much as the enemy. In the context of the thirteenth-century crusading spirit Rivers appears as most unnatural. "Restless minds" as his "find amid their *fellow men* / No heart that loves them, none that they can love" (III.4.33–35; my italics). "Fellow men" evokes an ideal brotherhood from which Rivers is separated by his incapacity to relate as man to man. Rivers denies the existence of a spiritual bond between men. The brotherhood of man entails reciprocity and co-operation, whereas Rivers's world stands for extreme individualism without the slightest hint that men might unite in common purpose:

> [*Rivers:*] . . . Bodies are like ropes:
> When interwoven, stronger by mutual strength.
> Thanks to our nature! *'tis not so with minds.*
> (III.5.47–49; my italics)

After his criminal desertion of Herbert, Mortimer can no longer think clearly. As Rivers is unravelling the story of his identical crime to Mortimer, Mortimer interjects: "We all are of one blood, our veins are filled / At the same poisonous fountain" (IV.2.56–57). He still believes in something uniting all men, although it has become a twisted unity. The "we" of the dialogue between Mortimer and Rivers is emphasized and made universal by "all", and "one" blood strengthens the notion of unity between men. "One blood" normally evokes a brotherhood and healthy coherence. Mortimer's crime, however, makes him link "veins" and "blood" (suggesting the pulsating life and vital principle) with the death-evoking "poisonous fountain". But there is hope, since the lines do prove at least a bond between men, a prerequisite for brotherhood. In Mortimer's mind the fountain has become "poisonous" because he was

---

[43] D. Brion Davis, *The Problem of Slavery in the Age of Revolution*, p. 29.
[44] First recorded in Cowper's *Task* (comp. 1783–84). See above, Introduction, n. 13.

not aware of the danger of evil, while a future insight into evil could prevent a crime against innocence and restore the fountain as a life-giving source. Man is basically good; only devilish beings that are "For unknown ends permitted to put on / The shape of man" (V.2.52–53) are capable of subverting the natural goodness. Three lines farther down Mortimer shouts in despair, "Oh monster! monster!", thus emphasizing the unnatural tone that dominates most of *The Borderers*. According to Lane Cooper's *Concordance* the singular form of "monster" occurs only eight times in Wordsworth's poetry of which five are found in *The Borderers* (1842)!—it appears seven times in MS. 15.

The criminal acts in *The Borderers* are, in Mortimer's words, "a plot, / A damned plot against the soul of man" (V.3.27–8). The "soul" here implies chiefly the seat of man's primary emotions and feelings, those sentiments of brotherhood and love that are suspended in *The Borderers*. Wordsworth asks himself what happens when traditional human values are replaced by abstract theories, which was the case in revolutionary France. Todd links *The Borderers* to Wordsworth's experience of the French Revolution and thinks that the "portrayal of the power of evil gives the play its political point".[45] Boulton's general discussion of Burke's *Reflections on the Revolution in France* is strikingly appropriate to *The Borderers* as well: "in France the revolutionists 'are so taken up with their theories about the rights of man, that they have totally forgotten his nature. Without opening one new avenue to the understanding, they have succeeded in stopping up those that lead to the heart.'[46] The moral consequences are disastrous: *the individual becomes the source of a private morality* and no corporate values remain; 'humanity and compassion are ridiculed as the fruits of superstition and ignorance'[47] . . ." (Boulton, p. 101; my italics). Between six and seven years after the *Reflections* had appeared, Wordsworth, in *The Borderers*, had begun to veer in the direction of his old enemy Burke, who died in July 1797.[48] In *The Borderers* nothing of Wordsworth's youthful idealistic revolutionary fervour remains. He warns us of the Rivers type of man in his "Prefatory Essay" to *The Borderers* (GCL I:52b: "probably composed at the same time as the first version" of *The Borderers*):[49]

---

[45] Todd, *Politics and the Poet*, p. 88.
[46] Quoted from Burke's *Works* (Bohn edn. [1854–89]) II, p. 337.
[47] Ibid., II, p. 341.
[48] Some time after 1820 Wordsworth introduced a eulogy on Burke into the 1850 *Prelude* VII.512–43 (1805 *Prelude*, p. xxxi).
[49] See further the section "Essay Prefaced to the Early Version (1797)" in Robert Osborn's edition of *The Borderers*.

It is his [Rivers's] pleasure and his consolation to hunt out whatever is bad in actions usually esteemed virtuous and to detect the good in actions which the *universal sense of mankind* teaches us to reprobate. While the general exertion of his intellect seduces him from the remembrance of his own crime, the *particular conclusions* to which he is led have a tendency to reconcile him to himself. His feelings are interested in making him a moral sceptic . . . (MS. 13; Reading Text ll. 11–18, *The Borderers,* Cornell U.P., in press; my italics).

The "universal sense of mankind" is what binds men together in one brotherhood. In the play Rivers is the detractor of those feelings. Sometimes people such as Rivers, if only temporarily, attain positions of political power, and as a result of their machinations the "universal sense of mankind" is suspended. The lesson brought home by *The Borderers* makes the play a defence of this universal feeling and its related universal human values, but it suggests as well that this universal sense may be skin-deep only and therefore needs constant strengthening. For the first time in Wordsworth's opus a member of the nobility, the Baron Herbert, is drawn sympathetically. Bearing in mind Wordsworth's attack on the nobility a few months earlier in the "Imitation of Juvenal", he has indeed widened his democratic sentiment, however little *The Borderers* is outwardly concerned with democratic issues.

The economic depression and a 75 per cent rise in the price of bread in 1795 (the price had remained virtually unchanged in 1792, 1793, and 1794)[50] must have hit the lower classes particularly hard and made high demands on man's active expression of brotherhood. Wordsworth's "Baker's Cart" (GCL I:55), probably written between 1796 and early 1797, highlights one aspect of the contemporary social scene, hunger:

> I have seen the Baker's horse
> As he had been accustomed at your door
> Stop with the loaded wain, when o'er his head
> Smack went the whip, and you were left, as if
> You were not born to live, or there had been
> No bread in all the land. Five little ones,
> They at the rumbling of the distant wheels
> Had all come forth, and, ere the grove of birch
> Concealed the wain, into their wretched hut
> They all returned. . . .
> (*PW* I, pp. 315–16)

The cart raises the children's expectations. We sense their longing but they return empty-handed into their "wretched" cottage. Hunger is not mentioned once. However, the implicit contrast between the "loaded

---

[50] Cone, *The English Jacobins,* p. 179.

wain" and the children's empty stomachs speaks for itself and points to the lack of brotherhood that makes innocent children the victims of painful hunger.

Wordsworth himself, at the beginning of 1797, experienced a small share of that poverty which he delineates here and which the female beggar of *The Borderers* (I.3) had suffered in her utter destitution. In a letter to Wrangham of [25 February 1797] he writes: "I have lately been living upon air and the essence of carrots cabbages turnips and other esculent vegetables, not excluding parsely the produce of my garden—" (*E.Y.*, p. 178).

At the end of March 1797 Wordsworth met Thomas Poole (Reed I, p. 195), Coleridge's neighbour at Nether Stowey. About eight times during the ensuing twelve months Wordsworth was to meet this radical farmer about whom Poole's cousin Charlotte complains in her diary: " 'I wish he would cease to torment us with his democratick sentiments . . .' " (quoted in Harper I, p. 306). On 16 July 1797 Wordsworth and his sister Dorothy moved into Alfoxden House, a few miles from Coleridge's home. Now began the most intimate contact with Coleridge which was to prove so fruitful for Wordsworth's poetic creativity. By coincidence this close relationship was inaugurated by the visit of a real leftist extremist, Thelwall, by now the "most notorious, if defeated, Jacobin in England . . ., and he was being *watched*. Coleridge and Wordsworth must have known perfectly well that he was being watched, but gave him the welcome of a comrade and a citizen nonetheless. . . ."[51] Thelwall stayed for about ten days at Nether Stowey and Alfoxden, discussing politics and literature with the two poets. If Wordsworth's conversation resembled the predominantly quiet thoughtful mode of his poetry at the time, the lively Coleridge and fiery Thelwall must have thought Wordsworth serene. One specimen of Thelwall's ardour for universal brotherhood and against slavery may suffice to illustrate his political commitment:

. . . man . . . looks in the face of his fellow creature; and he sees indeed a brother . . . the sooty African need lift his fettered hands no more to *remind* him that he is a MAN and a BROTHER!—He enfolds the universe in one large embrace, and finds an eternal source of rational gratification in contemplating the felicity, or labouring to mitigate the calamities of his fellow creatures.[52]

---

[51] Thompson, "Disenchantment or Default?", p. 160.

[52] Quoted in Wylie Sypher, *Guinea's Captive Kings: British Anti-Slavery Literature of the XVIII Century* (Chapel Hill: Univ. of North Carolina Press, 1942), p. 220, from Thelwall's *Moral Tendency of a System of Spies and Informers* (1795). Ellipses (except third), italics, and capitals in Sypher. For anti-slavery and some pro-slavery verse, see W. Sypher, pp. 220 ff.

A few days after Thelwall had left the district, a Dr. Lysons of Bath wrote to the Home Secretary about the suspicious behaviour of the Wordsworths (Reed I, p. 204). This denunciation well illustrates the tense political situation of 1797—fears of subversion, rumours of invasion—which, as is well known, resulted in the surveillance of Wordsworth, Coleridge, and Poole by a government spy in the middle of August to whom Alfoxden appeared the nest of a " 'gang of disaffected Englishmen' " (Moorman I, p. 331).[53] The spy left the area without having found any evidence of treason, but Wordsworth's association with Thelwall and the suspicion in general brought down upon Wordsworth the wrath of Mrs. St. Albyn, the mother of the infant owner of Alfoxden (Moorman I, p. 338): he was informed that he could not expect to have the lease for Alfoxden renewed after its expiry in the summer of 1798.

While work on *The Borderers* proceeded, Wordsworth composed the fragment "Argument for Suicide" (GCL I:51). Its first four lines strike a note of social protest:

> Send this man to the mine, this to the battle,
> Famish an aged beggar at your gates,
> And let him die by inches—but for worlds
> Lift not your hand against him . . .
> 			(*PW* I, p. 316)

The reiteration of "this" expresses the carelessness with which the fate of the little man is decided. The old beggar dies outside the gates of the well-to-do who maintain conventional "Christian" appearances but discard their social responsibility in disregarding the natural law that enjoins man to preserve life. Wordsworth indicts the kind of inaction which causes the death of one's fellow-man.

A part of "Lines Left upon a Seat in a Yew-Tree" (GCL I:20)[54] may be contemporaneous with the writing of *The Borderers*; the bulk of it, however, follows closely upon completion of MS. 15 of *The Borderers*. There are no traces of direct political thought in the Yew-Tree Lines that suggest the impact of the radical Coleridge and "democratick" Poole, and if Wordsworth was still harbouring revolutionary thoughts, he kept

---

[53] See also Harper I, pp. 320–29.
[54] Reed dates: "A few lines eventually used in this poem perhaps composed as early as mid-1787. Bulk of composition probably early 1797, perhaps after 8 Feb., and by July." The full title in Brett & Jones is "Lines Left upon a Seat in a Yew-Tree which Stands Near the Lake of Esthwaite, on a Desolate Part of the Shore, yet Commanding a Beautiful Prospect". For a recent detailed analysis of "Lines Left upon a Seat in a Yew-Tree", see Sheats, pp. 156–61. See also Chard, pp. 220–21.

them out of the poem. Although there is no evidence in the poetry and surviving letters, I wonder whether Wordsworth in early 1797 was as uninterested in partisan politics as we are led to believe on the basis of the extant sources. After all, he did lose the lease of Alfoxden House for political reasons and he was implicated in the spy episode. Would he have lost his lease, would he have been denounced by Dr. Lysons, merely on the basis of loose talk?[55]

In a way similar to Rivers in *The Borderers,* the solitary of the Yew-Tree Lines (Brett & Jones, pp. 38–40) leaves human society because of his hurt pride. The imagery of isolation expresses man's inner and outer separation from the human brotherhood:

> His only visitants a straggling sheep,
> The stone-chat, or the glancing sand-piper;
> And on these barren rocks, with juniper,
> And heath, and thistle, thinly sprinkled o'er,
> Fixing his downward eye, he many an hour
> A morbid pleasure nourished, tracing here
> An emblem of his own unfruitful life[.]
> (23–29)

The perception of the beauty of the natural scene (30 ff.) changes the solitary's barren existence into a state of peaceful contemplation. He now remembers those fellow-men who exerted "labours of benevolence" (36) and is thus linked in thought to the human brotherhood. In the last verse paragraph Wordsworth admonishes that

> . . . pride,
> Howe'er disguised in its own majesty,
> Is littleness; that he, who feels contempt
> For any living thing, hath faculties
> Which he has never used; that thought with him
> Is in its infancy. . . .

Where there is false pride and contempt, man's thought is stunted and infantile. The mature understanding of the wise man acknowledges that *"true knowledge leads to love"* (56; my italics). Knowledge is qualified

---

[55] Wordsworth's reading matter contradicts the impression of his being a Romantic recluse at the time. In spring 1797 Wordsworth received from Losh a "parcel of magazines and political pamphlets. It contained . . . Coleridge's *Conciones ad Populum* in which he protested against the Government's 'gagging Bills'; Burke's *Letters on a Regicide Peace* and *Letter to the Duke of Portland*; Coleridge's *Ode on the Departing Year,* a political poem . . .; some sermons against atheism by Estlin . . .; and Thomas Erskine's *View of the Causes and Consequences of the Present War.* These details are of interest because such a parcel must have been sent at Wordsworth's own request; they show how strong his interest still was in political matters . . ." (Moorman I, pp. 309–10).

by "true", for factual knowledge the solitary, in his youth "by genius nurs'd" (13; 1800 version: "by science nursed"), possessed in plenty; "true knowledge" is more an intuitive apprehension of values that are conducive to the inner well-being of man, such as "love". Love, in its thoughtful concern for others, is also a fertile ground for brotherhood. Where man's thought has reached the state of maturity, love and brotherhood are there to be discovered. Wordsworth, in the "Lines Left upon a Seat in a Yew-Tree", has reached a stage where brotherhood is part of the natural order. In comparison with the doubt of *The Borderers* the Yew-Tree Lines are more certain of an inherent sense of brotherhood. *The Borderers* suggests that the notion of fraternity may be skin-deep only and needs constant defence. The isolated Rivers had found no mental equilibrium neither through man nor nature; the solitary of the Yew-Tree Lines, after his isolated struggle, finds some kind of peace in the natural order.

Some work for Lyrical Ballads *(1st edition)*

In 1797 T. J. Mathias wrote in his *Pursuits of Literature* (Pt. III) that wherever "the freedom of the press exists . . . I must assert *that,* LITERATURE, *well or ill conducted,* IS THE GREAT ENGINE *by which, I am fully persuaded, all* civilized *states must ultimately be supported or overthrown!"*[56] Although literature was accepted as a vehicle of political ideas, the Yew-Tree Lines and the ensuing "Old Man Travelling" (GCL I:53a) and "Inscription for a Seat by a Road-Side, Half Way up a Steep Hill, Facing the South" (GCL I:56),[57] the two latter concluded by early June 1797, do nothing to "support" or "overthrow" a state. The following pages will show that Wordsworth was fully aware of the social issues of the day, but most of the 1797–1800 poetry is not concerned with the kind of political equality and fraternity that needs constant redefining by ideologues to suit new circumstances. From 1797 onward Wordsworth's concepts of brotherhood and implied equality escape temporary political commotions and are valid under more or less any form of government, for the day-to-day life of the common man—Wordsworth's hero—is more governed by deeply ingrained habits and customs than government-imposed ideas.

[56] Quoted in Lois Whitney, *Primitivism and the Idea of Progress in English Popular Literature of the Eighteenth Century* (Baltimore: The Johns Hopkins Press, 1934), p. 239. Points of omission, italics, and small capitals as in L. Whitney.

[57] de Selincourt entitles "Inscription for a Seat by the Road-Side Halfway up a Steep Hill Facing South" (*PW* I, p. 301).

War and its consequences are a secondary theme in "Old Man Travelling; Animal Tranquillity and Decay, A Sketch".[58] The poem illustrates well how important it is to use the earliest versions of Wordsworth's poetry if one wishes to bring out his direct or implied social criticism. The old man, asked what the object of his journey is, replies that he is going to take a last leave of his son, a mariner, "'Who from a sea-fight has been brought to Falmouth, / And there is *dying* in an hospital.'" (Brett & Jones, p. 107; my italics.) In the 1800 edition of the *Lyrical Ballads* Wordsworth replaced "dying" by "lying" and thus toned down considerably the implied protest against war. Patience has become more than second nature to the old man: it is integrated with his whole being. Younger students of the "Old Man Travelling" sometimes criticize Wordsworth for encouraging defeatism in it. This criticism is irrelevant. What makes the poem relevant and sound is the old man's total acceptance of a fact over which he has no control, his old age; the matter-of-factness with which he speaks about his son, again, has nothing to do with a loss of fighting spirit or a lack of parental affection but is another example of a mature stable old man who does not cling frantically to what cannot be retained. The poem makes us think about the human condition and prepares both mind and heart to grasp better Wordsworth's many appeals to values that keep society intact, of which brotherhood is one of the most important cohesive powers.

In an "Inscription for a Seat by the Road-Side" Wordsworth uses something as seemingly insignificant as a "turf" to invite the vigorous young man's empathy with the "weary homeless vagrants of the earth / Or that poor man, the rustic artisan" (*PW* I, p. 301) for whom the turf is a needful resting place. The young man would not need censuring for his "careless eye", which is inclined to overlook the significance of the turf, if he had learnt to respond to the spirit of caring consideration that emanates from "The Old Cumberland Beggar, a Description" (GCL I:53b and 53c), whose dignified old hero engenders feelings of brotherhood in everyone he meets.[59]

---

[58] "Description of a Beggar", the core of "The Old Cumberland Beggar" (GCL I:53c), was written at the same time (Reed I, pp. 184, 342).

[59] See Moorman I, p. 313, on the origin of "The Old Cumberland Beggar" and on its purpose to attack the "political economists" for their war against mendicancy. Woodring, *Politics in English Romantic Poetry*, pp. 95–96, places the poem in its socio-political context and concludes that in it Wordsworth's "stance is democratic, but no longer so fiercely, so absolutely, or so politically democratic as in 1794". Stephen Gill, "Wordsworth's Breeches Pocket . . .", *EIC*, 19 (1969), 385–401 (391), sees the poem as "Wordsworth's contribution to a public debate, not as a 'poem' in a restricted sense, but as a statement on public affairs. . . ." For a thoughtful sociological reading that establishes the

The Old Cumberland Beggar.—The first verse paragraph of "The Old Cumberland Beggar" (Brett & Jones, pp. 205-11) brings out the personal liberty of the old man:

> . . . In the sun,
> Upon the second step of that small pile,
> Surrounded by those wild unpeopled hills,
> He sate, and eat his food in solitude[.]
> (12-15)

His enjoyment of the caressing sun's warm rays and the peace and liberty conveyed by "unpeopled hills" form an implicit contrast with the closed-in work-house atmosphere of the dawning nineteenth century. The personal freedom of the beggar is of equal benefit to those he encounters on his rounds. His being softens their hearts into acts of brotherhood towards him: "The sauntering horseman-traveller does not throw / With careless hand his alms upon the ground" (26-27). "Sauntering" gives an impression of carelessness; thus to see the sauntering horseman circumspect comes as a pleasant surprise and is an effective contrast. The tollgate attendant "quits her work, / And lifts the latch for him [the beggar] that he may pass" (35-36). Even the usually hurried, noisy postboy "passes gently by, without a curse / Upon his lips, or anger at his heart" (42-43). Everywhere the presence of the beggar exerts a genuinely humanizing influence. The human sympathy shown towards him is not a grudging consideration towards old age; the no "anger at his heart" of the postboy, placed at the very end of the passage that portrays the beggar's impact on his fellow-men (22-43), proves that the little acts of love towards the old man come indeed from the heart.

There is no condescension towards the beggar, and Wordsworth does not glorify poverty: he calls the old man "*Poor* Traveller!" (58; my italics). Even the children do not tease the beggar (63-65). The seed of brotherhood is laid in them,[60] for they learn to respect the old man's right to receive the gifts of their community without begrudging him his personal freedom and basic human dignity:

> In childhood, from this solitary being,
> This helpless wanderer, have perchance receiv'd,
> . . .

"functional relationship" in "The Old Cumberland Beggar", see J. P. Ward, "Wordsworth and the Sociological Idea", *CritQ,* 16 (1974), 331-55 (337-41).

[60] For Wordsworth "The Child is Father of the Man" (from "My Heart Leaps Up . . .", comp. 1802). See also my discussion of childhood in the 1798-99 and 1805 *Prelude* (chs. 3 and 5).

> That first mild touch of sympathy and thought,
> In which they found their kindred with a world
> Where want and sorrow were. . . .
>
> (102–08)

Wordsworth chides the politicians who cannot grasp the cohesive function the beggar exerts on the community:

> . . . Statesmen! ye
> Who are so *restless* in your *wisdom*, ye
> Who have a broom still ready in your hands
> To rid the world of nuisances; ye *p*roud,
> Heart-swoln, while in your *p*ride ye contem*p*late
> Your talents, *p*ower, and wisdom, deem him not
> A burthen of the earth. . . .
>
> (67–73; my italics)

Restlessness is never the key to true wisdom. Restless minds are anathema to Wordsworth, as shown in his portrayal of Rivers and throughout his poetry. His prophetic rage over the politicians who according to the Fenwick Notes had begun their war against beggars at the time "The Old Cumberland Beggar" was composed (Brett & Jones, p. 306) gains additional force by the alliterative "p". Lines 73 ff. deduce from "Nature's law" a feeling of brotherhood for all that lives,[61] the "meanest of created things". There is a very interesting and significant difference between Wordsworth and Coleridge: in Wordsworth Nature suffices to fraternize, whereas in Coleridge it is the spirit of God in Nature that unites all in one brotherhood:

> 'Tis the sublime of man,
> Our noontide Majesty, to know ourselves
> Parts and proportions of one wondrous whole!
> This fraternises man, this constitutes
> Our charities and bearings. But 'tis God
> Diffused through all, that doth make all one whole.[62]

The "offices of charity" (82) towards the mendicant help establish, and uphold, the bond of brotherhood between the villagers. The phrasing brings across the ties of brotherhood: "inseparably link'd", "together binds" (79, 81).[63] The theme of the bond of brotherhood is resumed in

---

[61] On ll. 73–79 John Beer acutely observes that the "heart here is not simply the instrument of charity and courage which it had been in eighteenth-century poetry, but a badge of human equality . . ." (*Wordsworth and the Human Heart,* London: Macmillan, 1978, p. 116).

[62] S. T. Coleridge, "Religious Musings" (comp. 1794), in *Poetical Works,* 3rd impr., ed. E. H. Coleridge (1912; rpt. O.U.P. paperback, Oxford: Oxford U.P., 1974), pp. 113–14.

[63] On the "interrelatedness of all life", as illustrated by the beggar, see Woodring (referring to Karl Kroeber's *Artifice of Reality*), *Wordsworth,* pp. 56–57.

>   . . . all behold in him
>   A silent monitor, which on their minds
>   Must needs impress a *transitory* thought
>   Of self-congratulation . . .
>   (114–17; my italics)

Wordsworth is careful to point out that the state of self-congratulation among the distributors of charity is not permanent but "transitory". It seems to be necessary to single out "transitory thought" as much as I have drawn attention to the epithet "poor" in line 58 above, for despite the excellent defence of "The Old Cumberland Beggar" by Cleanth Brooks the poem is still being attacked for its alleged praise of poverty.[64] However, bearing in mind that the predominant socio-economic policies of the age were against the government's interference in a free economy, it is unhistorical to feel moral indignation over "The Old Cumberland Beggar". The Evangelicals too "did not find it recorded in the Gospels that poverty was an evil to be cured . . . 'The poor are always with you . . . Blessed are the poor.'"[65] Malthus's *Essay on the Principle of Population* . . . (1798) maintains that population always tends to increase more rapidly than the means of subsistence. No positive action was called for to relieve poverty. Vice, war, and pestilence maintain the balance between population and the means of subsistence.[66] Edmund Burke likewise preached the inevitability of poverty:

> To provide for us in our necessities is not in the power of Government. It would be a vain presumption in statesmen to think they can do it. The people maintain them, and not they the people. It is in the power of Government to prevent much evil; it can do very little positive good in this, or perhaps in anything else. It is not only so of the state and statesman, but of all the classes and descriptions of the rich: they are the pensioners of the poor, and are maintained by their

---

[64] Laurence Lerner, "What Did Wordsworth Mean by 'Nature'?", *CritQ*, 17 (1975), 291–308 (293), comments on ll. 150–54: "The old man is valuable to the village because he enables others to behave charitably, and so to benefit spiritually. Charity is for the sake of the giver, not the receiver; and the old man is being used as a means for the benefit of others. Wordsworth is pointing out the advantage of having someone poorer than you. Surely this is outrageous. . . . Wordsworth is prepared to praise poverty so that others may be the better for it." Contrast this with Cleanth Brooks, "Wordsworth and Human Suffering: Notes on Two Early Poems", in *From Sensibility to Romanticism: Essays Presented to Frederick A. Pottle*, eds. F. W. Hilles and H. Bloom (New York: Oxford U.P., 1965), pp. 373–87, in particular pp. 373, 375.

[65] D. C. Somervell, *English Thought in the Nineteenth Century*, 5th ed. (London: Methuen, 1947), p. 28.

[66] B. Sprague Allen, "Minor Disciples of Radicalism in the Revolutionary Era", *MP*, 21 (1923–24), 277–301 (285).

superfluity. They are under an absolute, hereditary, and indefeasible dependence on those who labor and are miscalled the Poor.[67]

Poverty was uncontested except by radicals such as Thomas Paine. Thanks to the evolving notion of a universal brotherhood of man, slavery and the slave trade began to be regarded as an evil in the eyes of God by religious people and as injustice by secular egalitarians. Since, on the other hand, poverty was here to stay, "The Old Cumberland Beggar" defends the beggar's human dignity and insists on his personal liberty. Wordsworth reacts against the plan to separate the beggar from ordinary human company:

> May never House, misnamed of industry,
> Make him a captive . . .
>
> (172–73)

Instead

> Let him be free of mountain solitudes,
> And have around him, whether heard or not,
> The pleasant melody of woodland birds.
>
> (176–78)

Wordsworth refers to the pleasure that man—including the "poorest poor"—derives from doing his occasional good deed (140–54). This passage carries a tone of religious conviction in its stress on the bond of brotherhood ("man is dear to man") and the universal equality and brotherhood implied in "we have *all* of us *one* human heart" [my italics]. Alan Grob comments on this that "Wordsworth's hope of general social reform is an ethical uniformitarianism".[68]

In Sweden more than in England much of private charity and individual moral responsibility has been replaced by State measures; however, now governmental countermeasures are being discussed to combat the anonymity of the State. Perhaps it sounds reactionary, but Wordsworth's "unletter'd Villagers" who "tender offices and pensive thoughts" (162–63) undoubtedly benefit emotionally and morally from their acts. The villagers are thoughtful and reflective; this distinguishes

---

[67] Edmund Burke, "Thoughts and Details on Scarcity" [originally presented to Pitt in 1795], in *The Works of the Right Honourable Edmund Burke*, vol. V (London: John C. Nimmo, 1899), pp. 133–34. See also Alfred Cobban, *Edmund Burke and the Revolt Against the Eighteenth Century: A Study of the Political and Social Thinking of Burke, Wordsworth, Coleridge and Southey* (London: George Allen & Unwin, 1929), pp. 192–94.

[68] Alan Grob, *The Philosophic Mind: A Study of Wordsworth's Poetry and Thought, 1797–1805* (Columbus: Ohio State U.P., 1973), p. 157. For the term "uniformitarianism" (used earlier by A. O. Lovejoy) in the context of the eighteenth century, see ch. 4, n. 36.

them from the unreal rural characters and village bumpkins of the Augustan Age and thus rings a democratic note, however often unhistoric interpretations may label "The Old Cumberland Beggar" as reactionary.

Alan Grob thinks that Wordsworth has embraced Godwin's rational benevolence in "The Old Cumberland Beggar".[69] This may be so. Ever since the composition of *Salisbury Plain* Wordsworth's love for humanity is individualized in his best poetry, and in "The Old Cumberland Beggar" the subtle individualization of the old man brings him nearer to our hearts. The poem opened on a note of personal liberty and it concludes with a eulogy of personal liberty (and for once the italics are not mine but in the *Lyrical Ballads* of 1798):

> And let him, *where* and *when* he will, sit down
> Beneath the trees, or by the grassy bank
> Of high-way side, and with the little birds
> Share his chance-gather'd meal, and, finally,
> As in the eye of Nature he has liv'd,
> So in the eye of Nature let him die.
> (184–89)

This chapter on 1795–97 has borne out that generally there is a vast improvement in Wordsworth's poetics over that of 1791–94. In *Adventures on Salisbury Plain* (comp. 1795) he no longer directly reflects the political radicalism of 1795 and he has broken away from the goriness of the Gothic school. We have noticed that in 1796, when Wordsworth temporarily returned to social and political directness (in "Imitation of Juvenal" and "The Convict"), the result was a deterioration in poetic quality. Again, as between 1791 and 1794, Wordsworth's development is not strictly chronological. I have attempted to show that *The Borderers* (comp. 1796–97) argues negatively for brotherhood and equality. *The Borderers* strikes a new note in its kindly treatment of the Baron Herbert; prior to this play Wordsworth had excluded on principle any members of the nobility from his idea of brotherhood. This chapter has illustrated the remarkable advance from the radical-fashionable sort of brotherhood of "The Convict"—via the doubtfulness in *The Borderers*—to the thoughtful kind of brotherhood and personal liberty of "The Old Cumberland Beggar". Wordsworth's timeless notions of brotherhood and equality, which escape the needs of the ephemeral political

---

[69] He refers particularly to ll. 90–97: "Where'er the aged Beggar takes his rounds, / The mild necessity of use . . .", etc. (Grob, *The Philosophic Mind*, pp. 160–61); see also A. Grob, "Wordsworth and Godwin: A Reassessment", *SIR*, 6 (1967), 98–119 (101–03).

manifesto, find their beginning in "The Old Cumberland Beggar". The importance of these concepts in their fundamental, permanent meaning will become apparent in the next chapter which is mainly concerned with poems that throw light on relationships between man and man in a society untouched by overcivilization.

CHAPTER 3

1798–1799

In the summer of 1797 the ardent revolutionary Thelwall had thought of renouncing public life,[1] and Wordsworth, as we have seen, had definitely withdrawn from public political commitment. The conservative counterreaction continued to gain momentum in 1798. For the *Anti-Jacobin* of 1 January 1798 liberty meant something very different from the *liberté* that the French armies spread across Europe:

> Thus Britons guard their ancient fame,
>   Assert their empire o'er the sea,
> And to the envying world proclaim,
>   One nation still is brave and free—
>
> Resolv'd to conquer or to die,
> True to their KING, their LAWS, their LIBERTY.[2]

The British Government's fear of subversion was understandable if seen, for instance, against the background of the inflammatory addresses and toasts delivered by the Opposition on the occasion of Charles Fox's birthday on 24 January 1798.[3] On the same day the Lemanic Republic

---

[1] Thompson, *The Making of the English Working Class*, p. 180.
[2] Quoted by Thompson, in *The Making of the English Working Class*, p. 86. The small capitals are in Thompson.
[3] Here, for example, is the Duke of Norfolk calling the health of Fox (implying by "freedom" freedom from the Tories): "'We are met, in a moment of most serious difficulty, to celebrate the birth of a man dear to the friends of freedom. I shall only recal[l] to your memory, that, not twenty years ago, the illustrious George Washington had not more than two thousand men to rally round him when his country was attacked. America is now free. This day full two thousand men are assembled in this place. I leave you to make the application.'" Then followed toasts to "the 'Rights of the People', 'Constitutional Redress of the Wrongs of the People', 'A speedy and effectual Reform in the Representation of the People in Parliament', 'The People of Ireland: and may they be speedily restored to the Blessings of Law and Liberty', there came the culminating point of the evening. Thanking the assembly for the applause that had been given to his conduct in the chair, the Duke of Norfolk called yet another toast to 'our Sovereign's Health, the Majesty of the People', and this almost republican sentiment was received with 'rapturous' acclamation. Few responsible people could have considered that the subsequent dismissal of the Duke from his Lord-Lieutenancy and Militia command was wholly undeserved." (Maccoby, *English Radicalism 1786–1832*, pp. 122–23).

was proclaimed in Geneva, and also in January the Irish rebellion broke out;[4] in the same month Ménard violated the national liberty of Switzerland with his 15,000 troops. Rome fell on 11 February, Berne on 5 March, and on 9 March 1798 France annexed the left bank of the Rhine. Many hitherto Jacobin intellectuals became disenchanted with the French.[5] Meanwhile Thomas Paine's *Rights of Man* was reputed to have reached a sales figure of 400,000 copies. The cheap edition of the *Rights of Man* sold "at least one hundred thousand copies";[6] T. J. Mathias wrote in 1797 that it was read by the peasantry "on mountains and moors and by the wayside".[7] It was indeed a time of reaction and counterreaction, an era which was bound to produce tension in sensitive minds.

Wordsworth's extant letters of the spring of 1798 do not reveal his reactions to these political events. However, the theme of national liberty must have occupied him during the period, for he was reading Henry Brooke's play *Gustavus Vasa* (1739), a play dealing with the liberation of Sweden from the Danish yoke (*E.Y.*, p. 210).[8] Artistically, the spring and summer of 1798 proved to be one of Wordsworth's most productive periods. One of the reasons for this may be that Wordsworth's boundless aspiration for liberty, reason, equality, and perfectibility clashed with a "peculiarly harsh and unregenerate reality" and that his creative impulse came out of this conflict.[9]

---

[4] On British and Irish sympathy with a possible French invasion in 1798, see Thompson, *The Making of the English Working Class,* pp. 186–87. The French attempt to invade Ireland in the autumn of 1798 failed.

[5] On the diminishing ranks of the Jacobins in 1798, see Thompson, *The Making of the English Working Class,* pp. 189–93.

[6] Quoted by J. H. Plumb, "Political Man", in *Man Versus Society in Eighteenth-Century Britain: Six Points of View,* ed. J. L. Clifford (Cambridge: Cambridge U.P., 1968), p. 17, n. 4, from P. S. Foner, ed., *The Complete Writings of Thomas Paine* (New York, 1945).

[7] Ibid., p. 17.

[8] Gustavus [Vasa] is mentioned in the 1805 *Prelude* I.211 as a subject worthy of poetic treatment. Another Gustavus Vasa (1745–97), an African spokesman for the anti-slavery movement, was widely known in the 1790s (*E.Y.*, p. 210, n. 2).

[9] Thompson, "Disenchantment or Default?", p. 152. Ibid., pp. 162–69, recreates the anti-Jacobin spirit of the spring of 1798, where Thompson makes particular reference to the persecution of the radical scholar and writer Gilbert Wakefield. Furthermore, Thompson thinks that the establishment of Britain's volunteer corps was somewhat compulsory and concludes that Coleridge and Wordsworth "were hopping the draft" (p. 168) when they went to Germany in the autumn.

The Ruined Cottage

In MS. B of *The Ruined Cottage* (GCL I:57e),[10] most of it probably written between 25 January and 5 March 1798, Wordsworth breaks for good with the political hyperbole of the *Descriptive Sketches* and the humanitarian eccentricity of "The Convict"; and probably no significant critic doubts the high artistic merits of *The Ruined Cottage*.[11] Jonathan Wordsworth notes that "Wordsworth's poetry from *The Borderers* through to *Tintern Abbey* [comp. July 1798] is vitally concerned with relationships . . .",[12] and Mary Jacobus observes that Wordsworth's interests during this period "are all with the human, the social, or the political . . .".[13]

Hardly any other motto could have been more appropriate for *The Ruined Cottage* than that of the inequality-castigating poet Robert Burns;[14] Wordsworth's selection of this democratic poet's verse—his ". . . Muse though homely in attire / May touch the heart"—is as indicative of Wordsworth's democratic stance as the choice of a simple country woman and a pedlar as the heroine and hero of the poem. Lines 70–74 repeat the veneration for Burns. Full of glee the narrator-poet and the pedlar "would repeat / The songs of Burns . . ."; some of them, we know, deal with liberty, equality, and fraternity.

---

[10] My quotations from MS. B are drawn from the Reading Text by James Butler, ed., *The Ruined Cottage* and *The Pedlar*, The Cornell Wordsworth (Ithaca, N.Y.: Cornell U.P., 1979), pp. 42–72.

[11] Even E. E. Bostetter, who criticizes the Wordsworth of 1797–98 for being aloof and detached, drawing "strength and even quiet satisfaction and pleasure from his observation of the suffering of others", finds praise for *The Ruined Cottage*: "it is in the description of the slow disintegration of Margaret and the accompanying disintegration of the cottage that the poem becomes truly great . . ." (*The Romantic Ventriloquists: Wordsworth, Coleridge, Keats, Shelley, Byron*, Seattle: Univ. of Washington Press, 1963, pp. 54 and 61).

[12] Jonathan Wordsworth, *The Music of Humanity: A Critical Study of Wordsworth's "Ruined Cottage", incorporating texts from a manuscript of 1799–1800* (New York: Harper & Row, 1969), p. 247. In the same book J. Wordsworth acutely observes that the "famous *Biographia Literaria* distinction between Coleridge and the supernatural, Wordsworth and the everyday, disguises the far more important one between Coleridge's interest in ideas, and Wordsworth's concern with people . . ." (p. 254).

[13] Jacobus, *Tradition and Experiment*, p. 62. Mary Jacobus remarks also on the difference between the understatement of *The Ruined Cottage* and the outspoken protest poetry of the 1790s (ibid., p. 143). Comparing *Salisbury Plain* with *The Ruined Cottage* she points out that Wordsworth has not become "a less humane poet, but that his vision is directed beyond topical issues to the permanent themes of loss, change, and mortality . . ." (ibid., p. 159). Finally Jacobus brings out the implicit socio-political radicalism of the Wordsworth of 1798 in contrasting his work with the conservative ballad tracts of the period (ibid., pp. 237–39).

[14] See also R. Noyes, "Wordsworth and Burns", *PMLA*, 59 (1944), 813–32; and *E.Y.*, p. 256.

Line 47 opens the life history of the pedlar: "I knew him—he was born of lowly race". The dash makes us pause, and thus the pedlar's low origins are fixed more firmly in our memories. This hawker "possessed / No vulgar mind *though* he had passed his life / In this poor occupation [as pedlar] . . ." (65–67). Line 74 continues the contrast: ". . . *Though* he was untaught, / In the dead lore of schools undisciplined, / . . . / To him was given an ear which deeply felt / The voice of Nature . . .". The pedlar was endowed with the gift of creative imagination, for "*Though* poor in outward shew, he was most rich" (86), and, finally, line 104 (containing yet another "though") concludes the pedlar's life history and personal qualities.[15] The well-balanced reiteration of "though" draws our attention to qualities that in the convention of the poetry of the period would exclude each other. The elements that cancel each other in the poetry of his predecessors, here concur: poor occupation + no vulgar mind; untaught + deep feelings; outwardly poor + rich with creative imagination—"So was he framed, though humble and obscure / Had been his lot . . ." (104–05). The reversal of the poetic convention is the poet's unobtrusive and subversive effort at working towards equality in a repressive society.

His extensive life experience has enabled the pedlar to develop fine human qualities: "much had he seen of men / Their manners, their enjoyments and pursuits, / Their passions and their feelings, chiefly those / Essential and eternal in the heart, / Which 'mid the simpler forms of rural life / Exist more simple in their elements / And speak a plainer language . . ." (59–65). Knowing the pedlar's varied life experience makes us more receptive to his later tale of Margaret and Robert and also more willing to accept his judgement. Lines 62–65 look forward to the democratic implications of the 1800 Preface to the *Lyrical Ballads*.[16]

The "dead lore" taught by the schools implies its converse, the real lore of men, which the hawker learnt from life. Although not trained in the theories of men, he has an eye that looks "deep into the shades of difference" (95). A forsaken spring makes him draw a parallel with the brotherhood of man; the tragedy of human suffering is evoked by "the waters", the element of life:

---

[15] Italics mine throughout this paragraph.

[16] "Low and rustic life was generally chosen because in that situation the essential passions of the heart find a better soil in which they can attain their maturity, are less under restraint, and speak a plainer and more emphatic language . . ." (*P.L.B.*, Brett & Jones, p. 245/*Prose Works* I, p. 124).

> The waters of that spring if they could feel
> Might mourn. They are not as they were; the bond
> Of brotherhood is broken—time has been
> When every day the touch of human hand
> Disturbed their stillness, and they ministered
> To human comfort. . . .
>
> (135–40)

These lines are central and set the scene for the pedlar's tale of Margaret's life of silent suffering.

In better times work had afforded Margaret and her husband a peaceful and contented life (172–84). By contrast the following lines deal with that curse of brotherhood, "the plague of war" (188), disease, and unemployment: "'twas now / A time of trouble; shoals of artisans / Were from their daily labour turned away / To hang for bread on parish charity" (205–08). Like fish ("shoals"), silent and helpless, the unemployed "hang" at the edge of the lake of the rich to receive their meagre charity. Todd says that Wordsworth in *The Ruined Cottage* is concerned with the "virtue and fortitude of man, not for his rights".[17] Perhaps this is how Wordsworth felt about the poem. However, in pointing to the socio-political circumstances that prevent man's enjoyment of peace, employment, family life, he implies man's rights to these preconditions for a happy life. In so far as *The Ruined Cottage* is an anti-war poem it is also a poem propounding brotherhood and some of the rights of man. Lines 213–43 are of particular relevance to our day. They witness to Wordsworth's psychological insight into how the social evil of long-term unemployment leads to the gradual decline of Robert's mental balance, for example, he does things haphazardly, does winter jobs in summer and vice versa; throughout, his behaviour is inconsistent.

Wordsworth's ideal countryman, such as the pedlar, is a captivating conversationalist. His tale is told in a spirit of brotherhood, "a countenance of love" (268). His moral seriousness warns us against holding "dalliance with . . . misery", however briefly we may be inclined "to draw / A momentary pleasure" (282–84) from a tale of misery. The pedlar's story is "a common tale / By moving accidents uncharactered" and "to the grosser sense / But ill adapted . . ." (290 ff.; compare with "Michael", l. 19: "[a story] ungarnish'd with events"). "Common" indicates the democratic subject matter. The hawker's account dispenses with the gross stimuli of the Gothic story and is "scarcely palpable / To him who does not think. . . ."

---

[17] Todd, *Politics and the Poet*, p. 90.

Line 297 resumes the story of Margaret. Like the sailor of *Adventures on Salisbury Plain* Robert is driven by poverty and unemployment into the army. *The Ruined Cottage* is as much an indictment of social injustice as the *Adventures on Salisbury Plain*. It is, however, more low-keyed. The psychology of suffering in *The Ruined Cottage* is that of a mature poet: we now enter the minds of those generations of women on the home-front whose sufferings Wordsworth individualizes through Margaret who had "lingered in unquiet widowhood, / A wife, and widow . . ." (483–84) before she wasted away. Wordsworth's quiet mode links wife and widow by that unobtrusive conjunction "and", but this contradiction engenders a tension that evokes fully all the uncertainties and worries of the "wife-widow", a pitiful state that excludes her from remarriage in most cases. These lines contain a store of human sympathy. Only an unthinking reader would not discern the silent cry for brotherhood in the moving tale of Margaret's suffering.

Margaret's decline is reflected in the step-by-step change of Nature from spring (434) to autumn (474) to winter (517). Margaret fades away like a flower. The language depicting her decline and change is rich in symbols:

> I turned aside
> And strolled into her garden. It was changed:
> The unprofitable bindweed spread his bells
> From side to side, and with unwieldy wreaths
> Had dragged the rose from its sustaining wall
> And bowed it down to earth . . .
>
> (370–75)

The excerpt comes early in the section dealing with Margaret's change. Thus if the "dragged-down rose" stands for Margaret and the "sustaining wall" for her husband, this passage foreshadows effectively the human misery to come.

The anti-war sentiments of *The Ruined Cottage* do not shout; but the criticism of social and political injustice is distinctly audible. Exactly like *Salisbury Plain* and *Adventures on Salisbury Plain* the poem raises the question of why there should be so much suffering. The censor could not have touched *The Ruined Cottage*; nevertheless, it is political dynamite, since it brings into the open one main cause of human sorrow: war. Instead of patriotic sabre-rattling Wordsworth sabotages the war effort.

Lyrical Ballads *(1st and 2nd editions)*

Not "genuine freedom" as in the sense of the "Prospectus to *The Recluse*" (below, ch. 4) but the enjoyment of more political liberty—besides their main purpose of learning German—may have been the reason why Wordsworth, his sister Dorothy, Coleridge, and Sara Coleridge had resolved to go to Germany. Wordsworth does not allude to political reasons when he mentions his German plans to James Losh in a letter of 11 March [1798] (*E.Y.*, p. 213).[18] Losh, however, a social reformer and an acquaintance of Wordsworth, records in his diary (entry 3 April 1798) an important talk with Southey and a Colonel Henry Barry. The " 'conversation turned principally upon the invasion of liberty. I [Losh] stated the probability of a stop being put to Southey's Joan of Arc, in that case he declared his intention of leaving the country. We all agreed that were there any place to go to emigration would be a prudent thing for literary men and the friends of freedom. . . .' "[19] This place may have been Germany for Wordsworth, both a writer and a friend of liberty. According to Todd "many Jacobins looked to Germany for the planting 'in hardier soil' of the tree of liberty to which the French had proved so false".[20]

In April 1798 Wordsworth "went to have his picture taken" by the painter William Shuter. Chard, p. 231, thinks that the painter was a liberal, since he, together with Holcroft and Thelwall, is mentioned in Godwin's diary (18 December 1794). During this spring as well—at the end of May—Wordsworth met one more liberal, William Hazlitt, who was one of the earliest critics to notice the implied socio-political radicalism of the *Lyrical Ballads* (see Introduction and below, p. 144) and who had the good fortune of reading some of Wordsworth's contributions to the *Lyrical Ballads* before they were anonymously published in the one-volume first edition of 1798.[21] More recent critics, for example Carl Woodring and David Perkins, also see the democratic ideas and questioning of the social order embedded in the poems of the *Lyrical Ballads*.[22]

---

[18] On the German trip, see also *E.Y.*, p. 216 (Dorothy to Richard Wordsworth, 30 April [1798]), and this chapter, n. 9.
[19] Quoted in Paul Kaufman, "Wordsworth's 'Candid and Enlightened Friend' ", *N&Q*, 207, N.S. 9 (Nov. 1962), 403–08 (405).
[20] F. M. Todd, "Wordsworth in Germany", *MLR*, 47 (1952), 508–11 (508).
[21] On Hazlitt and Wordsworth, see Chard, p. 236. Chard deals also with the socio-political significance of the *Lyrical Ballads* (ibid., pp. 244, 249–51).
[22] Woodring, *Wordsworth*, pp. 22–23; Perkins, *Wordsworth and the Poetry of Sincerity* (Cambridge, Mass.: The Belknap Press of Harvard U.P., 1964), p. 151. Robert Mayo, in his important article "The Contemporaneity of the *Lyrical Ballads*", *PMLA*, 69 (1954), 486–519 (495–96, 503, 506), stresses the "sentimental humanitarianism" of the poems. Mayo has been answered in Stephen Parrish's scholar-critical study *The Art of the Lyrical Ballads* (Cambridge, Mass.: Harvard U.P., 1973); Parrish's discussion of the terms "pastoral" and "lyrical ballad" is enlightening and especially relevant to understanding the

At about the same time as Wordsworth was writing MS. B of *The Ruined Cottage* he probably started work on "The Farmer of Tilsbury Vale", "A Character",[23] and "The Reverie of Poor Susan"[24] (GCL I:60); the two latter were to be included in the second volume/edition of *Lyrical Ballads* (1800). (Just as the first volume the second volume was a joint venture between Wordsworth and Coleridge; Coleridge's name, however, does not appear on the title page of the 1800 edition.) Like most of Wordsworth's contributions to the *Lyrical Ballads* all three poems centre on man. With the lighthearted tone of "The Farmer of Tilsbury Vale"[25] Wordsworth extends his hand of brotherhood to a farmer-debtor who had emigrated to London to escape his creditors. Isabella Fenwick notes that Wordsworth based this verse on a story told him by Mr. Poole of Nether Stowey and quotes Wordsworth as saying "I need scarcely add that he [Poole] felt for all men as his brothers" (*PW* IV, p. 447); on the evidence of this poem and "A Character", Wordsworth shared Poole's attitude. "A Character" wholeheartedly accepts man with all his contradictions; it is a poetic document of man's uniqueness and thus claims by implication man's right to personal liberty within a wider human brotherhood. "The Reverie of Poor Susan" strikes a sadder note. The poem deals first and foremost with a country girl's longing in the city for her native dwelling in one of Nature's beauty spots, but it also raises the question of which human activities made Susan leave her home. Is she a victim of industrialization, enclosure, poverty, dishonour? What circumstances prevent her from enjoying the right of living in her place of birth?

Some weeks after the bulk of work on *The Ruined Cottage* had been completed, Wordsworth concentrated on the *Lyrical Ballads* and composed the following poems: probably in March 1798 "To my Sister"[26] (GCL I:65) and "A Whirl-blast from Behind the Hill" (GCL I:68); between March and May "Goody Blake and Harry Gill"[27] (GCL I:66),

---

Lyrical Ballads (Parrish, pp. 158–59). On the social element, see also Moorman I, pp. 377–78. Mary Jacobus underscores Wordsworth's and Coleridge's attempt to go against the public taste of the period: Southey in his adaptation of the *Lyrical Ballads* is out to please whereas Wordsworth is out to rectify ("Southey's Debt to *Lyrical Ballads (1798)*", *RES*, N.S., 22 (1971), 20–36 (24–27, 35–36)).

[23] Brett & Jones, p. 214, entitle "A Character, in the Antithetical Manner".

[24] Brett & Jones, p. 170, entitle "Poor Susan".

[25] For a comment on Wordsworth's brotherly tolerance in general and the "Farmer" in particular, see Moorman I, p. 481. According to Moorman the poem belongs to the summer of 1800.

[26] Brett & Jones, p. 58, entitle "Lines Written at a Small Distance from my House, and Sent by my Little Boy to the Person to Whom They are Addressed".

[27] The full title in Brett & Jones, p. 54, is "Goody Blake, and Harry Gill, a True Story".

"The Complaint of a Forsaken Indian Woman", "Her Eyes are Wild",[28] "The Idiot Boy", "The Last of the Flock", "We are Seven", "Simon Lee"[29] (GCL I:67), and "The Thorn" (GCL I:69). Except for "A Whirl-blast . . ." all the poems deal to some extent with human relationships.

"Lines Written at a Small Distance from my House" ["To my Sister"] (Brett & Jones, pp. 59–60) expresses a "philosophy" of universal brotherhood and love:

> Love, now an universal birth,
> From heart to heart is stealing,
> From earth to man, from man to earth,
> —It is the hour of feeling.

The bond of affection between all men is illustrated by "heart to heart" and the interrelatedness between man and Nature (animate and inanimate) is brought out by linking man to earth and earth to man. Love and feeling are the key elements of the poem. Wise passiveness,[30] but only "for this one day" (15 and 39), and the "blessed power . . . about, below, above" will teach us greater insights into the essentials of life than "fifty years of reason". It may be necessary to point out that Wordsworth is not anti-intellectual. Even modern psychology would agree with the proposal to stop all intellectual pursuits for just that "one day", since this rest would clear the mind and make it subsequently more receptive.

An indictment of socio-economic injustice is implicit in "Goody Blake and Harry Gill" (Brett & Jones, pp. 54–58). The gleaning rights of cottagers had been restricted and farming property was more clearly defined in the 1790s, which made it more difficult to gather sticks for fuel.[31] Although Goody Blake spun all day and three hours at night, "It would not pay for candle-light", and "coals [were] dear". Goody Blake lacks one of man's basic needs, sufficient fuel, and thus

> When her old bones were cold and chill,
> She left her fire, or left her bed,
> To seek the hedge of Harry Gill.

---

[28] Brett & Jones, p. 83, entitle "The Mad Mother".

[29] Brett & Jones, p. 60, entitle "Simon Lee, the Old Huntsman, with an Incident in which He was Concerned".

[30] The idea of "wise passiveness" is important in Wordsworth. See, e.g., "Expostulation and Reply": "'Nor less I deem that there are powers, / 'Which of themselves our minds impress, / 'That we can feed this mind of ours, / 'In a wise passiveness." (Brett & Jones, p. 104.)

[31] On the injustice of enclosure and the attack on other customary rights, e.g., gleaning, access to fuel, see Thompson, *Making of the English Working Class*, pp. 238–43.

The contrast with the subsequent stanza is masterly. Harry Gill's needs are fulfilled and yet, to take vengeance on Goody,

> . . . oft from his warm fire he'd go.

The injustice is underlined by the juxtaposition of "old" Goody Blake's unqualified empty "fire", with "young" Harry Gill's qualified "warm fire". Goody's filching is against the law but she is morally justified. Although there is no equality of justice on earth, God's law is radical in treating "all" equally: "And kneeling on the sticks, she pray'd / To God that is the judge of all." Most of the poem has the tone of a morality and it finishes in that vein: "Now think, ye farmers all, I pray, / Of Goody Blake and Harry Gill".[32] The underlying thought of "Goody Blake and Harry Gill" is an appeal to equality and brotherhood. It is interesting to consider that Wordsworth himself and Dorothy gained first-hand experience in gathering sticks (including rotten boughs) and fir-apples for fuel in 1798.[33]

The most elemental of all bonds, mother and child, is partly the theme of "The Complaint of a Forsaken Indian Woman" and the main theme in "The Mad Mother". To choose an insane mother for the heroine of the latter poem is again an example of Wordsworth's democratic outlook. But more important than his choice of subject is his treatment of the mad mother: She arouses neither disgust nor excessive pity, nor is she a figure of fun. The poet describes her with the same gentle air of amusement that he uses to depict the warm-hearted mother and her half-witted son in "The Idiot Boy". Wordsworth himself commented on the democratic implications of "The Idiot Boy" in a letter to John Wilson of [7 June 1802] (*E.Y.*, pp. 354–55).[34] The Mad Mother ["Her Eyes are Wild"] is welcomed into Wordsworth's brotherhood, as much as the Old Cumberland Beggar was integrated in his community, and the Idiot Boy is welcomed most wholeheartedly into Wordsworth's ideal society. The boy experiences unconditional, pure motherly love; and there is neigh-

---

[32] Kenneth MacLean observes that the "name of 'farmer' was possibly as much scorned in the years around 1800 as that of 'capitalist' in some parts of our society today. . . ." (*Agrarian Age: A Background for Wordsworth* (1950), Yale Studies in English, vol. 115; rpt. Hamden, Conn.: Archon Books, 1970, p. 60.)

[33] *Journals of Dorothy Wordsworth: The Alfoxden Journal 1798, The Grasmere Journals 1800–1803.* Introd. Helen Darbishire. Ed. Mary Moorman (1958, 1971; new ed. and rpt. with corrections London: Oxford U.P., 1974), pp. 4, 6, 7, 9.

[34] See also Mary Jacobus, "Southey's Debt to *Lyrical Ballads (1798)*", *RES*, N.S., 22 (1971), 20–36 (24–27).

bourly love as well. These poems have no direct bearing on the universal brotherhood of man; nevertheless, the seed of worldwide *fraternité* can only grow and thrive when the world at large adopts a good portion of the emotions expressed by the mother of "The Idiot Boy".

Wordsworth's sense of wonder in "A Whirl-blast . . ." (Brett & Jones, p. 177) over the "wither'd leaves [that] skip and hop" in the calm makes him utter

> Oh! grant me Heaven a heart at ease
> That I may never cease to find,
> Even in appearances like these
> Enough to nourish and to stir my mind!

It is this sense of wonder that enables him to be fascinated by the mind of the little girl in "We are Seven" and which inspires him to see a story of gossip, tragedy, suffering, and pity in "The Thorn"; it is this feeling of awe that makes him grasp the moral lessons implicit in the meetings with an old leech gatherer and "Simon Lee, the Old Huntsman" (Brett & Jones, pp. 60–63).

The situation of Simon Lee is better than that of the female vagrant and her father in *Salisbury Plain,* who were expelled from their home (*SP,* sts. 23 and 24), and the woman who became the victim of the poor laws in *Adventures on Salisbury Plain*. Unlike the uprooted heroine in "Poor Susan", Simon Lee and his wife are firmly linked to their community (and this means especially much to the aged) exactly as the Old Cumberland Beggar forms part of a district. Simon's life is hard:

> . . . he's forced to work, though weak,
> —The weakest in the village[.]

On the other hand, the tenacity required of the former runner Simon now comes to the surface in his determination to cut the root of the old tree. Further, which seems to contradict the above quotation, Simon and his wife did not work only because they were forced to, since

> . . . though you with your utmost skill
> From labour could not wean them,
> Alas! 'tis very little, all
> Which they can do between them.

The subject matter of the poem is democratic, its language simple and matter of fact and in parts an imitation of common speech: "he is lean and he is sick". Simon Lee may still be able to scrape together a meagre living from the common land; enclosure has not yet caught up with him. However, it is not so clear—as MacLean and Brett & Jones say—[35] that Simon is capable of cultivating the land, for Wordsworth questions: "what avails the land to them, / Which they can till no longer?" Sure, however, is Simon Lee's stubborn pride in personal liberty and independence:

> One summer-day I chanced to see
> This old man doing all he could
> About the root of an old tree,
> A stump of rotten wood.

If this stubborn clinging to personal liberty and independence has been perhaps a little more pronounced in the English-speaking world than in many other parts, there may be a correlation between this Wordsworthian character Simon Lee and the firmly rooted political liberty of the United States and the old Commonwealth. The local brotherhood in "Simon Lee" is intact; in it there are the "little, nameless, unremembered acts / Of kindness and of love . . ." of the "Tintern Abbey" of a few weeks later, such as the "splitting of a log for old Simon Lee" (Moorman I, p. 403).

The Last of the Flock (GCL I:67; Brett & Jones, pp. 78–81) is an indictment of the economic plight many smallholders found themselves in towards the end of the 1790s.[36] Of all the poems written in 1798 "The Last of the Flock" contains the most overt social criticism. The concepts of liberty and equality can hardly be discerned in the poem, and there is little of brotherhood; however, the poem deserves a close look for its unidealized, naturalistic air.

The first stanza supplies the setting for the life drama of the shepherd.

---

[35] "The poem makes an interesting social comment regarding the enclosure of common land. Simon in old age is still able to live on and to cultivate a small piece of land to which he laid claim in his youth. Between 1700 and 1844, 1,765,711 acres of common land were enclosed by Act of Parliament and it is interesting to notice that Wordsworth, later in his life, succeeded in preventing the enclosure of Grasmere's commons." (Paraphrased in Brett & Jones, p. 284, from MacLean, *Agrarian Age*, pp. [20–21].)

[36] Brett & Jones, referring to Legouis's *Early Life of Wordsworth* (tr. Matthews), point out that the poem "illustrates Wordsworth's disagreement with the fundamental doctrine of Godwinian belief that property is the root of all evil", and, furthermore, they note that "Wordsworth is also pointing out the weakness of a system of parish relief which prevented a man from receiving any benefits while he still owned property, however little" (Brett & Jones, p. 291).

Wordsworth captures our attention from the outset (something one cannot say of his poetry in general):

> In distant countries I have been,
> And yet I have not often seen
> A healthy man, a man full grown
> Weep in the public roads alone.
> But such a one, on English ground,
> And in the broad high-way, I met;
> Along the broad high-way he came,
> His cheeks with tears were wet.

The widely travelled poet saw very seldom in foreign lands what he had hardly expected in his own country: a robust adult man shedding tears in public. The incongruity of the situation makes us thoughtful and inquisitive. Wordsworth, probably the most manly of English poets, must have had very strong feelings indeed about the plight of the smallholder to first bring out the soundness and strength of the man (3), followed by the anticlimactic contrast in line 4. For that kind of man to cry is bad, to cry in public is worse, and linking it to England is to kick Wordsworth's middle- and upper-class reader into awareness of the lot of the quickly vanishing class of smallholders.

In stanza 2 the poet asks the stranger in brotherly affection: "... 'My friend / 'What ails you? wherefore weep you so?'" Then and in the ensuing stanzas the shepherd's story is unfolded. Wordsworth is keen to enjoin that economic security be a prerequisite for human dignity and happiness. He illustrates in very simple terms the correlation between a sound economic basis and a sound human existence: "They [the lambs] throve, and we at home did thrive" (st. 4). The second part of the sentence stresses this connection by the emphatic "did" instead of the simple past tense "throve".

Stanza 5, exactly in the middle of the poem, is also central to Wordsworth's attack on the poor law. The parish officers tell the little peasant that he is "a wealthy man" (middle of st. 5) who ought to sell his flock before asking for relief. The injustice of the poor-law administration is underscored by their suggesting that the smallholder possesses the same kind of means ("wealthy") as a rich farmer, whereas the truth is that for the subsistence farmer selling his lambs is like losing his own blood, the essence of life: "It was a vein that never stopp'd, / Like blood-drops from my heart they dropp'd" (st. 7). The comparison with the human body underlines the very close connection between the smallholder and his little property, dramatically emphasized by the suddenness of the rhyming plosives in "stopp'd" and "dropp'd".

The stability of the family and the shepherd's affection for his children are enhanced by economic security:[37]

> Sir! 'twas a precious flock to me,
> As dear as my own children be;
> For daily with my growing store
> I loved my children more and more[.]
>
> (st. 9)

By contrast the natural affection between father and children is impaired by economic misery:

> I prayed, yet every day I thought
> I loved my children less[.]
>
> (st. 9)

His appeal to God to restore his love for his children is thwarted by the anger produced by poverty. (See also the inconsistent behaviour of Robert towards his children in *The Ruined Cottage*, ll. 237 ff., MS. B, Cornell ed.) The closest of human ties, the blood relationship, has thus been impaired by social injustice. The sailor-father of *Adventures on Salisbury Plain* (comp. 1795) who could not fulfil his family's most basic needs had committed unpremeditated murder. In "The Last of the Flock" of 1798 the rage is internalized: "To wicked deeds I was inclined, / And wicked fancies cross'd my mind" (st. 8). The shepherd has lost the peace of mind that the assurance of a regular income to a large extent guarantees.

One cannot say that the smallholder is one of Wordsworth's idealized rural characters: there are few if any feelings of brotherhood left in him. The poem witnesses to Wordsworth's insight into the negative impact of poverty on the human mind. Southey complained that Wordsworth "'should have condescended to write such pieces as *The Last of the Flock*'" (quoted in *E.Y.*, p. 268). This would hardly hold good today, for now most critics speak highly of "The Last of the Flock".

Work for the *Lyrical Ballads* progressed rapidly in the spring of 1798: all poems composed between early April and early July 1798 which deal with human relationships,[38] except "Peter Bell", were incorporated into the *Lyrical Ballads*. Very likely the poems were written in the

---

[37] In his *Conciones ad Populum* (1795) Coleridge comments directly on the link between affection and economic well-being (*Lectures 1795 on Politics and Religion*, eds. Lewis Patton and Peter Mann, The Collected Works of S. T. Coleridge, London: Routledge, and Princeton, N.J.: Princeton U.P., 1971, p. 45).

[38] Two poems only (and some fragments) deal with different subjects: "I Love Upon a Stormy Night" (GCL I:72) and "Away, Away, it is the Air" (GCL I:73).

following sequence: "Lines Written in Early Spring", "Anecdote for Fathers"[39] (GCL I:71), "Peter Bell",[40] "Andrew Jones" (GCL I:72), "Expostulation and Reply", and "The Tables Turned"[41] (GCL I:74). "Lines Composed a Few Miles above Tintern Abbey"[42] (GCL I:75: completed on 13 July 1798) was the last to be included in *Lyrical Ballads* (1798).

In "Lines Written in Early Spring" (Brett & Jones, p. 69) Wordsworth contrasts the beauty and harmony of Nature in spring with the disorder in human affairs. He implies that the "link" which exists between himself and Nature could be achieved by all and that it could be extended to interhuman relationships and thus produce the contrary of man's present disunity, a genuine brotherhood:

> To her fair works did nature link
> The human soul that through me ran;
> And much it griev'd my heart to think
> What man has made of man.

The lost political leader—by now twenty-eight years old—reiterates the same thought and concludes the poem on a sad note: "Have I not reason to lament / What man has made of man?"

"Anecdote for Fathers" (Brett & Jones, pp. 64–66), that delightful poem on child psychology, is more optimistic. After continually trying to elicit a five-year-old boy's reasons for preferring one place to another the poet receives a lie in response to his continual adult reasoning. The little boy's answer is an eye-opener to the poet who, in the final stanza, acknowledges the mystery of a child's world, the individual child's right—should I say his liberty?—to live in the world of childhood. He learns more from the direct contact with one child than from the educational theories fashionable at the time. There is a distinct democratic tone in the adult accepting the child as teacher:

> Oh dearest, dearest boy! my heart
> For better lore would seldom yearn,
> Could I but teach the hundredth part
> Of what from thee I learn.

---

[39] Brett & Jones, p. 64, entitle "Anecdote for Fathers, Shewing How the Art of Lying may be Taught".

[40] I have not dealt with "Peter Bell", since no transcript of the early text was available to me.

[41] Brett & Jones, p. 105, entitle "The Tables Turned; an Evening Scene, on the Same Subject".

[42] Brett & Jones, p. 113, entitle "Lines Written a Few Miles Above Tintern Abbey, on Revisiting the Banks of the Wye During a Tour, July 13, 1798"

These lines firmly close the door on the hierarchical order and decorum of the eighteenth century.

However tolerant Wordsworth may be of madmen, petty thieves, or gipsies, he vehemently reacts against anti-social behaviour when the moral code is transgressed by the strong, as in "Andrew Jones" (Brett & Jones, pp. 174–75). A man such as Andrew Jones, who finds an excuse for seizing a penny before a crippled beggar manages to pick it up, is for Wordsworth a danger to the soundness of the local brotherhood, especially since he fears that the villain's children will follow in their father's footsteps. Although Wordsworth is against the press-gang elsewhere, his narrative "I" in "Andrew Jones" strikes a different note:

> I hate that Andrew Jones: he'll breed
> His children up to waste and pillage.
> I wish the press-gang or the drum
> With its tantara sound would come,
> And sweep him from the village!

The poet's instinctive moral sense makes him react against Andrew Jones; and a healthy moral sense also informs "Expostulation and Reply" (Brett & Jones, p. 104), the lines directed against abstract moral philosophy.[43] The "primary passions" of man—affection, pity, gratitude, kindness—Wordsworth felt had been ignored or even disparaged by modern books of philosophy (Moorman I, p. 381). Seen in this context, "Expostulation and Reply" and its accompanying piece "The Tables Turned"[44] (Brett & Jones, pp. 105–06) assume key importance in the *Lyrical Ballads,* for the "primary passions" that link man into a true brotherhood are the main theme of the *Ballads.*

Tintern Abbey.—The composition of "Tintern Abbey" (GCL I:75; Brett & Jones, pp. 113–18) comes towards the end of the first third of Wordsworth's golden decade, 1795–1805. The poem opens on a note of remembrance, couched in the convention of an eighteenth-century descriptive landscape poem (1–23). But soon the tone becomes reflective

---

[43] In the "Advertisement to *Lyrical Ballads*" he says that the "lines entitled Expostulation and Reply, and those which follow ["The Tables Turned"] arose out of conversation with a friend [Hazlitt] who was somewhat unreasonably attached to modern books of moral philosophy" (*Prose Works* I, p. 117).

[44] Paul Sheats defends the language of "Expostulation and Reply" and "The Tables Turned": the speaker "is a dramatic character . . . his language is appropriate to the debate, a genre that sanctions hyperbole, ellipsis, and condensation . . ." Sheats counters another misinterpretation of "The Tables Turned": "Wordsworth is not seeking to substitute an unthinking and instinctive communion with nature for the life of reason proper to man, but is rather pointing to the proper use of reason. . . ." (*The Making of Wordsworth's Poetry,* pp. 208–10.)

and the restoring impact of the natural scenery is acknowledged (24–31); the beautiful landscape evokes

>   feelings too
>   Of unremembered pleasure; such, perhaps,
>   As may have had no trivial influence
>   On that best portion of a good man's life;
> 35   His little, nameless, *unremembered* acts
>   Of kindness and of love. Nor less, I trust,
>   To them I may have owed another gift,
>   Of aspect more sublime; that blessed mood,
>   In which the burthen of the mystery,
> 40   In which the heavy and the weary weight
>   Of all this unintelligible world
>   Is lighten'd . . .
>   [my italics]

Nature engenders feelings of inner joy, perhaps unconsciously strengthened by the accumulation of the good man's "little, nameless, unremembered acts / Of kindness and of love" (35–36). Once again Wordsworth points to what he had illustrated in earlier poems: securing an old man a lift (*ASP*, st. 5) or the villagers' consideration for the Old Cumberland Beggar. In Wordsworth there is no doubt about the correlation between these good deeds and a "good man's life", for Nature alone would not be sufficient to evoke inner joy in him.

Thanks to the feeling of permanence conveyed by the beautiful natural scenery the burden of the incomprehensible world is eased (40–42), and the mind stays ordered amid the "fretful stir / Unprofitable, and the fever of the world" (53–54), such as the French Revolution, wars, and suppression of civil liberties. A balanced mind is the prerequisite for clear thinking and thus, implicitly, also a good basis for bringing order into social and political disorder.

Alan Grob is right in regarding "Tintern Abbey" as "implicitly a gesture of protest directed toward the existing social order".[45] In adult-

---

[45] Grob continues: "As an alternative to that order, the poem offers us the life pattern of its hero, a developmental process that is presented as both exemplary and, given the surroundings and circumstances in which it takes place, as necessary. According to the poem's empirical premises, such a process is, of course, universally accessible and universally beneficial, available to any and all who would submit themselves to the circumstances and surroundings that had determined the life and behavior of its hero and who would thereby participate in bringing about a true reformation of man and society. The progressive—indeed, virtually millen[n]ial—suppositions that *Tintern Abbey*, like most of Wordsworth's autobiographic poetry of this period, indirectly sets forth are suppositions common to most of those who, in the eighteenth century, advocated an empiricism that traced all human knowledge back to sensory and hence external origins. . . ." (*The Philosophic Mind*, p. 31.)

hood Nature is more than a fulfilment of self-centred private emotions. She assumes public significance by making man hear the "still, sad music of humanity"; and the awareness of the human condition, one can hope, makes him see the importance of and strive for liberty, equality, and fraternity. Eighteenth-century uniformitarianism[46] implies, and Wordsworth teaches, that man in general could understand the moral force of Nature, the "anchor of my purest thoughts, the nurse, / The guide, the guardian of my heart, and soul / Of all my moral being" (110–12). Wordsworth forestalls unbelief—"If this / Be but a vain belief", etc. (50–58)—by reasserting three times "how oft"/"how often" he felt the beneficial communion with Nature.

After his lines of grateful praise to Nature, Wordsworth addresses his sister Dorothy. The lesson contained in this final, individualized address has a general meaning, exactly as in most of Wordsworth's other poems. In the same way as Wordsworth teaches his sister that Nature never betrays the heart that loves her, the right kind of education could teach men—and some of them successfully—that Nature

> . . . can so *inform*
> The mind that is within us, so impress
> With quietness and beauty, and so feed
> With *lofty thoughts,* that neither evil tongues,
> Rash judgments, nor the sneers of selfish men,
> Nor greetings where no kindness is, nor all
> The dreary intercourse of daily life,
> Shall e'er prevail against us . . .
>   (126–33; my italics)

Wordsworth is no dreamer who refuses to see the evil in human affairs. Instead he points out how to overcome low-mindedness, how to retain one's "lofty thoughts". To feel and understand the moral import of "Tintern Abbey" we ought to listen to the voice of Nature, in solitude, far away from the din of the city and the motorway. That experience, I think, would silence many an anti-Wordsworthian. By the summer of 1798 Wordsworth had learnt to distinguish from among the multitude of life's impressions those that are essential for a moral life, as opposed to those that are trivial and impermanent.

The "Advertisement to *Lyrical Ballads*"[47] (*Prose Works* I, pp.

---

[46] For definition, see ch. 2, n. 68.

[47] The "Advertisement" is not included in Reed's General Chronological List. Owen and Smyser have found no precise evidence for dating it but assume that it was "written after the first published mention of *Lyrical Ballads,* 30 April 1798 (*E.Y.,* p. 216) and certainly before 13 September 1798 . . ." (*Prose Works* I, p. 111).

116–17) sums up the democratic subject matter of the 1798 volume and foreshadows the democratic tone of the 1800 Preface to *Lyrical Ballads*. The very first sentence of the "Advertisement" asserts: "It is the honourable characteristic of poetry that its materials are to be found in every subject which can interest the human mind...." (*Prose Works*, p. 116.) "[E]very subject" points to Wordsworth's poetic theory of democratic egalitarianism. The implicit democratic approach used in selecting subjects is extended to the language, for Wordsworth goes on to say that he has chosen "the language of conversation in the middle and lower classes of society". His interest in man is substantiated by his appeal to his readers to ask themselves whether the *Lyrical Ballads* contain "a natural delineation of human passions, human characters, and human incidents". Indeed, the reiteration of "human" in the "Advertisement" points to what concerns him so much—his love for man—and this is also what he has expressed in the slender first volume of *Lyrical Ballads*, irrespective of what some critics say.[48]

The publication of the first edition of the *Lyrical Ballads* coincided with Wordsworth's, Dorothy's, and S. T. Coleridge's departure for Germany in mid-September 1798.[49] The Wordsworths had been forced to leave Alfoxden at the end of June 1798, as will be recalled, probably for political reasons. While they were still at Alfoxden, France annexed Geneva (April 1798). Shortly before the Wordsworths and Coleridge visited their radical friend Thelwall, however, at the beginning of August (Reed I, p. 245), Nelson had stopped the French expansion for the time being: on 1 August the French fleet was destroyed off Aboukir (Battle of the Nile).

On 18 September 1798, approximately six years to the day on which he may have attended the celebration in honour of the Republic in Orleans (Reed I, p. 136), Wordsworth's German plans materialized: he, his sister, and Coleridge set foot in the country of the subsiding *Sturm und Drang* movement whose proponents advocated a revolt against

---

[48] For example, David Ferry on "Tintern Abbey": "He [Wordsworth] has not, be it noticed, developed a love for *men*, for other human beings, but rather for the 'mind of man', for himself or for the mind of man considered abstractly" (*Limits of Mortality*, p. 110; Ferry's italics).

[49] Later on S. T. Coleridge referred to this trip in "Satyrane's Letters" where he pokes fun at the pretence of equality and brotherhood in a drunken Danish fellow traveller who "declaimed, like a member of the Corresponding Society, *about* (not concerning) the Rights of Man, and assured me that, notwithstanding his fortune, he thought the poorest man alive his equal. 'All are equal, my dear friend! all are equal! Ve are all Got's children....'", etc. (*Biographia Literaria*, ed. J. Shawcross, Clarendon Press: Oxford, 1907 [1st ed. 1817], vol. II, p. 139. The italics are in Shawcross.)

literary conventions. Loyal English periodicals fulminated against German Jacobin literature, for they were aware of its political implications; and they also fulminated against German universities which were known for their Jacobinism and infidelity.[50] Thus Wordsworth may have nurtured the hope of experiencing once more a little of the republican excitement he had felt in the France of 1790–93.[51] But as so often happens, the intellectual atmosphere of another country is not always what it is reputed to be. Wordsworth found among the liberal faction in Germany

a counter to his own suspicion of England's international position; with them it was England who was the hope of the world, the only bulwark against French military ambition. England was to Germany "The Great Nation", and Coleridge found that Nelson's victories only increased the enthusiasm of the continental Anglophiles. Klopstock, Bürger and Wieland had all turned from France to England as the nation which now held out the only hope for the lovers of rational liberty, and the only model for reformers.[52]

Hence when Wordsworth and Coleridge visited Klopstock in September, they encountered a humane old man instead of a political hothead. Wordsworth's stay in Germany resulted in his moving yet further away from radicalism, culminating later, in 1803, in his absolute certainty that England was the "only light / Of Liberty that yet remains on Earth".[53]

Meanwhile at home in Britain the more Paine's *Rights of Man* and similar works circulated, the more freedoms were restricted. The Newspaper Act of 1798 and legislation of 1799 regulating the printing industry restricted the freedom of the press considerably.[54] In addition William Pitt increased the tax on British newspapers from 1½d. to 2½d. per copy and prohibited the import of foreign newspapers.[55]

We shall look in vain into Wordsworth's poetry in our search for his reactions to these and other public events during 1798–1800 (although his teaching voice is, by the end of 1798, firmer than it had been in the first part of 1798). He conveys implicit general socio-political truths through his poems and, most notably, through the Preface to the

---

[50] Todd, *Politics and the Poet*, p. 101.

[51] Wordsworth's visit to France in the autumn of 1793 is not certain, but probable (see Reed I, p. 147).

[52] Todd, *Politics and the Poet*, p. 106. For further details also F. M. Todd, "Wordsworth in Germany", *MLR*, 47 (1952), 508–11.

[53] "October, 1803" ["One might believe that natural miseries"], in *Poems in Two Volumes, 1807*, ed. Helen Darbishire, 2nd ed. (Oxford: Clarendon Press, 1952), p. 152.

[54] Maccoby, *English Radicalism 1786–1832*, pp. 128–31.

[55] Neville Williams, *Chronology of the Modern World, 1763–1965* (1966; rev. ed. Harmondsworth: Penguin, 1975), p. 79.

Lyrical Ballads (below, ch. 4).[56] I concur with Sheats, pp. 247–49, and Chard, p. 256, for whom the Wordsworth of 1798 is above all the poet of *caritas*, in other words brotherhood. But brotherhood, if not in line with Pitt's policies, could be misinterpreted. Some bad newspaper verse of November 1798 reflects the intolerant atmosphere in England:

> Careless of late, I danced the ways
> Of *Godwin's* metaphysic maze,
>   And laughed at ties of honour;
> From *Paine* I learn'd my rights to know,
> And plighted faith with *Fox and Co.,*
>   *Fitzgerald* and *O'Connor.*[57]

The erosion of liberty continued in 1799: political associations were forbidden on 12 July,[58] Habeas Corpus was suspended, and the Combination Acts of 1799 and 1800 drove underground the incipient unionization of labour.[59] The *Anti-Jacobin* pursued its diatribes against the ideas of the radicals, among them brotherhood:

> Reason, philosophy, fiddledum, diddledum;
> Peace and fraternity, higgledy piggledy[.][60]

By coincidence George Washington, the champion of America's national liberty and democracy, died in the same month, December 1799, that Napoleon Bonaparte became First Consul for ten years. Under Napoleon's rule the French were to succeed in their military offensives in Austria and Italy throughout 1800. In France itself many newspapers were suppressed and theatrical censorship was established during that year; one year after his taking office as First Consul a plot to assassinate Bonaparte was discovered, which gave him an excuse to deport democratic republicans to Guiana. French *liberté* had destroyed itself; the "ancient liberties" of Englishmen as well were curtailed one by one.

---

[56] There is a parallel between the endeavours of Wordsworth the romantic poet and what Edward Allen Whitney calls the "highly personal and individual" efforts of late-eighteenth-century humanitarians ("Humanitarianism and Romanticism", *HLQ*, 2 (1938–39), 159–78 (163)).

Sheats concludes that "Wordsworth's persevering assault on the literary conventions of his age proceeded on political and social grounds as well" (*The Making of Wordsworth's Poetry*, p. 246).

[57] Quoted in Brinton, *The Political Ideas of the English Romanticists*, p. 44, from *The Times* (8 Nov. 1798); italics in Brinton. Wordsworth was an adherent of Fox (see his letter to Fox below, pp. 133–35).

[58] Williams, *Chronology*, p. 80.

[59] Woodring, *Politics in English Romantic Poetry*, p. 19. See also Goodwin, *The Friends of Liberty*, pp. 454–60.

[60] Quoted in Brinton, *The Political Ideas of the English Romanticists*, p. 29.

Even humanitarian reforms, such as prison reform, suffered from the concentration of resources on the war.[61]

Against this dire background, it is all the more surprising to trace liberty, equality, and fraternity in Wordsworth, whose mature craftsmanship enabled him to embed in his poetry ideas, which, in the world of politics, had suffered temporary suppression and distortion by a fearful Tory Government.

As mentioned earlier, Wordsworth's visit to Germany was inaugurated by some meetings in Hamburg with Friedrich Gottlieb Klopstock, the author of *Der Messias*. The "Conversations with Klopstock"[62] (GCL I:76; *Prose Works* I, pp. 91–95) are probably the first matter he penned during his German stay. Lines 12–15 and 56–57 deal directly with political events: the attempted but frustrated "liberation" of Ireland by the French between August and September 1798 and Nelson's victory in the Battle of the Nile. Wordsworth records in the manner of an uncommitted neutral observer: "We began a conversation in french upon the events which had just taken place in Ireland"; "We talked of admiral Nelson's rumoured victory; he was all [? faith]. I had my doubts."[63]

"The Conversations" illustrate that Wordsworth extended his demand for high poetic standards to other areas of taste. For example, he criticizes Klopstock for not having been "influenced by poetic ideas" in his choice of his home "amongst a range of commonplace houses" (3–4), and he disapproves of Klopstock's unsuitable wig (37–40). All this goes to show that Wordsworth's simplicity in poetic style in 1798—which many of us regard as the best style nowadays—does on no account preclude him from being a man of taste. When, finally, Wordsworth frowns on Wieland's *Oberon* for its emphasis on "animal gratification" he adds the voice of a teacher and moralist to that of the aesthete:

I [Wordsworth] thought the passion of love as well suited to the purpose[?s][64] of poetry as any other passion, but that it was a cheap way of pleasing to fix the attention of the reader through a long poem on the mere sexual enjoyment. Well, but, said . . . he, you see that such poems please every body. I answered that *it was the province of a great poet to raise people up to his own level, not to descend to theirs.* (124–30; my italics.)

---

[61] One notable private act of brotherhood though must not be forgotten: the establishment of Robert Owen's model factory at New Lanark in 1800.

[62] "Probably written 26 Sept. 1798 or shortly after" (GCL I:76); Reed entitles "Record of Conversations with Klopstock, in MS Journal 5". For textual data and general notes, see *Prose Works* I, pp. 89–90, 96–98.

[63] Square brackets in *Prose Works* I, p. 92.

[64] Square brackets in *Prose Works*.

The italicized sentence implies that Wordsworth would not confuse political democracy and equality with a vulgarization of literature that panders to popular taste. Wordsworth is a democrat but no popularizer in the negative sense of the word.

At about the same time as Wordsworth recorded his conversations with Klopstock he wrote the unfinished "Essay on Morals"[65] (GCL I:77; *Prose Works* I, pp. 103–04). The essay is directed against abstract philosophy in general and singles out two such very different philosophers as Godwin and Paley.[66] Moral philosophy should be expressed in terms which the common man understands: "I [Wordsworth] know no book or system of moral philosophy written with sufficient power to melt into our affections[?s], to incorporate itself with the blood & vital juices of our minds . . ." (18–21; square brackets in *Prose Works*). "Incorporate" suggests that philosophy and the experience of man ought to fuse into a unity. The demand that philosophy should not detach itself from life is implicitly democratic.[67]

Probably between October 1798 and February 1799 Wordsworth composed a whole sheaf of poems for the second volume of *Lyrical Ballads* (1800),[68] some work for *The Prelude,* in particular Books I and II (GCL I:63),[69] a couple of minor poems, and the poems of the "Matthew" cycle (some printed in the *Lyrical Ballads*). As in the spring at Alfoxden so now in Germany Wordsworth's "creative breeze" was quite a strong, continual wind.

The prayer to "genuine freedom" in the "Prospectus to *The Recluse*" (below, GCL II:119) is foreshadowed by the implicit emphasis on the importance of man's free will in "Ruth" (GCL I:79). Here the young

---

[65] Reed entitles "Fragment of a Moral Essay, in MS Journal 5".

[66] For a perceptive analysis of the "Essay on Morals", see Grob, "Wordsworth and Godwin", *SIR,* 6 (1967), 98–119. Grob thinks that "Wordsworth's purpose in his essay on morals was not to combat the theory of rational benevolence nor, for that matter, any other single system of ethics but rather to expose the liabilities and dangers inherent in all theoretical discussions of moral problems" (p. 115). Compare also the anti-abstract tone of the "Essay" with "Expostulation and Reply" and "The Tables Turned" (GCL I:74) above. See further Owen and Smyser's Commentary, *Prose Works* I, pp. 105–07, and Geoffrey Little, "An Incomplete Wordsworth Essay upon Moral Habits", *A Review of English Literature,* 2 (1961), 9–20.

[67] For Wordsworth's similar request concerning poetic language, see my discussion of the 1800 *P.L.B.* below ("Poetry sheds no tears . . .", Brett & Jones, p. 254).

[68] For dates of individual poems, see GCL I:79–83; 86–88: "The Danish Boy" ["Fragment": Between two sister moorland rills], "Ruth", "To a Sexton", "Matthew", "The Fountain", "The Two April Mornings"; "Three Years She Grew in Sun and Shower", "The Brothers", "To M. H.".

[69] See below, pp. 120–23.

soldier acts voluntarily against his better judgement when he imitates the Indians:

> But ill he liv'd, much evil saw
> With men to whom no better law
> Nor better life was known;
> *Deliberately* and *undeceiv'd*
> Those wild men's vices he receiv'd,
> ...
> His genius and his moral frame
> Were thus impair'd, and he became
> The *slave* of low desires[.]
> (Brett & Jones, p. 185; my italics)

The young soldier is not a "wild man".[70] Thus, acting against the moral law of civilized society whose values he has imbibed results in his moral enslavement.[71] In 1798–99 Wordsworth insisted that man was a free agent, a prerequisite for morality; but he had alluded to man's free will as early as 1795, for although the female vagrant of *Adventures on Salisbury Plain* had suffered much from the injustice of society, she did not stay with the gipsies, where she would have had an excellent opportunity of revenging herself on society: "But ill it suited me, in journey dark / O'er moor and mountain, midnight theft to hatch; / . . . / The black disguise, the warning whistle shrill, / And ear still busy on its nightly watch, / Were not for me, brought up in nothing ill / . . . /" (*ASP*, st. 59). In 1795 Wordsworth did not censure half so much the ways of the wild gipsies as he now does the wild vices of the Indians. Hence even if the female vagrant had permanently embraced the customs of the gipsies, her action would not have been as immoral as that of Ruth's lover.

In late 1798 and early 1799 Wordsworth reflected on the lessons we can extract from the world of the dead. Thus "To a Sexton" (GCL I:79) portrays how the human brotherhood continues beyond death, exactly as in "The Brothers" (GCL I:87, below) of 1799–1800. In another reminiscence on death, "Matthew"[72] (GCL I:79a), Wordsworth depicts the ideal character of man in whom liberty and restraint are balanced:

---

[70] Wordsworth deviates here from the romantic convention of idealizing the "noble savage".

[71] For a parallel between the young soldier's lack of self-control and the social havoc generally caused by misdirected self-interest in society, see Chard, p. 254.

[72] The original longish title begins thus: "In the School of —— is a Tablet on Which are Inscribed", etc. (Brett & Jones, p. 190).

> If Nature, for a favorite Child
> In thee hath temper'd so her clay,
> That every hour thy heart runs wild
> Yet never once doth go astray[.]
> (Brett & Jones, p. 190)

Mental health shines forth from Matthew, the hero of this poem: he is endowed with "the oil of gladness" and a "spirit . . . profound". We discern the same kind of sanity in the other "Matthew" cycle poems.

Probably the most thoughtful and poetically skilful stanza on the right balance inherent in Nature's education was written a few weeks later for "Three Years She Grew in Sun and Shower" (GCL I:86), where Nature's ideal proportion of liberty and discipline is reflected in the contrasting balance of the vocabulary:

> Myself [Nature] will to my darling be
> Both *law* and *impulse,* and with me
> The Girl in rock and plain,
> In earth and heaven, in glade and bower,
> Shall feel an overseeing power
> To *kindle* or *restrain.*
> (Brett & Jones, p. 198; my italics)

On the one hand, we get the juxtaposition of "law ↔ impulse" and "kindle ↔ restrain", and the opposition is strengthened by both pairs, consisting of first a Germanic and second a Romance word.[72a] On the other hand, there is the repeated contrast between the lines themselves:

This illustrates the interrelatedness of Nature's balancing forces. Nature's education on no account means wildness and licence. Obedience to her laws,[73] as seen in "The Fountain"[74] (GCL I:79b), would entail happiness and freedom for man as well:

[72a] Professor Birgit Bramsbäck has further suggested the *noun–verb* relationship: law/impulse–kindle/restrain.

[73] "The words 'nature' and 'reason' are both found, at various periods of Wordsworth's writing, associated with 'law', often in phrases such as 'the law of reason' and 'nature's law' " (Joseph Warren Beach, "Reason and Nature in Wordsworth", *JHI*, 1 (1940), 335–51 (339)). In the same article (p. 341) Beach refutes Babbitt's assertion of Wordsworth's falling into " 'an inarticulate ecstasy before the wonders of nature' ".

[74] Brett & Jones, p. 194, entitle "The Fountain, a Conversation".

> With Nature never do *they* [the birds] wage
> A foolish strife; they see
> A happy youth, and their old age
> Is beautiful and free[.]
> (Brett & Jones, p. 195; italics in Brett & Jones)

The artificial hierarchy which separates young and old and which impairs the free dialogue between them is done away with in "The Fountain" (we remember the same democratic spirit in "Anecdote for Fathers" above, GCL I:71):

> We talk'd with open heart, and tongue
> Affectionate and true,
> A pair of Friends, though I was young,
> And Matthew seventy-two.
> (Brett & Jones, p. 194)

Much in the five elegies on Matthew (MS. 18A), later revised and published in 1842 as "Address to the Scholars of the Village School of ——" (GCL I:79f), brings out the "democratic" personality of the perfect village teacher who "handled book or spade" (elegy II) and through whom a bond is formed between the various members of the community. In a number of neatly copied lines, which are connected to but not certainly contemporaneous with the fair copy of elegy III,[75] Wordsworth appeals, significantly, to the lower strata of society to mourn the death of the schoolmaster: reaper, mower, milkmaid, blind sailor, poor half-witted boy, shepherd, angler, woodman, sick man. In elegy II Wordsworth delineates a teacher whom many people in the educational discussions of the 1970s favour, a man who is integrated into his community through his activities outside school and who teaches more than mere book-learning:

> Learning will often dry the heart,
> The very bones it will distress,
> But Mathew had an idle art
> Of teaching love and happiness.
> (Elegy II, MS. 18A)

Like the democratic and fraternal lines in "Nutting" (GCL I:83), which lead us to the origins of Wordsworth's feelings of brotherhood—

> I was early taught
> To look with feelings of fraternal love
> Upon those unassuming things which hold
> A silent station in this beauteous world
> (MS. verse 56)[76]

---

[75] The transcript was supplied to me by Stephen Gill.
[76] Transcript of "Nutting" by Stephen Gill.

—"A Poet's Epitaph"[77] (GCL I:80; Brett & Jones, pp. 212–13) continues to inculcate the poet's message of democratic simplicity: "In common things that round us lie / Some random truths he [the poet] can impart". The politician's fervour for abstract political theories is challenged by Wordsworth's exhortation in stanza 1 "to love one living man; / *Then* may'st thou think upon the dead" [italics in Brett & Jones]. Wordsworth's disillusion with the current political situation in Europe is apparent in this stanza. In the lines connected with elegy III of the "Matthew" cycle Wordsworth had enumerated occupations and people dear to him. "A Poet's Epitaph" reverses this and lists the professions of the upper strata of society (lawyer, physician, philosopher), chiding them as not being worthy of coming near the poet's grave. Except for the poet himself, only the soldier—provided he lays his sword aside and leans upon a peasant's staff—is welcome to visit the poet's grave. Wordsworth has nothing against the profession of the soldier, as long as he does not fall victim to the pomp of militarism. The combination of "soldier" and "peasant's staff" evokes the idea of a democracy's citizens army.

Intermingled with the serious matter of late 1798 and early 1799 we find a piece of humorous empathy, "Written in Germany on One of the Coldest Days of the Century" (GCL I:80; Brett & Jones, pp. 203–04). However, the trivial theme of a fly's last minutes is transformed by Wordsworth's imaginative sympathy:

> No Brother, no Friend has he [the fly] near him, while I [the poet]
> Can draw warmth from the cheek of my Love[.]

The vocabulary of human relationships (note also the personal pronoun referring to an insect) connects the lot of the apparently insignificant fly with the need for human brotherhood that man feels in his hour of adversity. We have an instance of this in the woman's longing for her tribe and child during her last hours in "The Complaint of a Forsaken Indian Woman" (above, GCL I:67). Despite its humorous tone the words and the thought place the verse on the little fly among the poems of brotherhood and democratic subjects:

> Yet, God is my witness, thou small helpless Thing,
> Thy life I would gladly sustain
> Till summer comes up from the South, and with crowds
> Of thy brethren a march thou should'st sound . . .

---

[77] For a parallel between this poem and Theocritus, "Epigram XIX", see *PW* IV, p. 414.

Wordsworth's first, more detailed attempt to define what liberty actually is might have been written during his stay in Germany. So far, especially between 1791–94, he had written much about liberty without defining it; he was mostly concerned with political liberty as evidenced in *Descriptive Sketches,* "A Letter to the Bishop of Llandaff", and in the letters to Mathews. Now, in the fragment "There is an Active Principle Alive in All Things" (GCL I:84a; MS. 18A),[78] we get several definitions. The first line strikes the keynote of the fragment, the limitless all-pervasive activity of the universe. The "active principle" is in "all things, in all natures"; lines 12–16 conclude that this "is the freedom of the universe, / Unfolded still the more, more visible, / The more we know, and yet is reverenced least / And least respected in the human mind, / Its most apparent home. . . ." Next we are enjoined to make an active moral contribution in life, but it is conceded that our freedom of action is restricted by the inherent laws of our own nature (24–29) (see also "Three Years She Grew in Sun and Shower", above, GCL I:86). This demand for positive efforts leads to one of Wordsworth's most assured assertions of what liberty entails:

> There is *one only* liberty, *'tis his*
> Who by *beneficence* is circumscribed;
> *'Tis his* to whom the power of *doing good*
> Is law and statute, penalty, and bond,
> His prison, and his warder; *his* who finds
> His freedom in the joy of virtuous thoughts.
>   (39–44; my italics)

"One only" strongly emphasizes the ensuing qualities which are essential to liberty. After this forceful, restricting linguistic signal the reiterated "'tis his" further continues to give weight to what leads to liberty: "beneficence" and "doing good". Both are closely related and thus emphasize the importance of being *actively* kind (which implies a spirit of brotherhood).[79] Finally, but in a softer tone, the liberty of the mind is evoked by "virtuous thoughts".

But the active exertion of love for man is Wordsworth's first priority—although man's freedom is never as free as "is the light of heaven" (60); and his freedom of action ought not to be misused, for his existence is not formed for "wishes that debilitate and die / Of their own weak-

---

[78] The revised version of this fragment was incorporated into Book ix of *The Excursion* (see *PW* V, pp. 286 ff., *Apparatus criticus*). My text is derived from the transcript of MS. 18A by Stephen Gill.

[79] Compare this also with the earlier "little, nameless, unremembered acts / Of kindness and of love" (above, "Tintern Abbey", GCL I:75).

ness..." (63–64). "There is an Active Principle..." evinces how hard Wordsworth has struggled with the concept of liberty. In the final analysis it seems to me that the stress on an active exertion of man's capacities in the service of liberty leads to effective political reform.

"There is a Law Severe of Penury" (GCL I:84b; MS. 18A),[80] another fragment, exposes the evil of child labour.[81] It shares the angry tone of his earlier protest poetry, thus appealing to legislators to change radically those conditions that run counter to a free and normal development of the child's mind. The benumbed state resulting from child labour prevents the older child from enjoying the liberty that is his right by nature. For him

> ... liberty is not and cannot be
> But wheresoe'er he turns his steps the boy
> Is still a prisoner when the wind is up
> Among the clouds, and in the antient woods
> Or when the sun is rising in the heavens
> Quietly calm[.]

The necessity of child labour to ward off penury is one of the worst consequences of economic inequality and has made the boy a mental captive, incapable of appreciating the beauty or the restoring impact of Nature. Worse, the handicap will last for life; his deprived childhood has rendered him an emotional and social cripple, who may be so passive as to be unaware of the injustice inherent in a society that lacks political liberty:

> The limbs increase but liberty of mind
> Is gone for ever, and the avenues
> Of sense impeded this organic frame,
> So joyful in its motions, soon becomes
> Dull to the joy of its own motions dead[.]

The Brothers.—The Wordsworths returned to England in late April/ early May 1799,[82] and between that date and the early winter of the same year Wordsworth composed little apart from some work on the

---

[80] The revised version of this fragment was incorporated into Book viii of *The Excursion* (see *PW* V, pp. 274 ff., *Apparatus criticus*). My text is derived from the transcript of MS. 18A by Stephen Gill.

[81] "[Wordsworth] was perhaps drawn into a special interest in the evils of child-labour in factories by conversations with John Thelwall, who visited him at Alfoxden in 1797" (de Selincourt, *PW* V, p. 471).

[82] Reed I, p. 267. But see Stephen Parrish: "[Wordsworth] had come back to England with Dorothy at the beginning of May [1799]..." (*The Prelude, 1798–1799*, The Cornell Wordsworth, Ithaca, N.Y.: Cornell U.P., and Hassocks, Sussex: Harvester Press, 1977), p. 27.

1798–99 *Prelude*. Shortly after they had moved from Sockburn-on-Tees to Grasmere (on 20 December 1799), where they resided until they moved to Rydal Mount in May 1813, William probably began work on his last major poem of the year, "The Brothers" (GCL I:87; Brett & Jones, pp. 135–50),[83] which was not completed until early 1800, thus concluding the old and ushering in the new century.[84]

Throughout, the plain setting of "The Brothers" and its simple language reinforce the feelings of brotherhood and equality. At the beginning the "homely Priest" (16) observes that there is "neither epitaph nor monument, / Tomb-stone nor name . . ." (13–14) in the village cemetery. The same idea is repeated by Leonard in his conversation with the Priest: "Here's neither head nor foot-stone, plate of brass" (171). In contrast to the usual perpetuation of inequality in life in the shape of unequal monuments for the dead this churchyard knows of no distinctions. The "dead man's home / Is but a fellow to that pasture field" (174–75). "Fellow" suggests that the equality and extended brotherhood between Nature and man continues beyond death. In a living, healthy community there is no need for names and epitaphs, for the memory of the dead is kept alive by reminiscing on their lives "by our fire-sides" (180); thus the deceased continue their membership in the local brotherhood, best expressed in the words of Leonard: "Your dalesmen, then, do in each other's thoughts / Possess a kind of second life . . ." (185–86).

Due to the dire economic circumstances of the period the hero of "The Brothers", Leonard, had been forced to leave his native district and his beloved brother for life at sea. Although Wordsworth's socio-political criticism is indirect in "The Brothers", the implied theme is lasting and effective, for it brings into focus the highly developed sensitivity of the poem's lower-class hero and the active sense of brotherhood among the humble village folk. The village parson too is integrated into the community, exactly as the teacher was in the Matthew poems. In one instance Wordsworth is not only democratic in spirit but,

---

[83] "The Brothers" and "Michael" were Wordsworth's and Coleridge's favourite poems in the *Lyrical Ballads*. On Wordsworth's socio-political interpretation of the two poems in his letter to Charles James Fox, see below, ch. 4 (under section "Michael"). "Coleridge described *The Brothers* as 'that model of English pastoral, which I have never yet read with unclouded eye'" (Brett & Jones, p. 299, from *Biographia Literaria* II, p. 62n.).

[84] "Nowhere is Wordsworth's dramatic achievement better illustrated than in 'The Brothers'. Within its limits the poem is an impressive compound of dramatic irony, pathos, and psychological realism, a fine example of Wordsworth's mature technique. . . ." Stephen Parrish, "Dramatic Technique in the *Lyrical Ballads*", *PMLA*, 74 (1959), 85–97 (96–97).

in the context of 1799–1800, quite radical: he credits the two lower-class brothers with the skill to "write, aye and speak too, as well / As many of their betters . . ." (284–85). Hence the brothers are raised to the same intellectual level as their superiors in rank and station. Both of them are "brother Shepherds" (73) in two explicit senses of "brother", first related by the same parentage and second sharing the same work; they are also implicitly united in the bond of brotherhood to the other villagers.

The vocabulary of brotherhood is interspersed throughout the poem: "brother fountains" (144), "kindred", "fellow" (e.g. in "fellow tale", l. 341); and the idea of brotherhood is put into practice when Leonard's brother finds himself without parents and relatives:

> He was the child of all the dale—he liv'd
> Three months with one, and six months with another:
> And wanted neither food, nor clothes, nor love[.]
> (353–55)

The orphan enjoys more than what is guaranteed by the most progressive poor law: "love". Enumerating it in the same line as the other basic needs proves what importance Wordsworth attaches to the fulfilment of this primary need. We are probably right in assuming that Leonard's thoughtful sensitivity was fostered by his childhood spent with his loving grandfather Walter Ewbank, also a character similar to Matthew. When Leonard is convinced that his brother is dead and that he led a virtuous life which lacked neither food nor love, he is content and, unobtrusively, unsentimentally, he bids farewell to his brother's grave (424–25). Declining the Priest's "homely fare", he continues his journey into the calm of an evening instead of choosing the joyous public welcome that could have been his:

> If there was one among us who had heard
> That Leonard Ewbank was come home again,
> From the great Gavel,[85] down by Leeza's Banks,
> And down the Enna, far as Egremont,
> The day would be a very festival[.]
> (315–19)

The brotherhood felt in the hearts of those rugged villagers, who will eventually rest in their simple "egalitarian" churchyard, would be audibly expressed by the glad peal of the village's two bells.

---

[85] For Wordsworth's note on the meaning of "Gavel", see Brett & Jones, p. 146.

The 1798–99 Prelude

Scholars' acknowledgement of a two-part *Prelude* has recently made 1799 an important date in Wordsworthian studies;[86] for the end of the year saw the completion of the first *Prelude,* some work for which had been done in 1798 (GCL I:63). Wordsworth's seven-month stay with the family of his future wife, the Hutchinsons of Sockburn, would not have engendered any ideas of radical political reform; and when Coleridge, who had returned from Germany in the summer, joined Wordsworth on a long walking tour through the Lake District in November 1799, their conversation probably centred on the scenes and life of William's childhood and early youth, the subject of the 1798–99 *Prelude.* Indeed, for the whole seven-month period there is only one piece of biographical evidence that indicates an opportunity for discussing politics at length and that was with Thomas Clarkson, who, according to Dorothy Wordsworth, " 'took such pains about the slave-trade' " (Moorman I, p. 475) and whom Coleridge and William visited at the end of their excursion (Reed I, p. 280). Thus both the time span the two-part *Prelude* covers and the relative lack of political stimulus explain in some degree why the first *Prelude* is nearly devoid of thoughts on liberty. (Compare this with the importance of "liberty" in the 1805 *Prelude,* ch. 5.)

However, the 1798–99 *Prelude* probably best explains Wordsworth's early life in terms that make it possible to uncover the roots of what was later to develop into his commitment to liberty, equality, and fraternity. The child is no outcast, "bewildered and depressed: / Along his infant veins are interfused / The gravitation and the filial bond / Of nature that connect him with the world" (1798–99 *Prelude,* II.291–94,[87] p. 61, Cornell ed.). The "filial bond", suggesting both the ties with a mother and Nature, engenders the basic trust that in later life creates the firm bond between the individual and society.

The outer environment too determines man's mental equilibrium. In his praise of his "Beloved Derwent! fairest of all Streams!" Wordsworth links the soothing impact of the river's tempering "cadence" with our

---

[86] My quotations from this *Prelude* are drawn from the Reading Text by Stephen Parrish, ed., *The Prelude, 1798–1799,* The Cornell Wordsworth (Ithaca, N.Y.: © Cornell U.P., and Hassocks, Sussex: Harvester Press, 1977), pp. 43–67. *The Prelude, 1798–1799* was published in its entirety for the first time in 1974 by *The Norton Anthology of English Literature* (3rd ed.) under the title "The Two-Part *Prelude* (1799)", edited by Jonathan Wordsworth and Stephen Gill. Most of the 1798–99 *Prelude* was later incorporated into Books I and II of both the 1805 and the 1850 *Prelude.*

[87] The roman numerals I and II in the discussion of the 1798–99 *Prelude* denote the "First Part" and "Second Part" of this poem.

"human waywardness" (I, p. 43). The order and harmony in the outer environment of the infant help to strengthen the young man against the unreasonable and erratic elements in some of the "fretful dwellings of mankind" (I.13, p. 43). While the bird-snaring and boat-stealing scenes (pp. 44-46) indicate that Nature's guidance and formal education had not turned Wordsworth into a model child, the definite moral signposts in the society of the 1780s were distinct enough to engender a bad conscience in the young "libertarian" and they guided him on to the path of social responsibility. This was the beginning of the growth of morality. Indeed, one wonders if Wordsworth would ever have developed his ardent love for liberty if he had been a model child. For which child is more liable to become an adult tool of a dictatorship or a defender of democracy, the Wordsworthian child in whom education "kindles or restrains" (see above, GCL I:86) or the fully disciplined model child?

William's childhood experience of "games *confederate*" (I.157-58, p. 47), when he was a member of a "noisy crew" and of "a *race* in happiness and joy" (I.202, 204, p. 48; my italics), plants the seed of fraternal feelings. The boys' "quiet independence of the heart" and "diffidence and modesty" (II.72, 75, p. 56) are fertile ground for a democratic spirit. There is a correlation between the capacity of losing a game in good spirits and the acceptance of democratic decisions in adult life:

> . . . In such a race,
> So ended, disappointment could be none,
> Uneasiness, or pain, or jealousy;
> We rested in the shade *all* pleased alike,
> Conquered *and* conqueror. Thus our selfishness
> Was mellowed down, and thus the pride of strength
> And the vain-glory of superior skill
> Were interfused with objects which subdued
> And tempered them . . .
> (II.63-71, p. 56; my italics)

The general agreement expressed by "all" is very much emphasized by the afterthought "Conquered and conqueror", and the apparently insignificant conjunction "and" establishes equality between both loser and winner.

Lines II.465-96 (p. 66)[88] echo the thought on the origin of moral strength from Nature in "Tintern Abbey" (above, GCL I:75: ll. 109-12 and 126-33): his native mountains and Nature strengthen the poet to be content with "modest pleasures" and to overcome the "little enmities

---

[88] See also I.165 ff.

and low desires" and "selfishness disguised in gentle names". We may infer that, equipped with these moral qualities, political man too would find it less difficult to work effectively for the implementation of the concepts of the French Revolution or the ideas of Britain's reforming societies.

Sometimes the young William retires from the uproar of the games confederate (p. 47) and then—as early as the period of boyish days and "their glad animal movements" ("Tintern Abbey")—there are moments when the earth and "common face of Nature spake to [him] / Rememberable things . . ." (I.419–20, p. 53). The "common" aspect of Nature recalls and looks forward to the democratic and egalitarian subject matter of Wordsworth's poetry. (See also II.216 ff.) Some lines (II.446–64, p. 65) in the passage dealing with Wordsworth's habit of seeing brotherhood everywhere[89] have been adapted from *The Pedlar*.[90] A few lines earlier Wordsworth ascribes to himself as a seventeen-year-old the task to speak

>   Of that interminable building reared
>   By observation of affinities
>   In objects where no brotherhood exists
>   To common minds . . .
>   (II.433–35, p. 65)

Besides the democratic and egalitarian tone we here discern the teaching voice, for the cold reasoning intellect—however brilliant—finds some of Wordsworth's relationships trivial or ridiculous. A mind which does not acknowledge the dignity of or is condescending towards the characters of "The Idiot Boy" or "Simon Lee" is a common mind that Wordsworth wishes to rectify. In the final analysis the philosophy of the interrelatedness of all life leads to a democratic and humanitarian outlook on life and by extension to a love for animals and plants, to "the great social principle of life / Coercing all things into sympathy" (II.438–39, p. 65).

In the 1805 *Prelude* Wordsworth is even more certain about man's capacity to see the unity of all:

---

[89] See also Havens, *The Mind of a Poet*, pp. 332–33.
[90] Jonathan Wordsworth, *The Music of Humanity*, pp. 236–37, compares *The Pedlar* lines with "Tintern Abbey". On the implied brotherhood in the Wordsworth of 1798–99, see J. Wordsworth's chapters on the "One Life", ibid., pp. 184–232.

> The mind of Man is fram'd even like the breath
> And harmony of music.[91] There is a dark
> Invisible workmanship that reconciles
> Discordant elements, and makes them move
> In *one* society . . .
> (1805 *Prel*. I.351–55; my italics)

The belief in man's ability to make sense of life strikes a note of hope that makes human progress feasible. The poetry and the thought of the corresponding passage in the 1798–99 *Prelude* are not as impassioned:

> The mind of man is fashioned and built up
> Even as a strain of music . . .
> (I.67–68, p. 44)

The passionate love William had for his childhood friend John Fleming (II.382–83, p. 64)[92] was a prototype for such later and closer affinity with Coleridge in later life ("In many things my brother . . .", II.508, p. 67). Wordsworth's biography witnesses to his capacity for a few close friendships, and if his relationships with strangers and acquaintances were somewhat aloof, they are characterized by thoughtfulness. The last word of the 1798–99 *Prelude* is "mankind", and although this refers to Coleridge's role for mankind, the 1805 *Prelude*, as will be shown, bears out how deeply concerned Wordsworth is for this human brotherhood.

The examination of Wordsworth's work of 1798–99 has revealed that he now is more consistent in thought and poetic mode than in earlier periods. He does not fall back into simplistic diatribes against sociopolitical injustices. The tone of the fragment "There is a Law Severe of Penury", which is the only piece resembling his early protest poetry, is low-keyed if we compare it with "The Convict". Wordsworth's contributions to social and political change are implicitly subversive as the discussion of *The Ruined Cottage* has shown: for example, ascribing to the lower-class pedlar a fine sensitivity to man and Nature. *The Ruined Cottage* is as much an attack on war and social injustice as *Salisbury Plain* and *Adventures on Salisbury Plain*. However, its criticism is less overt. *The Ruined Cottage* substantiates further what we have observed

---

[91] Experiences "unpleasant and even harmful in themselves are necessary if our natures are to have depth and beauty, just as discords are necessary to rich harmonies in music" (Havens, *The Mind of a Poet*, p. 299).

[92] A note to the 1850 *Prelude* identifies the friend referred to in these lines as John Fleming (*The Norton Anthology of English Literature*, 3rd ed., p. 215n.).

in the earlier chapters, namely that the more indirect Wordsworth's socio-political criticism is, the better is his poetry.

I have attempted to illustrate Wordsworth's appeal to brotherhood in the poems of the *Lyrical Ballads* and have pointed out the democratic implications of the *Lyrical Ballads,* through, for example, their choice of character, their serious poetic treatment of simple folk and half-wits, and their linguistic features. I have also drawn attention to the egalitarian spirit inherent in the "Matthew" cycle poems. We have seen that Wordsworth's democratic outlook in the poems written between 1798 and 1799 is paralleled by his prose such as the well-known "Advertisement to *Lyrical Ballads*" and the lesser known, incomplete "Essay on Morals". An important change in Wordsworth's concept of liberty is discernible in 1798–99: he has added the element of restraint to liberty (e.g., in "Three Years She Grew in Sun and Shower" and "The Fountain"). The close reading of the fragment "There is an Active Principle Alive in All Things" has supplied us with the key to what Wordsworth actually means by liberty. We have noted that the fragment (probably comp. 1798–1800) is his earliest detailed definition of liberty and that the active practice of love towards one's fellow-man is for him the most important kind of liberty. On the basis of the 1798–99 *Prelude* I have attempted to establish to what extent Wordsworth's childhood may have led in later life to a commitment to liberty, equality, and fraternity.

The following chapter will deal with the remainder of the poems included in the second edition of the *Lyrical Ballads* with special emphases on "Hart-Leap Well" to illustrate how Wordsworth extends his brotherhood to the animal kingdom, and on "Michael" to exemplify Wordsworth's notion of the ideal brotherhood of a small community. "Michael", one of Wordsworth's most important poems, will enable us to see that Wordsworth was above all interested in man's inner moral struggle in 1800—in contrast with the outer struggle against society's institutions between 1791 and 1795/6 or if we include "The Last of the Flock", 1798. Further, I shall examine in detail Wordsworth's rhetorical devices in the Preface to the *Lyrical Ballads* (1800 and 1802 versions) to show that the Preface is much more than a statement of poetic theory; I hope to illustrate that it is a document that advocates the spirit of brotherhood and equality. Last but not least I shall study the new socio-political vocabulary of the 1780s and 1790s and relate my findings to Wordsworth's poetic theory and his verse (see also Appendix); my attention paid to the vocabulary may prove to be a clue in dating the "Prospectus to *The Recluse*" more accurately.

CHAPTER 4

1800

Unlike most of the poems composed between 1797 and 1799 much of the work done in 1800 (primarily for the second volume of *Lyrical Ballads*) is not as directly concerned with human relationships. This does not mean, however, that Wordsworth has given up his democratic stance. Be it his praise for simple rural architecture, the story of a little broom, or one of the "Poems on the Naming of Places" (see below, GCL II:16, 18, 24) his loving concern for humanity continues to be implicit in these little pieces. And as we can see from Dorothy's journals many a beggar afforded the newly founded Wordsworth household the opportunity of putting their theory of loving care into practice.[1] Except three,[2] all poems that were included in the *Lyrical Ballads* (1800) were probably completed by mid-October 1800 at the very latest and most of them probably in the summer.[3]

Soon after the Wordsworths had moved into Dove Cottage their beloved brother John arrived for an eight-month visit (Reed II, p. 59). Coleridge's first visit to Dove Cottage took place between April and May (Reed II, p. 61), and after Coleridge had settled at Keswick in the summer he came eight more times to Grasmere; Wordsworth visited Keswick five times and Dorothy twice before the end of December (Moorman I, p. 478). Thus in 1800 Wordsworth was surrounded by those dearest to him, and his personal contentment was probably enhanced by his success as a poet.[4] His domestic bliss is to some degree reflected in the happy tone of "The Pet-Lamb"[5] (GCL II:13; Brett & Jones, pp.

---

[1] For examples of alms-giving and meetings with destitute people in 1800, see *Journals of Dorothy Wordsworth* (1971 ed./1974 rpt.), pp. 16, 17, 25, 26, 28, 43–44, 51.

[2] The exceptions are: GCL II:9 ("There is an Eminence,—of These Our Hills" [not included in this thesis]); "A Narrow Girdle of Rough Stones and Crags" and "Michael" (see below, GCL II:24 and 30).

[3] "It is remotely possible that any poem for vol. II, unless specifically shown by other evidence to date later, had been virtually completed by early June . . ." (Reed II, p. 75n.).

[4] "The *Lyrical Ballads,* in spite of Wordsworth's apprehension, were all sold by the beginning of June 1800. Perhaps their ultimate success was in part due to an excellent review which appeared in October 1799 in the *British Critic* . . ." (Moorman I, p. 486).

[5] Brett & Jones entitle "The Pet-Lamb, a Pastoral".

200–02), where his love for children fuses with a brotherhood extended to animals.

So far all of Wordsworth's poems about children have proved that he is diametrically opposed to the cliché that children should be seen but not heard. He comes across as a defender of children's rights in pointing out that their freedom should not be unduly restricted. His relationship with children is one of dialogue, and where their actions necessitate censure, as in "The Idle Shepherd-Boys" (GCL II:20; Brett & Jones, pp. 164–67), it is pronounced in a benevolent manner: "And gently did the Bard / Those idle Shepherd-boys upbraid, / And bade them better mind their trade."

Bearing in mind the history of the Jews in the twentieth century, many modern readers probably appreciate better the "Song for the Wandering Jew" (GCL II:15; Brett & Jones, p. 178) than Wordsworth's contemporaries did. Earlier, Wordsworth had treated Roman Catholics and gipsies sympathetically (*Descriptive Sketches* [1793], *PW* I, ll. 654–55; *Adventures on Salisbury Plain* [Cornell Wordsworth], st. 56) within the context of larger poems. To the Jew he devotes an entire poem and thus makes a modest contribution to the emancipation of Jews, and to racial equality in general. Stanzas 1, 2, and 4 are introduced by "Though" pointing to the apparent homeless state of torrents, chamois, sea-horse; and three times a "Yet" points to a home that these seemingly homeless enjoy. The raven too enjoys an abode (st. 3). Consequently the final stanza, in depicting the real homelessness of the Jew, comes as a climactic contrast:

> Day and night my toils redouble!
> Never nearer to the goal,
> Night and day, I feel the trouble,
> Of the Wanderer in my soul.

In the order of Nature there is a place of rest for animals and torrents, whereas the Wandering Jew, a man, is excluded from that order that cares for every creature. Mary Moorman is right in saying that the "Song for the Wandering Jew" "deserves to be better known than it is . . ." (Moorman I, p. 480).

"Written with a Pencil upon a Stone in the Wall of the House (an Outhouse), on the Island at Grasmere"[6] (GCL II:16; Brett & Jones, p. 172) was composed at approximately the same time as the poem on the Jew. In raising the status of the little rural building, Wordsworth again uses

---

[6] Brett & Jones entitle "Inscription, For the House (an Outhouse) on the Island at Grasmere". Reed's title is that of 1815 (*PW* IV, p. 198, *Apparatus criticus*).

"yet" (5, 13) to underscore its unexpected worthiness. The unknown village builder and his "rude edifice" have as much right to poetic praise as the famous architect in the "great city". The democratic sentiment is striking; moreover, sometimes the unadorned functional building is the spot where one poet has "Fair sights, and visions of romantic joy" (29), a place where the creative imagination of the Romantic era rules. In "Written with a Slate Pencil upon a Stone, the Largest of a Heap Lying Near a Deserted Quarry, upon One of the Islands at Rydal"[7] (GCL II:17; Brett & Jones, pp. 189–90) we also discern Wordsworth's democratic spirit when he chastises the architecture that is an expression of social pride. The pompous buildings in "snow-white splendour" of the rich newcomers to the Lake District are anathema to Wordsworth, and he points warningly to the pile which remains of a planned "little dome / Or pleasure-house". (Cf. with proud architecture in "Hart-Leap Well", ll. 57–74, below, GCL II:21.)

The fable of "The Oak and the Broom"[8] (GCL II:18; Brett & Jones, pp. 157–60) is another of Wordsworth's unobtrusive but revolutionary pieces.[9] One of the "simple truths" (l. 1) that Andrew gleans from Nature is that things can turn out contrary to expectations. The slender, sleepy broom thanks the wise, mighty oak for warning it of the rocks that might crush it one day and observes:

> Frail is the bond, by which we hold
> Our being, be we young or old,
> Wise, foolish, weak or strong.
>
> Disasters, do the best we can,
> Will reach both great and small;
> And he is oft the wisest man,
> Who is not wise at all.
>
> (58–64)

The contrasting pairs "young or old", etc.—and especially line 62 in which "both" emphasizes the disasters to which "great and small" are subject—stress the equality of mankind before a levelling fate. Doubting the wisdom of the man who, like the old oak, may seem wise in the eyes of the world but is not (63–64), carries a democratic undertone. The sense of home and the feeling of being completely integrated in the

---

[7] Brett & Jones: "Lines, Written [etc.] . . . Rydale".
[8] Brett & Jones entitle "The Oak and the Broom, a Pastoral".
[9] On the implicit moral lesson for man of "The Oak and the Broom" and "The Waterfall and the Eglantine" (GCL II:18), see Chard, pp. 239 and 242. Mary Moorman thinks that the two fables are "conscious reminiscences of Langhorne's *Fables of Flora*, one of which bears the title *The Wilding and the Broom*" (Moorman I, p. 480).

goings-on of Nature make the broom content (65–90). (Contrast this with the misery caused by homelessness in, e.g., *Adventures on Salisbury Plain*.)

One can couch the events of the final stanza in political terms: The strong, well established principles (represented by the oak) are overthrown by the winds of change. The weak "little careless Broom" proves to be more flexible and resistant; it can help to rebuild a new order. Although the oak here happens to represent protection and fatherliness, its overthrow implies that political change and progress can be brought about even if those in power seem as strong and irresistible as the mighty tree.

The happy ending for the broom is of particular relevance if we bear in mind that this poem was preceded by "The Waterfall and the Eglantine" (GCL II:18; Brett & Jones, pp. 155–56) in the 1800 edition of *Lyrical Ballads*. The eglantine is at the mercy of the tyrannous flood. It is "living, as a child might know, / In an unhappy home" (9–10). The poem calls forth our feelings of sympathy with the oppressed briar. (The allusions to children in stanzas 1 and 2 are yet another example of Wordsworth's love for them.) The tyrannous waterfall destroys the briar. However, its destruction makes us side with liberty against tyranny; and placing the happily ending "Oak and the Broom" after the verse of the eglantine's downfall is dramatically effective, restoring thus the balance of hope for the weak.

Hart-Leap Well.—According to Wordsworth "Hart-Leap Well"[10] (GCL II:21; Brett & Jones, pp. 127–33) was written easily and quickly (Brett & Jones, p. 298). However speedily composed, it nevertheless documents Wordsworth's profound thought on man and beast as members of the one creation and their right to life within this order. Sir Walter's pride is in opposition to that order and prevents him from seeing that, in causing the hart's death, he tampers with Nature. His pride precludes him from extending feelings of brotherhood to the hart. Sir Walter erects a pleasure-house and an arbour to commemorate the death of this "gallant brute". However, neither playful architecture nor sentimental admiration will restore the hart's life. The hubris of "Till the foundations of the mountains fail / My mansion with its arbour shall endure" (73–74) is revenged by the ironic contrast of "You see these lifeless stumps of aspin wood, / Some say that they are beeches, others elms, / These were the Bower; and here a Mansion stood, / The finest palace of a hundred realms" (125–28).

---

[10] On the origin of and for excellent interpretations of "Hart-Leap Well", see Moorman I, pp. 454–56, and Beer, *Wordsworth and the Human Heart* (1978), pp. 144–50.

Much of Part Two of "Hart-Leap Well" comments on Sir Walter's act as seen through the eyes of a shepherd who acknowledges the brotherly bond between man and beast. Whereas the knight had "gaz'd upon the spoil with silent joy" (36), the man of the people is endowed with imaginative sympathy. In talking about the hart he employs a vocabulary usually applied to human beings: "What thoughts . . ." (141), "What *cause* the Hart might have to *love* this place, / And come and make his *death-bed* near the well" (147–48; my italics). Lines 149–56 continue to credit the hart with human qualities, thus underlining the fraternal feelings between man and the animal kingdom.

As a consequence of the knight's act the place of human callousness "seem'd as if the spring-time came not here, / And Nature here were willing to decay" (115–16). As in the *Ancient Mariner* Nature's rhythm stops until all that is reminiscent of the crime is gone. The extended brotherhood of the *Ancient Mariner,* "He prayeth well who loveth well / Both man and bird and beast" (Brett & Jones, p. 34), is also the concluding lesson of "Hart-Leap Well":

> Never to blend our pleasure or our pride
> With sorrow of the meanest thing that feels.[11]
> (179–80)

The "milder day" for beast and man ("Hart-Leap Well", 175) was still a vision of future times. When Wordsworth composed "A Narrow Girdle of Rough Stones and Crags" (GCL II:24; Brett & Jones, pp. 223–25), probably in the autumn of 1800, he described the world as a place that sometimes lacked brotherhood and forced a man to work despite illness:

> . . . we saw a man worn down
> By sickness, gaunt and lean, with sunken cheeks
> And wasted limbs, his legs so long and lean
> . . .
> Too weak to labour in the harvest field,
> The man was using his best skill to gain
> A pittance from the dead unfeeling lake
> That knew not of his wants. . . .
> (64–66, 69–72)

Here Nature is not benevolent, which is exceptional in Wordsworth. There is a sense of impotence, for how can a "dead unfeeling lake" grant a pittance? And worse, "pittance" carries the undertone of allowance as though the peasant depended on the good will of the lake.

---

[11] This is similar in thought to "who feels contempt / For any living thing", etc. of the Yew-Tree Lines above, pp. 80–81.

In that autumn of 1800 the Wordsworths had more than one reason to converse about the disagreeable qualities and "manners of the rich—avarice, inordinate desires . . .",[12] etc. However, the human brotherhood existing in some local communities—as we have seen in "The Brothers"—may one day become a genuine worldwide brotherhood and prove as firm and stable as the hope emanating from the "brotherhood / Of ancient mountains" ("To Joanna", GCL II:26; Brett & Jones, p. 221). A society permeated with fraternal feelings can kindly tolerate a dotard-pilferer whose daughter feels responsible enough for him to repair the little damage done by the old man, as in "The Two Thieves" (GCL II:19; Brett & Jones, pp. 175–77).

A few days before William had finished the bulk of the Preface to the *Lyrical Ballads*[13] Dorothy described the qualities of her neighbours in a letter of 10 and [12] September [1800] to Mrs. John Marshall: "We are very comfortably situated with respect to neighbours of the lower classes, they are excellent people, friendly in performing all offices of kindness and humanity and *attentive* to us *without servility*—if we were sick they would wait upon us night and day" (*E.Y.*, p. 298; my italics). This excerpt is similar to the praise Wordsworth has for the "low and rustic life" in his Preface; Dorothy's dislike of servility evokes its opposite, the proud kind of independence that her brother likes so much in his rural characters. The brotherhood expressed by their neighbours in performing offices of kindness is shown to them by people enjoying that amount of personal liberty and independence which is so important for human dignity.

Michael.—"Michael"[14] (GCL II:30; Brett & Jones, pp. 226–40), the tragic story of a tenacious independent shepherd, is very much coloured by Wordsworth's Grasmere experience.[15] It was the last poem written for the second volume of the *Lyrical Ballads*. Its composition was probably begun in early October and certainly concluded by 19 December 1800. Work on this poem, which contains Wordsworth's most important "views" (Moorman I, p. 506), was to be time-consuming and

---

[12] *Journals of Dorothy Wordsworth* (1971 ed./1974 rpt.), p. 41.

[13] I deviate here from a strictly chronological arrangement and shall discuss the Preface after "Michael".

[14] Brett & Jones entitle "Michael, a Pastoral Poem".

[15] See also Kenneth MacLean whose comment on Dorothy's *Grasmere Journal* could equally well apply to "Michael": it is "the story of Westmorland and Cumberland—a story of an ancient rural society falling into decay . . ." (*Agrarian Age*, p. 89). On similar lines, see V. G. Kiernan's Marxist interpretation of "Michael" and the earlier "The Brothers" ("Wordsworth and the People", pp. 256–57).

painful.[16] The last poem of the *Lyrical Ballads*, like so many others in the collection, is permeated by a democratic spirit through its selection of "low" subject matter, a story "ungarnish'd with events" (19),[17] and its plain but versatile shepherd hero, "Intense and frugal, apt for all affairs" (45). Like the schoolmaster of the Matthew poems, Michael is no narrow specialist; and, similar to Matthew or the adult in "Anecdote for Fathers", old Michael, in contact with his son Luke, is characterized by a spirit of equality: they "Were as companions . . ." (208), "in us the old and young / Have play'd together . . ." (364–65).

The "history / Homely and rude" (35) endows the shepherd with the same kind of deep appreciation for the natural scenery as the pedlar in *The Ruined Cottage* (GCL I:57e, above). The pointed address to the middle- and upper-class reader is unmistakable:

> And *grossly* that man errs, who should suppose
> That the green Valleys, and the Streams and Rocks
> Were things indifferent to the Shepherd's *thoughts*.
> (62–64; my italics)

"Grossly" emphasizes the error of denying this capacity to a plain uneducated man. The choice of "thought" (instead of a presumed blind lower-class "feeling"), connoting Michael's intelligent mental activity, makes inroads into what was supposed to be an activity of the educated classes. The undertone of these three lines is radically democratic in its implicit questioning of so-called class characteristics.

A few lines further down Wordsworth repeats and fortifies the bond with Nature: "these fields, these hills / Which were his living Being, even more / Than his own Blood . . ." (74–76). Here Wordsworth makes his strong love for Nature explicit through Michael's words; the strength of his feeling explains why in some other instances he discerns a brotherhood between man and Nature, or wishes to build a bridge of fraternization between Nature and man.

---

[16] Its laborious growth can be retraced in Moorman 1, pp. 490–500. For its democratic subject matter (in the extended meaning), see ibid., p. 490.

MS. Verse 18 contains a half-jocular ballad version of "Michael". Knowing and appreciating the tragic theme of "Michael" one is as shocked about the funny text as Helen Darbishire was in 1959 when it was first shown to her. For its transcription and facsimile, see Stephen Parrish, "*Michael* and the Pastoral Ballad", in *Bicentenary Wordsworth Studies in Memory of John Alban Finch*, ed. Jonathan Wordsworth (Ithaca, N.Y., and London: Cornell U.P., 1970), pp. 71–75. Jonathan Wordsworth, "A Note on the Ballad Version of 'Michael'", *Ariel*, 2 (1971), 66–71, throws light on the history of its composition.

[17] This is similar to the "common tale / By moving accidents uncharactered" of *The Ruined Cottage* (ll. 290 ff.).

When the liberty of his "patrimonial fields" (234) is endangered—"patrimonial" evoking the moral obligation towards his ancestors—Michael chooses an image from one of Nature's most unrestricted phenomena, the wind, to express the virtually religious import the freedom of his property has for him:

> . . . the land
> Shall not go from us, and it shall be free,
> He [Luke] shall possess it, free as is the wind
> That passes over it . . .[18]
> (254–57)

The religious tone is emphasized by the threefold reiteration of "shall", in a sense reminiscent of the language of the Bible, as though Michael wants to invoke the help of forces independent of the human will.

More evident, however, than liberty is the solidarity of local brotherhood in "Michael". Isabel, Luke's mother, reminisces on past acts of brotherhood. The beneficiary then was a "parish-boy" who went to London to make his fortune: "at the church-door / They made a gathering for him, shillings, pence, / And halfpennies, wherewith the Neighbours bought / A Basket, which they fill'd with Pedlar's wares" (269–72).

The community spirit manifests itself in more than mere material proofs of brotherhood. When Luke leaves his native village

> . . . all the Neighbours as he pass'd their doors
> Came forth, with wishes and with farewell pray'rs,
> That follow'd him 'till he was out of sight.
> (437–39)

As the village community in "The Brothers" would have extended a hearty welcome to Leonard so here the villagers bid farewell to Luke, and we can be certain that, although he is absent, they talk about him at their firesides as they did about Leonard in "The Brothers". The local brotherhood in "Michael" is still intact. There is not a trace of gloating over the misfortune of the old man when his promising son gives himself to evil courses. The pity for Michael is universal in his locality: ". . . 'Tis not forgotten yet / The pity which was then in every heart / For the Old Man . . ." (471–73).

---

[18] In May 1800 Dorothy Wordsworth recorded a conversation that throws light on the increasing economic inequality: "John Fisher . . . talked much about the alteration in the times, and observed that in a short time there would be only two ranks of people, the very rich and the very poor, for those who have small estates says he are forced to sell, and all the land goes into one hand. . . ." (*Journals of Dorothy Wordsworth* (1971 ed./1974 rpt.), p. 19.)

The height of happiness in Michael's life story earlier in the poem is reflected in the repeated joyful alliteration of "light" and "life" (119–46). In the final verse paragraph, by contrast, there is darkness and no human life; "great changes have been wrought / In all the neighbourhood" alludes to the transformations that have taken place and that may be inimical to the social coherence of the local brotherhood. The end of "Michael" forebodes the changes in the countryside. As a young man Michael had "toil'd and toil'd" until "the land was free" (387–88). In view of enclosures and industrialization his tenacious efforts to free the land from debt would probably have been in vain if he had begun his life work in 1800.

"Michael" draws no parallels with an earlier happy golden age (as *Descriptive Sketches,* comp. 1791–92) nor with prehistoric man's basic equality in sharing equally the adversities and hardships of existence (as *Salisbury Plain,* comp. 1793). "Michael" is set entirely in the present and resembles in this respect much of Wordsworth's production between 1797 and 1800. As in the *Adventures on Salisbury Plain* (comp. 1795–96) his heroes are still drawn from the lower classes, but their struggles are different. The sailor-murderer and the old father of *Adventures on Salisbury Plain* had tried to obtain justice in the courts, and when that failed both reacted against society. Old Michael's fight is quieter, an inner moral struggle. "Michael" extends the seventeenth- and eighteenth-century theories of natural rights: a little landed property is not only a matter of secure material welfare but it is also important in strengthening family affections.[19]

In a letter of 18 December 1800 to his publisher, Longman and Rees, roughly contemporary with the completion of "Michael", Wordsworth said that he did not add certain poems to the second volume of the *Lyrical Ballads,* since "some of them being connected with political subjects I judged that they would be injurious to the sale of the Work" (*E.Y.,* p. 309). Giving precedence to commercial considerations in selecting his poems is not an agreeable trait in Wordsworth. (However, his dire financial situation is a mitigating factor.) The letter implies that Wordsworth did not see the socio-political significance of the *Lyrical Ballads,* since for him "political" apparently meant overtly political.

However, only four weeks after the letter to Longman, Wordsworth took a highly political step; he sent the *Lyrical Ballads* with an accompanying letter to Charles James Fox, who at that time was alone among the

---

[19] See also Parrish, *The Art of the* Lyrical Ballads, pp. 182–83, and my analysis of "The Last of the Flock", above GCL I:67.

leading politicians in his struggle for political measures encouraging brotherhood and equality.[20] In the letter Wordsworth draws Fox's attention to "The Brothers" and "Michael" and hopes they will make their contribution in bringing about political change for the better. These poems

> may in some small degree enlarge our feelings of reverence for our species, and our knowledge of human nature, by shewing that our best qualities are possessed by men whom we are too apt to consider, not with reference to the *points in which they resemble us,* but to those in which they manifestly differ from us. I thought . . . that the two poems might co-operate, however feebly, with the illustrious efforts which you have made to stem this and other evils with which the country is labouring . . . (*E.Y.*, p. 315; my italics).

The italicized words point to the importance Wordsworth attaches to men's basic equality at a time when the differences between men were overrated in order to justify an unequal treatment of people. The letter is proof enough that Wordsworth at the end of 1800 and the beginning of 1801 is still interested in public issues; but he is more concerned with the direct impact of politics on the individual than in the early 1790s, for his retirement from the intellectual circles and debates had brought him nearer to the people and enabled him to share the concrete experiences of the Michaels of northern England:

> They are small independent *proprietors* of land here called statesmen, men of respectable education who daily labour on their own little properties.[21] . . . Their little tract of land serves as a kind of permanent rallying point for their domestic feelings, as a tablet upon which they are written which makes them objects of memory in a thousand instances when they would otherwise be forgotten. It is a fountain fitted to the nature of social man from which supplies of affection, as pure as his heart was intended for, are daily drawn. . . . (*E.Y.*, pp. 314–15; Wordsworth's emphasis.)

In "A Letter to the Bishop of Llandaff" (comp. 1793) Wordsworth had propounded the redistribution of excessive wealth (*Prose Works* I.34.132–36) for reasons of greater economic justice, but as alluded to earlier, now Wordsworth sees the correlation between the "patrimonial

---

[20] Between "1797 and 1802, Fox appeared to provide the only shelter for reform" (Thompson, *The Making of the English Working Class*, p. 491).

[21] Thompson examines the large landowners' views on the smallholders: "At a time when Wordsworth was extolling the virtues of old Michael and his wife, in their struggle to maintain their 'patrimonial fields', the very much more influential *Commercial and Agricultural Magazine* regarded the 'yeoman' in a different light: 'A wicked, cross-grained, petty farmer is like the sow in his yard, almost an insulated individual, who has no communication with, and therefore, no reverence for the opinion of the world.' " (*The Making of the English Working Class*, p. 243.)

fields" and, to use a modern expression, the quality of life which is hampered by excessive economic inequality. "Michael" does not call for revolutionary political action. Indeed, Wordsworth has come a long way from the embittered indictment of the monarchy and aristocracy and the advocacy of liberty, equality, and fraternity in their strictly political sense of "A Letter to the Bishop of Llandaff". Some of that letter's political theory, however, is still discernible in Wordsworth's Preface to the *Lyrical Ballads* of 1800, transformed, and fused there with his poetic theory into an indissoluble unity.

Preface to the Lyrical Ballads

Critics and scholars from Jeffrey down to Harper, Moorman, Todd, and Woodring acknowledge the socio-political radicalism of Wordsworth's theory of poetic language and subject matter in the Preface to *Lyrical Ballads* (1800 and 1802 editions),[22] but no detailed work on the political implications of the *P.L.B.* in general nor on the concepts of equality and brotherhood that are embedded in it has been done. Throughout the Preface[23] Wordsworth reiterates that a selection and an imitation of the "language of men" ought to be the language of poetry. In Franklyn Bliss Snyder's list of Wordsworth's forty-six most frequently used words[24] "man" comes third, preceded by (1) love and (2) heart. In Josephine Miles's later study "man" is placed in the top frequency column together with "live/life", "love", and "see/sight".[25] Snyder's and Miles's findings for the poetry are also borne out for the Preface, namely that man/men, in many cases engendering the notion of the "brotherhood of man", appears very frequently in it. The cornerstones of democracy—

[22] "The theories in the *Preface to the Lyrical Ballads* (1800), even more than the poems themselves, had been attacked by Jeffrey because that influential critic discerned their liberal democratic implications . . ." (Ernest Bernbaum, *Guide Through the Romantic Movement*, 2nd ed. [1st ed. 1930], New York: Ronald Press, 1949), p. 86. The *P.L.B.* "heralds one of the most splendid triumphs of democracy" (Harper I, p. 425). "There is more in the preface than a criticism of bad poetry. In it we see Wordsworth the man of action, the social reformer, and critic of the bad customs of his day . . ." (Moorman I, p. 495). See also Woodring, *Wordsworth*, p. 143; and Todd, *Politics and the Poet*, pp. 111–12.

[23] My text (1800 and 1802 versions) is derived from Brett & Jones, pp. 241–72. Page references to the relevant passages in Owen and Smyser, *Prose Works* I (1974), are given in square brackets. For a detailed annotation of the Preface, see W. J. B. Owen, ed., *Wordsworth's Preface to Lyrical Ballads* (Copenhagen: Rosenkilde & Bagger, 1957; vol. IX of *Anglistica*); and *Prose Works* I, pp. 167–88.

[24] Franklyn Bliss Snyder, "Wordsworth's Favorite Words", *JEGP*, 22 (1923), 253–56.

[25] Josephine Miles, *The Vocabulary of Poetry: Three Studies*. [Study 1:] *Wordsworth and the Vocabulary of Emotion*. Univ. of California Publications in English, vol. XII, No. 1 (1942), p. 171, Table 4.

fraternity and equality—can be clearly discerned in one of the key passages of the 1802 *P.L.B.*:

What is a Poet? . . . He is a man speaking to men: a man, it is true, endued with more lively sensibility, more enthusiasm and tenderness, who has a greater knowledge of human nature, and a more comprehensive soul, than are supposed to be common among mankind; a man pleased with his own passions and volitions, and who rejoices more than other men in the spirit of life that is in him . . . (Brett & Jones, pp. 255–56, [138]).

The answer to the question "What is a Poet?" stands out in its entirely unadorned simplicity: "He is a man . . ."[26] This undramatic statement has an effective dramatic impact;[27] its brevity and simple vocabulary bring out forcefully the actual basic equality and brotherhood of men. The communicative power of the poet is expressed by the word "speaking" which acts as a copula uniting "man . . . to men". We accept the poet as one of us, as a man and nothing more. He is part of the brotherhood of man and what he wishes to communicate to us in this capacity is surely of relevance to us, his fellow-men.

Having established the poet as a man in brotherhood and equality, the answer continues: the colon after men demands a long pause (and a prolonged enunciation of "man") and we are told "a man, [pause] it is true, [pause] . . ."; while this second instance of "man", in the same line, may reinforce our feelings of brotherhood, Wordsworth's pauses prepare us to accept the ensuing modifications. Wordsworth's persuasive technique leads us to a more kindly paraphrase of that famous sentence from *Animal Farm,* namely that all men are equal but in the function of a poet man is more equal than his fellows. Wordsworth does this masterfully, for he neither negates his original answer nor restricts it by a "but" or a "however". He just qualifies it by comparatives ("more" and "greater") which take nothing away from the feeling of brotherhood. On the contrary, he reasserts the theme of universal brotherhood: "among mankind; a man . . .". Further on (1802 *P.L.B.*, p. 261, [142]) the basic brotherhood and equality of man is taken up again; the poet is not different "in kind from other men, but only in degree. . . ."

This poet, then, chooses as his principal subject matter the low and

---

[26] David Perkins, in discussing the concept of sincerity in Wordsworth, notes the difference between the older view of the poet as a "maker" and Wordsworth's view as the poet being "a man speaking to men": "Wordsworth would have a poet speak not from the traditions of a craft, but from his full experience and *concern* as a man" [my italics]. (*Wordsworth and the Poetry of Sincerity,* p. 13.)

[27] It is reminiscent of Kent's answer in *King Lear.* "*Lear:* . . . How now, what art thou? *Kent:* A man, sir" (I.iv.9–10; *Riverside Shakespeare,* 1974 ed.).

rustic life, "because in that situation the essential passions of the heart find a better soil in which they can attain their maturity . . ." (1800 *P.L.B.*, p. 245, [124]). The ideal conditions under which the rustic can develop his essential passions are by implication set out as an example to all men. The situation of the exemplary rustic is also an ideal situation in which is engendered "a far more philosophical language than that which is frequently substituted for it by Poets, who think that they are conferring honour upon themselves and their art in proportion as they separate themselves from the sympathies of men . . ." (1800 *P.L.B.*, pp. 245–46, [124]). In this passage Wordsworth reproves the poets for separating themselves from the "sympathies" of men and thereby from the ideal brotherhood of man. Instead of showing a linguistic solidarity with those who are worthy of it, they adopt "arbitrary and capricious habits of expression". The word "think" in the quotation has a slightly caustic tone, and "their art" seems rather ironic. Wordsworth implies that art and the brotherhood of man are closely interrelated; to detach yourself from that great fraternity is inimical to poetic creativity.

Poetry sheds no tears "such as Angels weep", but natural and human tears; she can boast of no celestial Ichor that distinguishes her vital juices from those of prose; the same human blood circulates through the veins of them both. (1800 *P.L.B.*, p. 254, [134].)

On a first reading we note how well the juxtapositions of celestial and terrestrial elements work in this excerpt. The effect of contrast is reinforced by a carefully chosen vocabulary. Poetry is not distant, separate, incomprehensible, as the expression "angels" suggests. "Human tears" are common to all men and therefore the language of poetry ought to be accessible to all men. The "celestial Ichor" of supposed poetry is contrasted with the "same human blood" of both good poetry and prose. Ichor suggests the inaccessibility of the gods. Human blood implies relationships and the epithet "same" strengthens the notion of the same blood flowing in all human veins, making us one band of brothers. The ethereal fluid of the gods, ichor, is contrasted with the human blood, the symbol of the warmth of human life, and thereby the bond is made between a vital language of poetry and prose and the common life of man. All in all, Wordsworth implies a democratizing of the literary genres which is reinforced by a quotation from the republican poet Milton ("such as Angels weep", *Paradise Lost* I.620).

In referring to personifications in poetry Wordsworth says "I have wished to keep my Reader in the company of flesh and blood, persuaded that by so doing I shall interest him . . ." (1802 *P.L.B.*, p. 250, [131]).

Again, the expression "flesh and blood" can be set off against "ichor" mentioned earlier on. "Flesh and blood" suggests the idea of the brotherhood of man. The poet identifies himself with his fellow-men;[28] it is his wish "to bring his feelings near to those of the persons whose feelings he describes . . ." (1802 *P.L.B.*, p. 256, [138]). "Near" expresses the closeness and intimacy the poet hopes to achieve between himself and those who inspire him with the subject matter of his poetry. This identification with the human heart makes the poet deal with those feelings that are shared by all men whose primary affections are still intact. It underlines the sense of community and excludes subject matter that separates man from man.

However, this does not mean that Wordsworth is, for instance, against science as such, for if

> the time should ever come when what is now called Science, thus familiarized to men, shall be ready to put on, as it were, a form of flesh and blood,[29] the Poet will lend his divine spirit to aid the transfiguration, and will welcome the Being thus produced, as a dear and genuine inmate of the household of man. . . . (1802 *P.L.B.*, p. 260, [141].)

"Familiarized" implies that when the linkage is made between science and what could be called the common frame of reference of all men (Wordsworth uses once more the expression "flesh and blood"), then it is part of our consciousness and ready for poetic treatment. The "divine spirit" of the poet suggests a parallel with the biblical idea of the incarnation, i.e. putting on flesh and blood, or God becoming man, spirit transformed to Nature. In short, "Science" putting on "flesh and blood" is close to the "Word" becoming "Flesh".[30] Much as the earlier passage (above, p. 136) has implied the poet's superiority, the rhetorical trick here of ascribing a "divine spirit" to the poet-man sets him a little apart from ordinary men. The final part of the quotation contains an accumulation of words that trigger off deeply rooted emotions of love ("dear") and the feeling that the "genuine inmate" is not an alien intruder but a welcome brother in that "household" (connoting

---

[28] "The notion of imaginative identification with others, and hence of the author with his characters, is common in the late eighteenth century" (*Prose Works* I, p. 177). This notion of imaginative identification is, in my opinion, an important prerequisite for feelings of brotherhood.

[29] In "believing that science can eventually put on such a form and offer mankind such service, Wordsworth differed considerably from his contemporaries . . ." (Grob, *The Philosophic Mind*, p. 184). See also Owen and Smyser's Commentary to *P.L.B.*, *Prose Works* I, p. 181 (note on ll. 430–1).

[30] I am indebted to Frank Jordan, Miami University, Oxford, Ohio, for suggesting the biblical parallel.

warmth and intimacy) of human brotherhood. The "divine spirit" of the poet will build the bridge between science and the heart of mankind.

Wordsworth is uncompromising in his search for that kind of truth which is meaningful to all men. The poet joins together and brings out the fundamental fraternal relationship that exists between the lawyer, physician, mariner, astronomer, etc. He contrasts this unifying role with that of the scientist:

> The Man of Science seeks truth as a remote and unknown benefactor; he cherishes and loves it in his solitude: the Poet, singing a song in which all human beings join with him, rejoices in the presence of truth as our visible friend and hourly companion. . . . the Poet binds together by passion and knowledge the vast empire of human society, as it is spread over the whole earth, and over all time. . . . (1802 *P.L.B.*, p. 259, [141].)

The passage following the colon rings with the element of universal brotherhood: "a song in which *all* human beings"; "vast empire of human society"; "whole earth" [my italics]. For the poet, truth is a "visible friend"; on the other hand, the scientist in "his solitude" ("his" underlines Wordsworth's disparaging attitude) seeks truth as a "remote and unknown benefactor". This contrast is by itself effective but is heightened by the term "friend", an old Germanic word of time-honoured usage; whilst the Latinate "benefactor" suggests a hierarchical relationship, "friend" implies a relationship based on equality. The last sentence is very Wordsworthian in tone: the poet endeavours to bring together all men into one all-comprising, everlasting brotherhood, for "human society . . . is spread over . . . all time".

Since the poet is not different in kind from other men, he "must descend from this supposed height" (1802 *P.L.B.*, p. 261, [143]).[31] The image of descent, whether from a heaven of some sort (religion) or from a throne in an imperial palace (politics) or from the classical hierarchy of genres indicates that the proper place of the poet is among men. The democratization of both genres and poet is extended to the democratization of subject matter within poetry. Wordsworth chooses "subjects from common life" (1800 *P.L.B.*, p. 267, [150]) and "ordinary things" (1802 *P.L.B.*, p. 244, [123]) and he defends his theory by referring to the poets of former times: "poems are extant, written upon more humble subjects, and in a more naked and simple style than what I have aimed

---

[31] In Wordsworth's letter to John Wilson of [7 June 1802] "descend" points to his democratic sentiment. Wordsworth complains that "we err lamentably if we suppose" "gentlemen, persons of fortune, professional men . . . to be fair representatives of the vast mass of human existence . . .", and few of higher rank "descend lower among cottages and fields and among children" (*E.Y.*, p. 355).

at ..." (1800 *P.L.B.*, p. 263, [144]). He warns his reader that he does not intend to adhere to the rules of contemporary poetic decorum[32] (*P.L.B.*, pp. 243-44, [122, 123]: "It is supposed ..."); instead he repeats Joshua Reynolds's dictum that "an *accurate* taste in Poetry ... is an *acquired* talent, which can only be produced by thought ..."[33] (1800 *P.L.B.*, p. 271, [156]). Wordsworth does not demand more from his audience than he requests earlier in the Preface from the poet, namely to think "long and deeply" (1800 *P.L.B.*, p. 246, [126]). Unlike Lord Kames, who automatically disqualifies from aesthetic judgement "those who depend for food on bodily labour",[34] he does not stipulate a certain class or occupation as his readership and demonstrates thus his democratic stand. Wordsworth stresses the liberty of his reader to "decide by his own feelings genuinely, and not by reflection upon what will probably be the judgment of others" (1800 *P.L.B.*, p. 270, [154]).

In the Preface Wordsworth tries to change poetic taste and to make his middle- and upper-class readers reassess their ideas about the lower classes. His teaching voice leaves no doubt that each of his poems in the *Lyrical Ballads* "has a worthy *purpose*"[35] (1800 *P.L.B.*, p. 246, [124]). Bearing in mind that the concept of "general truth" appears throughout

---

[32] Comparing Dr. Johnson's praise of Shakespeare's comic characters with Wordsworth's choice of humble characters, M. H. Abrams observes: "Wordsworth ... was quite in agreement with Johnson that the poet properly concerns himself with the general and uniform ... he merely differed in regard to the place these qualities are best exemplified in real life. This difference, however, led in practice to a drastic break with traditional poetic decorum. To Wordsworth, a mad mother, an idiot boy, or a child who cannot know of death were as appropriate subjects for serious poetry as Achilles or Lear. The poetic representation of these people was not intended to be a shift from the universal and normal to the deviant and abnormal, as some critics have charged from his day to this. On the contrary, by a simple extension of the most widely held premise of neo-classic thought—an extension for which there was ample precedent even in Johnson's lifetime—Wordsworth turned in his poetry to those feelings and thoughts whose very presence in peasants, children, and idiots is what proves them to be the property, not of the cultivated classes alone, but of all mankind ..." (*The Mirror and the Lamp*, p. 107). See also below, n. 36.

[33] Wordsworth had referred to Reynolds in the "Advertisement to the *Lyrical Ballads* [1798]". For the text, see *Prose Works* I, pp. 116-17.

[34] Quoted in Abrams, *The Mirror and the Lamp*, p. 109. On the poet's audience, see Abrams's comparison between Dr. Johnson, Lord Kames, and Wordsworth; this comparison underlines Wordsworth's democratic stance (ibid., pp. 108-09).

[35] Wordsworth reiterates "purpose" a number of times; it is the only term that he italicizes twice in the otherwise very sparingly italicized Preface. In his letter of [7 June 1802] to Wilson, commenting on the *Lyrical Ballads*, his purpose becomes apparent: "a great Poet ought to ... rectify men's feelings, to give them new compositions of feeling, to render their feelings more sane pure and permanent, in short, more consonant to nature, that is, to eternal nature, and the great moving spirit of things. He ought to travel before men occasionally as well as at their sides. ..." (*E.Y.*, p. 355.)

the Preface, Wordsworth's didacticism assumes yet greater significance. His perception of general truth, as Owen has observed, makes Wordsworth to some extent an eighteenth-century man.[36] Directly after a paragraph condemning poetic diction Wordsworth announces that "the most valuable object[s] of all writing whether in prose or verse" are "the great and *universal* passions of men, the most *general* and interesting of their occupations . . ." (1800 *P.L.B.*, p. 262, [144]; my italics). Again, there is an equalization between the genres: "poetry *or* prose". More striking, though, is the fundamental equality implied in "universal passions of men". Wordsworth's poetry, since "well adapted to interest mankind permanently" (the phrase, in the best of the rhetorical tradition, occurs both near the beginning and the end of the Preface), helps to break down the barriers that hamper human brotherhood; the poet "carrying every where with him relationship and love" prepares the ground for the brotherhood of man (1802 *P.L.B.*, p. 259, [141]).

Wordsworth's notion of generality reaches its peak with his proposal to use a "selection of the real language of men"/"the language really spoken by men" as the language of poetry; in this respect he differs very much from the neo-classicists. The generality of Wordsworth's language is evident, since the poet does not speak with the tongue of a specialist, for example, as a "lawyer, a physician, a mariner, an astronomer or a natural philosopher, but as a Man" (1802 *P.L.B.*, pp. 257–58, [139]); the poet "must express himself as other men express themselves" (1802 *P.L.B.*, p. 261, [143]).[37] As in earlier instances here too the equality between writer and audience is asserted.

Although "vocabulary" is only of minor importance in Wordsworth's meaning of "language" in the context of the Preface,[38] the influx of

---

[36] Owen discusses Wordsworth's notion of general truth (and what Lovejoy, in the eighteenth-century context, labels "uniformitarianism") (Owen, *Wordsworth's Preface to Lyrical Ballads*, pp. 83–98). Owen points also to Wordsworth's divergence from the neo-classic point of view: "in Wordsworth's hands, the argument that agreement between the poet and some men is sufficient proof that he has attained general truth, that those who agree with him are, obviously, the pure in heart, and that those who do not are, as obviously, the sophisticated Public, prejudiced, lacking in true taste, and aberrant from 'nature'" (ibid., p. 99). See also Josephine Miles, "Wordsworth: The Mind's Excursive Power", in *The Major English Romantic Poets: A Symposium in Reappraisal*, ed. C. D. Thorpe *et al.* (Carbondale: Southern Illinois U.P., 1957), p. 35. [I have not had access to the expanded version of this article in *Eras and Modes in English Poetry*, Berkeley, Univ. of California Press, rev. ed. 1964.]

[37] On the "language of men", see, e.g., Abrams, *The Mirror and the Lamp*, pp. 110 ff.

[38] "*Language* in the Preface means 'characteristic rhetoric', 'idiom', 'style', 'a way of saying things': ideas which include those of vocabulary and word-order, but which are not wholly defined by one or both of these" (Owen, *Wordsworth's Preface to Lyrical Ballads*, p. 158).

words into English with a socio-political content during the years of political reform and turmoil led me to examine whether Wordsworth used these specialist terms in his poetry—especially since "A Letter to the Bishop of Llandaff" (comp. 1793) and the letters to Mathews (comp. 1794) testify to his acquaintance with the political terminology—or whether he adhered to the non-specialist "language of men". I therefore selected from the *Chronological English Dictionary*[39] all politically coloured words that were first found in English between 1786 and 1805 (see Appendix) and checked them against the Wordsworth *Concordance*.[40] This check reveals that these words are not used in Wordsworth's early poetry (1793–1806). Many of the words are as clumsy and cacophonous as the political vocabulary of the 1970s. Truly, Wordsworth's poetic ear was too fine for him to use terms merely on account of the egalitarian or current progressive values they may have connoted. Carl Woodring has reached the same conclusion about the Romantics in general: "Except for Byron with tongue in cheek, none of the major English Romantics employed the phraseology common to the pamphlets of the day. . . ."[41]

M. H. Abrams rightly says that in Wordsworth's Preface "the controlling and interrelated norms are the essential, the elementary, the simple, the universal, and the permanent".[42] This also applies partly to Wordsworth's poetic vocabulary, since it is not modish in the least. Permanent as well are the kinds of liberty, equality, and fraternity—be they overt or embedded—throughout the period from *The Borderers* (MS. 15) (comp. 1796–97) to the last poem in my chronological arrangement, the "Prospectus to *The Recluse*" (see end of this chapter); even before 1796, in *Adventures on Salisbury Plain* (comp. 1795), we could discern that Wordsworth was no longer interested in an ephemeral revolutionary *fraternité*. Concerning a reform of poetic language Wordsworth was more radical than the anarchist philosopher Godwin.[43] In a letter to Mathews of June 1794 Wordsworth had propounded general rules for the social order that are "applicable to all times and to all places" (*E.Y.*, p.

---

[39] T. Finkenstaedt, E. Leisi, and D. Wolff, eds., *A Chronological English Dictionary* (Heidelberg: Carl Winter, 1970).

[40] Lane Cooper, *A Concordance to the Poems of William Wordsworth* (London: Smith, Elder, 1911). *Note:* The *Concordance* is based on the one-volume edition of Wordsworth's poems (Thomas Hutchinson, ed., *Wordsworth: Poetical Works,* Oxford [1907 imprint according to Lane Cooper's Preface]). The Hutchinson text gives only the final versions of Wordsworth's poems and thus does not include the 1805 *Prelude.*

[41] Woodring, *Politics in the Poetry of Coleridge,* p. 38.

[42] M. H. Abrams, ed., *Wordsworth: A Collection of Critical Essays* (Englewood Cliffs, N.J.: Prentice-Hall, 1972), p. 1.

[43] Todd, *Politics and the Poet,* p. 100.

124). In the Preface of 1800 and 1802 he proposes a general poetics, the basis of which, however, according to Christopher Wordsworth,

"may be found in his *political* principles; these had been democratical, and still, though in some degree modified, they were of a republican character. At this period he entertained little reverence for ancient institutions as such; and he felt little sympathy with the higher classes of society. He was deeply impressed with a sense of the true dignity of the lower orders, and their sufferings; and his design was to endeavour to recover for them the rights of the human family, and the franchise of universal brotherhood, of which . . . they had been robbed by the wealthy, the noble and the few." (Quoted in Todd, *Politics and the Poet,* p. 100, from Christopher Wordsworth, *Memoirs of William Wordsworth* [1851].)[44]

The first edition of *Lyrical Ballads* had been sold by the beginning of June 1800. A little more than six months later (about 25 January 1801)[45] the second edition came out and it had been enlarged with a second volume (Moorman I, p. 501). Publication of the second volume had been delayed by work on what ought to be regarded as the crown of the second edition, the Preface and "Michael".

As we have seen, the poems that make up the two little volumes are quite a mixed bag: there is the overt social criticism of "The Last of the Flock", the rectifying happy "Idiot Boy", the philosophical "Tintern Abbey", the serene, virtually religious "Michael", etc.; but all of the poems are united by the portrayal of man's primary passions; and in none of them is Wordsworth condescending or satirical. The variety of content and form corresponds to the variety of places in which the poems were written: southern England, Germany, northern England. Ever present though during their composition were Wordsworth's financial worries, and when he and Dorothy retreated to Grasmere it was not a withdrawal from the real world into a state of Arcadian bliss. Wordsworth's own little financial worries during his first years there will have made it easier for him to sympathize with the big worries of his rural neighbours. This may partly explain his artistic success in conveying to us the fundamental and simple emotions—the "primary passions" of man—which are the main theme of the *Lyrical Ballads* and which also link man into one brotherhood.

The *Lyrical Ballads* were received with praise and hatred,[46] and

---

[44] Although Christopher Wordsworth is not a very reliable biographer, his observation is right in this respect. Todd concurs as well.

[45] The year on the title-page is "1800".

[46] For the attitudes of the leading periodicals, see Patricia Hodgart and Theodore Redpath, eds., *Romantic Perspectives: The Work of Crabbe, Blake, Wordsworth, and Coleridge as Seen by Their Contemporaries and by Themselves* (London: George G. Harrap, 1964). See especially pp. 81 ff.

concerning their socio-political implications opinion was as divided as it is today: for example, *The British Critic,* reviewing the 1798 volume, saw no "offensive mixture of enmity to present institutions, except in one or two instances, which are so unobtrusive as hardly to deserve notice".[47] A few years later Jeffrey's well-known diatribes began in the *Edinburgh Review.* In a letter of May 1803 de Quincey was full of love and admiration for the *Lyrical Ballads.*[48] Charles James Fox was quite pleased with them, and Wordsworth himself was eager to tell his brother Richard that he had received "high encomiums on the poems from the most respectable quarters, indeed the highest authorities . . . and [from] people of consequence in the state" (*E.Y.,* p. 337 [June 1801]). From the same letter we learn that at that time the *Lyrical Ballads* had nearly sold out. Thus Wordsworth was not too unpopular, despite his originality. The best early criticism on the egalitarian implications of the *Lyrical Ballads* is still Hazlitt's *Spirit of the Age* (1825) (see also above, Introduction): Wordsworth's "popular, inartificial style gets rid . . . of all the trappings of verse, of all the high places of poetry . . ."; "Kings, queens, priests, nobles, the altar and the throne, the distinctions of rank, birth, wealth, power . . . are not to be found here . . ."; and two pages farther on: Wordsworth "has struck into the sequestered vale of humble life, sought out the Muse among sheep-cotes and hamlets and the peasant's mountain-haunts, has discarded all the tinsel pageantry of verse, and endeavoured (not in vain) to aggrandise the trivial and add the charm of novelty to the familiar . . . ".[49]

The limited scope of this thesis does not allow S. T. Coleridge to assume his rightful place in it.[50] He had admired Wordsworth from the time of reading the *Descriptive Sketches,* and Wordsworth relied on Coleridge's critical judgement ever since the time he submitted *Salisbury Plain* to him for comment. During the Alfoxden period (1797–98) Cole-

---

[47] Quoted in John Hayden, ed., *Romantic Bards and British Reviewers: A Selected Edition of the Contemporary Reviews of the Works of Wordsworth, Coleridge, Byron, Keats and Shelley* (London: Routledge & Kegan Paul, 1971), pp. 7–8, from *The British Critic* (Oct. 1799). Contrast this with a modern view. For example, Chard instances David Perkins (*Wordsworth and the Poetry of Sincerity*) to support his idea that the *Lyrical Ballads* were partly intended to direct their readers "towards a more liberal . . . response to life" (Chard, p. 255).

[48] J. E. Jordan, *De Quincey to Wordsworth: A Biography of a Relationship* (Berkeley and Los Angeles: Univ. of California Press, 1962), p. 30.

[49] William Hazlitt, *The Spirit of the Age: Or Contemporary Portraits* (1825; Menston, Yorks.: Scolar Press, 1971 [reprinted from 1st edition]), pp. 234 and 236.

[50] Two recent studies on the interaction between Coleridge and Wordsworth are John Beer's *Wordsworth and the Human Heart* (London: Macmillan, 1978) and *Wordsworth in Time* (London: Faber, 1979).

ridge, the co-author of *Lyrical Ballads,* and his friends William and Dorothy were like one soul.[51] Wordsworth shared with him the same kind of political radicalism and a corresponding disillusion over the events in France. Coleridge was the constant driving force that virtually compelled Wordsworth to write *The Prelude.*

We will see that the mostly implicit democratic ideas of the *Lyrical Ballads* find a more overt socio-political expression in the 1805 *Prelude,* in particular in Books VI, IX, and X (see next chapter); but let us first turn to the "Prospectus to *The Recluse*", the verse that was intended for Wordsworth's three-part major philosophical poem of which only *The Excursion* was published in his lifetime and *The Prelude* posthumously.

Prospectus to The Recluse

The "Prospectus" (MS. 1) (GCL I:62 and GCL II:119),[52] eventually used by Wordsworth as the Preface of *The Excursion* (1814), places first in its first line its most important subject, "Man"; here "man" is used generically, thus implying the fundamental equality between all human beings. Second follows Nature and third man's more organized activities ("human Life"):

> On Man, on Nature, and on human Life
> Thinking in solitude, from time to time
> I find sweet passions traversing my soul
> Like music: unto these, where'er I may
> I would give utterance in numerous verse[.]
> (1–5)

As the Preface reveals Wordsworth's ideas on the poetry of the *Lyrical Ballads,* so the "Prospectus" enables us to trace Wordsworth's ideas before he embarked on the never completed *Recluse.* Lines 8–11 announce that the subject of personal liberty is to become a major theme in the projected poem:

> Of th'individual mind that keeeps [*sic*] its own
> Inviolate retirement, and consists
> With being limitless, the one great Life;
> I sing; fit audience let me find though few.

The liberty of the individual mind is the basis of all other liberties. When most other liberties have been abolished, the permanent freedom of the

---

[51] I have been influenced by Moorman I to say "like one soul".
[52] My work is based on the transcription of MS. 1 by Beth Darlington, ed., *Home at Grasmere:* Part First, Book First, of *The Recluse,* The Cornell Wordsworth (Ithaca, N.Y.: Cornell U.P., and Hassocks, Sussex: Harvester Press, 1957), pp. 257–63.

"individual mind" remains, made indestructible by "inviolate" and free from all bounds by "limitless". It is the kind of liberty that strengthens man against slavery, even though he be behind prison walls. Like Milton, that earlier bard of liberty, Wordsworth does not intend to pander to public taste (11).[53] Although Wordsworth insists on standards in his readers that may separate the poet from the multitude, his subjects are democratic, derived from the "growth of common day" (40) and based on humble matter (64). He wishes to sing about the human brotherhood (43), depicting their good and evil ways, and he prays for wisdom (46) and the gift to discern general truth:

> . . . teach me to discern, and part
> Inherent things from casual, what is fix[e]d
> From fleeting, that my song may live, and be
> Even as a light hung up in heaven to chear
> The world in times to come. . . .
> (59–63)

We recall that Wordsworth's constant struggle for general truth characterizes also his treatment of liberty, equality, and fraternity since 1797. For him these concepts are not subject to temporary political commotions, for he has learnt to differentiate between "what is fixed from fleeting". He concludes the "Prospectus" with a fervent prayer to God to instruct him "in genuine freedom" (76):

> . . . O great God
> To less than thee I cannot make this prayer
> Innocent mighty spirit let my life
> Express the image of a better time
> Desires more wise and simpler manners, nurse
> My heart in *genuine freedom,* all pure thoughts
> Be with me and uphold me to the end.
> (71–77;[54] my italics)

The appeal to God and in particular Wordsworth's passionate emphasis on inner freedom—liberty of mind—strike a very new note in his thought. In the boy of "There is a Law Severe of Penury" (above, GCL I:84b), written between 1799 and late October 1800, "liberty of mind / Is gone for ever". The final lines of the "Prospectus", on the other hand, are similar in thought and vocabulary to a passage in the 1805 *Prelude*

---

[53] "[F]it audience let me find though few" is from Milton's address to Urania, *Paradise Lost,* Book vii.30–31.

[54] For typographical reasons it was necessary to deviate slightly from Beth Darlington's transcription, *Home at Grasmere,* p. 262. The changes do not affect the sense.

("For this alone is genuine Liberty", XIII.119)⁵⁵ that was written at the earliest in January 1804 and certainly by 12 March 1804 (Reed II, p. 15, subsection 8a). Nowhere else in Wordsworth's poetry do we find the combinations "genuine Liberty" (1804) or "genuine freedom" (?1800–1806).⁵⁶ Furthermore, my material on the poetry of 1801 and 1802, not included in this thesis for reasons of space, permits me to say that Wordsworth was not much concerned with inner liberty until the implied inner freedom of "Nuns Fret Not at Their Convent's Narrow Room" (GCL II:93: "perhaps composed c. late 1802"); as regards liberty Wordsworth's first concern was with personal, political, and national liberty up to the autumn of 1802. Hence these findings might contribute to narrowing down the dating span of the "Prospectus to *The Recluse*" to as early as 1802.⁵⁷

As we have seen, in the "Prospectus" "liberty" strikes a new chord. For that reason and because of the uncertain date I let the "Prospectus to *The Recluse*" close the chronological pattern of this thesis. In forming part of the final section of *Home at Grasmere*, Part First, Book First, of *The Recluse*, the "Prospectus" is as much a prelude to Wordsworth's *magnum opus* as *The Prelude* was to be "a sort of portico to the Recluse" (*E.Y.*, p. 594). Let us now, in the next and final chapter, turn to *The Prelude*, this "portico" Wordsworth felt he needed to open before starting on *The Recluse*, which was to "give pictures of Nature, Man, and Society" (*E.Y.*, p. 212).

---

⁵⁵ From "the Deity" (106) derive "chearfulness in every act of life / Hence truth in moral judgements and delight / That fails not in the external universe. [New verse paragraph.] Oh! who is he that hath his whole life long / Preserved, enlarged, this freedom in himself? / For this alone is genuine Liberty[.]" (1805 *Prelude* XIII.106, 114–19, rev. Gill; cf. also with the parallel *Prelude*, 2nd ed., eds. de Selincourt and Helen Darbishire [Oxford: Clarendon Press, 1959], p. 486, since Gill omits three lines before l. 114.)

⁵⁶ I have not paid attention to synonyms of "genuine" in my vocabulary study.

⁵⁷ Beth Darlington sums up the scholarship on the dating of the "Prospectus" and concludes that "while it is not possible to pinpoint the exact date of composition of the Prospectus, the period between spring, 1800, and early spring, 1802, appears the likeliest time" (*Home at Grasmere*, p. 22). The most recent work on the dating is by Jonathan Wordsworth, who concludes that there "seems to be little doubt that the Prospectus was written *c*. January 1800" ("On Man, on Nature, and on Human Life", *RES*, N.S., 31 (1980), 17–29 (28)).

CHAPTER 5

The 1805 *Prelude*

Origin of liberty, equality, and fraternity in Wordsworth

By 1800 the most formative of Wordsworth's experiences were over. He had already written one version of his autobiography, the 1798–99 *Prelude* (see ch. 3), in which we have traced some of the experiences that may have led to his commitment to liberty and equality in early manhood. Before turning to the text of the 1805 *Prelude* let us examine what critics have to say on the origin of Wordsworth's conceptions of liberty, equality, and fraternity.

Chard, pp. 16–41, in his survey of the most important scholarship on the foundation of Wordsworth's liberalism, points out that early scholars were inclined to romanticize Wordsworth's childhood,[1] whereas certain "recent scholars have gone to the other extreme, resorting to a psychoanalytical interpretation in their efforts to plant the seeds of Wordsworth's radicalism in his childhood experiences" (Chard, p. 16). A letter from Dorothy Wordsworth to Jane Pollard in the summer of 1787 points to the injustice to which the Wordsworth children had been subjected.[2] But we have to remember that although all the Wordsworth children suffered from similar kinds of deprivations, only William revolted—unless we regard Dorothy's aiding and abetting Wordsworth in his aspirations for a poetic career as a revolt. It is too facile to believe that a love for liberty, equality, and fraternity is solely determined by certain biographical events. I think that the clues to Wordsworth's championship of political liberty can be found in what might be called his inherent need for personal liberty and independence, which we can detect as early as his boyhood (to judge by the 1798–99 *Prelude*), and in an accumulation

---

[1] See, e.g., Harper I, p. 89.

[2] "Many a time have [William, John, Christopher,] and myself shed tears together, tears of the bitterest sorrow, we all of us, each day, feel more sensibly the loss we sustained when we were deprived of our parents, and each day do we receive fresh insults, you will wonder of what sort; believe me of the most mortifying kind . . ." (*E.Y.*, p. 3). However, I concur with Chard, who finds that Dorothy was "at the mercy of her guardians to a much greater extent than her brothers" and that, so far, scholars have been too ready to see Wordsworth through the eyes of Dorothy (Chard, pp. 21–22).

of environmental influences (for example schooling) that were conducive to a development of political radicalism.

Mary Moorman interprets Wordsworth's childhood and his time at Cambridge as happy periods: "The equalitarianism of Cambridge life, where no differences of rank or wealth or university status affected the social intercourse of the students, even in that aristocratic age, was in many ways a happy prolongation of the freedom and fellowship of the little 'republic' of schoolboys and shepherds he had left behind at Hawkshead." (Moorman I, p. 103.)[3] Carl Woodring, on the other hand, says that Wordsworth at Cambridge "was an indigent sizar, or scholarship boy, while the chief privileges and pleasures, along with many academic advantages, went to the well-born . . ."[4] I am inclined to agree with Woodring. Schneider too, in his detailed study of Wordsworth's period at Cambridge, sees William as a socially handicapped student and concludes that Wordsworth's sudden change from the high estate at Hawkshead to the low estate at Cambridge "had an extremely important bearing on his development into the poet we know".[5] F. M. Todd also deals with the political significance of Wordsworth's life experience as a youth and adult.[6] Kurt Lienemann's pioneering study of Wordsworth's reading permits us to infer the development of Wordsworth's political radicalism from political and philosophical works;[7] and Carl Woodring states that Wordsworth's concept of liberty was influenced by Milton, Thomson, Dyer, Beattie, Collins, Goldsmith, Burns, and Cowper. He thinks that Wordsworth's "admiration for these poets was increased only partly by their treatment of personal and political liberty; he inherits their love rather than their argument. He certainly does not follow John Dyer or the many other Tories infected with Whiggery who, like the

---

[3] On similar lines, see Chard, p. 38, and Havens, *The Mind of a Poet,* p. 352 (ll. 512–33). Cf. also 1805 *Prelude* IX.226–36.

[4] Woodring, *Wordsworth,* p. 4.

[5] Ben Ross Schneider, Jr., *Wordsworth's Cambridge Education* (Cambridge: Cambridge U.P., 1957), p. 47. Schneider is invaluable on the political radicalism at Cambridge during 1780–1800. See particularly pp. 11, 113–14, on the free-thinking democratic spirit; pp. 74–76, on political virtue and the immorality of tyranny (linked to Wordsworth's study of Cicero); pp. 115–17, on the struggle of the Cambridge dissentients for freedom of religion and equality; p. 155, for reasons of dissent at Cambridge. For Wordsworth's study of Cicero, consult also Jane Worthington, *Wordsworth's Reading of Roman Prose* (New Haven: Yale U.P., 1946).

[6] *Politics and the Poet* (1957). On the probable breeding ground of Wordsworth's republican and democratic sentiments, see especially pp. 17–19 (domestic oppression, Lonsdale debt), 24–26 (radical friends and acquaintances), 27–30 (reading matter).

[7] Kurt Lienemann's *Die Belesenheit von William Wordsworth* (Berlin: Mayer & Müller, 1908) supplies lucid lists of Wordsworth's historical and political (pp. 172–83) and philosophical (pp. 187–94) reading matter.

outright Whigs, found liberty inextricably locked in embrace with the glories of commerce."[8]

Let us now see what Wordsworth himself has to say in the 1805 *Prelude* on the origin of his interest in liberty, equality, and fraternity before we examine how he regards these concepts in his retrospective view of his experience of the French Revolution. Most of Books III–XIII was written between early 1803 and May 1805;[9] by March 1804 Wordsworth had written the first five books[10] of *The Prelude,* the poem that we nowadays look upon as the finest and most original long narrative poem since *Paradise Lost.* Addressed to his intimate friend Coleridge, "For whom I thus record the birth and growth / Of gentleness, simplicity . . ." (VI.271–72),[11] the poem has in many parts the lofty tone of epic poetry. Wordsworth's purpose to describe the origin and development of "gentleness" (considerateness which implies brotherhood) and "simplicity" (which implies democratic feelings) announces his overt treatment of brotherhood and equality in *The Prelude.*

The source of these concepts is found "In simple childhood . . . / On which thy [Man's] greatness stands . . ." (XI.331–32). In the 1798–99 *Prelude* (Cornell ed., p. 61) Wordsworth had referred to the importance of mother-love in infancy. He resumes this theme in the 1805 *Prelude* and adds the picture of his own mother which, however, could stand for any woman who enjoys the naturalness of motherhood and who rears her children more according to her motherly instinct than in terms of

---

[8] Woodring, "On Liberty in the Poetry of Wordsworth", *PMLA,* 70 (1955), 1033–48 (1036).

[9] Reed II, pp. 628–55, gives a detailed chronology of the composition of *The Prelude.*

[10] Some scholars are certain that Wordsworth's initial plan was to write a five-book *Prelude.* See Jonathan Wordsworth, "The Five-Book *Prelude* of Early Spring 1804", *JEGP,* 67 (1977), 1–25.

[11] This and all subsequent quotations from *The Prelude* (1805) are drawn from E. de Selincourt, ed., *The Prelude or Growth of a Poet's Mind,* 2nd ed., corrected by Stephen Gill (1933; Oxford: Oxford U.P., 1970). In the meantime a new edition (Norton Critical Edition) of the 1805 text has been published: *The Prelude: 1799, 1805, 1850,* eds. Jonathan Wordsworth, M. H. Abrams, and Stephen Gill (New York: Norton, 1979). An edition of the 1805 text for the Cornell Wordsworth series (gen. ed. Stephen Parrish) is being prepared by Mark Reed.

The 1805 and 1850 parallel text is printed in the standard variorum edition by E. de Selincourt, ed., *The Prelude,* 2nd ed. revised by Helen Darbishire (1926; Oxford: Clarendon Press, 1959). The 1805 and 1850 texts are also printed in J. C. Maxwell, ed., *The Prelude: A Parallel Text* (Harmondsworth: Penguin, 1971). Maxwell's edition (pp. 31–32) supplies a comprehensive list of general studies on *The Prelude.* The most complete study (670 pp.) on *The Prelude* is by Raymond Dexter Havens, *The Mind of a Poet: A Study of Wordsworth's Thought with Particular Reference to* The Prelude (Baltimore: The Johns Hopkins Press, 1941).

trendy systems of child education (V.266–71).¹² The mother places her trust in God, "Who fills the Mother's breasts with innocent milk, / Doth also for our nobler part provide, / Under his great correction and controul" (V.272–74)—for He has implanted in the child and mother the "kindling or restraining" forces of Nature that we have observed in "Three Years She Grew in Sun and Shower" (above, GCL I:86). The calm presence of Wordsworth's mother in his early childhood may have had a steadying impact on his artistic temper and may have been instrumental in later shaping the quiet mode of the mature poet. The stability and clearsightedness Wordsworth had gained by 1800 is reflected in the masterful manner with which in *The Prelude* he links the life of the individual to a wider social and political life.

After the death of his mother the "lowly Cottages" (I.525) of Hawkshead—and most notably Ann Tyson's cottage—became William's home at the age of eight. The "plain and seemly countenance" with which the simple abodes deal out their "plain comforts" (I.531–32) prepares the way for his democratic and egalitarian philosophy of life.¹³ His "first human love" (VIII.178) extends to the people of his childhood whose lives are "severe and unadorn'd", intent on "little but substantial needs" (VIII.207, 209). On his vacation from college a few years later his love for the simple people has become that thoughtful kind of love which was to inspire him with the democratic subject matter of the *Lyrical Ballads*:

> [Then] I read, without design, the opinions, thoughts
> Of those plain-living people, in a sense
> Of love and knowledge; with another eye
> I saw the quiet Woodman in the Woods,
> The Shepherd on the Hills. With new delight,
> This chiefly, did I view my grey-hair'd Dame [Ann Tyson]
> (IV.203–08)

As in the previous example here too "plain" indicates Wordsworth's veneration of the democratic simplicity of the villagers. ("Plain" and "simple" are among Wordsworth's favourite adjectives in *The Prelude*.) His childhood was influenced by "mountain liberty" (IX.242) and by an egalitarian environment where neither boy nor man was "vested with

---

¹² de Selincourt discusses Wordsworth's and Rousseau's educational ideas in an elaborate note to ll. 226 ff. (1805 *Prelude*, pp. 265–66). See also Havens, *The Mind of a Poet*, p. 135.

¹³ "Wordsworth's predilection for democratic politics had its origins partly in the circumstances of his early life" (Schneider, *Wordsworth's Cambridge Education*, p. 152).

attention or respect / Through claims of wealth or blood . . ." (IX.225–26).[14]

The democratic example given by the adults is reinforced by Hawkshead Grammar School, whose educational policy can accommodate

> A race of real children, not too wise,
> Too learned, or too good; but wanton, fresh,
> And bandied up and down by love and hate,
> Fierce, moody, patient, venturous, modest, shy[.]
> (V.436–39)

Indeed, this is the microcosm of a democratic society reflecting the interplay within the pluralistic adult world; the vocabulary ("wanton", "fresh", etc.) strongly suggests a tone of liberty. Towards the end of the verse paragraph Wordsworth places an important imperative: "Simplicity in habit, truth in speech, / Be these the daily strengtheners of their minds!" (V.445–46). "Truth in speech" implies freedom of speech, for where truth can be uttered there usually is absence of fear and thus a fertile soil for the development of habits of democracy and liberty in adult life. A model school for model children[15] would not have afforded Wordsworth the opportunity of practising democratic "independence, to stand up / Among conflicting passions, and the shock / Of various tempers . . ." (XIII.310–12). In the Cumberland and Westmorland of Wordsworth's formative years manners were more "erect, and frank simplicity" was more pronounced than in other parts of England (IX.220–21). Again at the emphatic end of a verse paragraph (Book III: "Residence at Cambridge") Wordsworth concludes that education should be pervaded by a "healthy, sound simplicity, / A seemly plainness, name it as you will, / Republican or pious" (405–07). "Simplicity" and "plainness" are strengthened by "Republican", connoting the abolishment of aristocratic privilege, and hence advocating an education in the spirit of equality.

---

[14] See also Woodring, *Wordsworth*, p. 3.

[15] "One feature of the child's training that [Wordsworth] particularly stressed is freedom [V.224–78, 380–89]. Fortunate were he and Coleridge both as men and as poets in that instead of being 'noosed' they were left free to wander [e.g. V.235–37] . . . This is what would be expected of a person so self-willed as Wordsworth . . . and one who, as his poetry reveals, gained immeasurably from unusual liberty in unregulated sports and in wandering about at all hours alone or with other boys. Such wandering was not merely physical, for he observed: 'my earliest days at school . . . were very happy ones, chiefly because I was left at liberty . . . to read whatever books I liked.' Nor was his insistence on freedom merely an expression of personal desires, for in later years he voiced his 'utter distrust of all attempts to nurse virtue by an avoidance of temptation'." (Havens, *The Mind of a Poet*, pp. 378–79; ellipses within single quotation marks by Havens.) On Wordsworth's need for freedom, see further Havens, p. 348 (note on l. 355), and especially pp. 407–08.

Prelude: *Origin of liberty, equality*

Long before the radical officer Beaupuy had kindled Wordsworth's love of *liberté* or before Wordsworth had read the political "Pamphlets of the day" (IX.97),[16] the base of his love of freedom had been laid in his Lake District, which is for him

>   the Paradise
> 145   Where I was rear'd; in Nature's primitive gifts
>   Favor'd no less, and more to every sense
>   Delicious, seeing that the *sun* and *sky*,
>   The *elements* and seasons in their change
>   Do find their dearest Fellow-labourer there,
> 150   The heart of Man, a district on all sides
>   The fragrance breathing of humanity,
>   *Man free, man working for himself, with choice
>   Of time, and place, and object;* by his wants,
>   His comforts, native occupations, cares,
> 155   Conducted on to individual ends
>   Or social, and still follow'd by a train
>   Unwoo'd, unthought-of even, simplicity,
>   And beauty, and inevitable grace.
>   (VIII.144–58; my italics)

Here shines the same sun of gladness and mountain liberty that had enhanced the personal liberty of the Old Cumberland Beggar among the "wild unpeopled hills" (above, GCL I:53b,c). "Sky" suggests openness, immensity, freedom; the "elements" an incessant free movement. This accumulation of terms connoting freedom adds weight to the independent situation of the inhabitant of the Lake District: "Man free" (VIII.152) who determines the when, where, and how of his work (VIII.153) exactly as the Old Cumberland Beggar was, in a way, master of his own situation ("And let him, *where* and *when* he will, sit down" ["O.C.B.", l. 184]).[17]

Before alluding to his unwillingness to follow the discipline of the university curriculum at Cambridge, Wordsworth uses some strong images of liberty that underline his deeply rooted need for freedom:

---

[16] "Among the many pamphlets issued at this time . . ." are for instance "those of the royalist Peltier, the *constituant* Drouet (*Voilà ce qu'il faut faire*), and the extremists Marat and Robespierre (on universal suffrage); also the anonymous *Grande Visite de Mademoiselle République*, and *Deux Brutus au peuple français*" (1805 Prelude, p. 291, note l. 97). Havens, *The Mind of a Poet*, p. 499 (note ll. 106–7), implies that the pamphlets had no great impact on Wordsworth.

[17] Contrast this with the misery in other parts of England, e.g., child labour, in "There is a Law Severe of Penury" (above, GCL I:84b).

> ... I, bred up in Nature's lap, was even
> As a spoil'd Child; and rambling like the *wind*
> As I had done in daily intercourse
> With those delicious rivers, solemn *heights,*
> And mountains; ranging like a *fowl of the air,*
> I was ill tutor'd for captivity[.]
> (III.358–63; my italics)

The poet's free childhood is reinforced by the images of the swift wind and the bird. The "wind" is a central image in Wordsworth;[18] see for instance "Michael" ("the land" shall be "free as is the wind") and the very beginning of *The Prelude*.

Luckily enough, Wordsworth encountered mostly the better side of the adult world during his boyhood: for him the rustic was "Man Ennobled" (VIII.410–11); William's "heart at first was introduced / To an unconscious love and reverence / Of human nature . . ." (VIII.412–14).[19] He absorbed early in life the values of "grace", "honour", "power", and "worthiness" (VIII.416). His sense of realism makes him point out that his ideal characters, however, are not the figures from the classical and Elizabethan pastoral (Corin and Phyllis), and he forestalls the criticism that his ideal conception of the shepherds in his youth is a "shadow, a delusion" (VIII.431).[20] Wordsworth is right in emphasizing the importance of having met in his youth men who "did at the first present themselves / Before my untaught eyes thus purified" (VIII.438–39). The highly ethical and experiential approach to liberty, equality, and fraternity in the 1805 *Prelude* is undoubtedly partly due to the moral rectitude that he discerned in the adults of his childhood and youth;[21] remembering them later is a safeguard against a twisted view of life, and, generally applied, the best guarantee for a lasting reform of society, a bulwark "Against the weight of meanness, selfish cares, / Coarse manners, vulgar passions . . ." (VIII.454–55), against the anar-

---

[18] For further images of freedom, see Woodring, "On Liberty in the Poetry of Wordsworth", *PMLA*, 70 (1955), 1033–48 (1043).

[19] For the important mental benefits Wordsworth has derived from the upright shepherds in later life, see Chard, p. 25.

[20] Havens remarks on the corresponding passage in the 1850 *Prelude* that the "conception of man thus formed is not a delusion; we are all introduced to knowledge through seeing the idealized before the sordid" (*The Mind of a Poet*, p. 453).

[21] Havens observes that "Wordsworth's assertion that we are led to knowledge by seeing life at first not as it really is but idealized seems to me inconsistent with his praise of the rough-and-tumble experience in a public school . . ." (*The Mind of a Poet*, p. 463). Havens is wrong, for besides the rough and tumble we find love, patience, modesty, and shyness among that "race of real children" in Wordsworth's school (V.432–49). (See also above, p. 152.)

chistic mind of Rivers [Oswald] and moral relativism in general. Wordsworth's development from the theories of men in 1792 to the portrayal of lived morality in the *Lyrical Ballads* may illustrate the point.

Another influence that strengthened Wordsworth against the "loathsome sights / Of wretchedness and vice . . ." (VIII.65–66) which he witnessed in London was Nature. To her he owed "High thoughts of God and Man . . ." (VIII.64).[22] Nature had taught him to practise brotherhood towards his "Fellow-beings" and to extend it beyond the "bosom of [his] Family" and his circle of "Friends and youthful Playmates" (VIII.73–74) some years before he came under the impact of the concept of the brotherhood of man propagated by the French Revolution.

Through the friendship with Beaupuy during his second visit to France (1791–92) Wordsworth's ideas on liberty, equality, and fraternity became more systematic.[23] Their conversations covered important fields of political theory:

> Of civil government, and its wisest forms,
> Of ancient prejudice, and chartered rights,
> Allegiance, faith, and laws by time matured,
> Custom and habit, novelty and change[.]
> (IX.330–33)

"Chartered rights" may refer to Beaupuy's illustrating for Wordsworth the origin and slow growth of political liberty and legal justice by the example of England's Magna Carta (1215) and the Bill of Rights (1689) or the American Declaration of Independence (1776) and the contemporary American Bill of Rights (1789–91), but most certainly the discussion centred on the French declaration of the *Droits de l'homme* (1789), that document of socio-political "novelty and change", and the poet acquainted himself with the traditionalist views of "laws by time matured, / Custom and habit". One may speculate whether this and in particular the expression "ancient prejudice" owe something to Burke. If so, Wordsworth attributes something to the conversations with Beaupuy

---

[22] On the origin of Wordsworth's "love of Man" from "love of Nature", see Perkins, *Wordsworth and the Poetry of Sincerity*, p. 115, and Geoffrey H. Hartman, *Wordsworth's Poetry, 1787–1814*, 2nd ed. (1964; rpt. New Haven and London: Yale U.P., 1971), pp. 233–38. See also my discussion of "Tintern Abbey", above (GCL I:75).

[23] Schneider, referring to Wordsworth's concern with liberty, equality, and fraternity, correctly observes that Wordsworth's "republicanism . . . experienced a *confirmation*, not a *conversion*, in France in 1792" (*Wordsworth's Cambridge Education*, p. 151; Schneider's italics). For Wordsworth's reading at this time, see also Owen and Smyser's Commentary to "A Letter to the Bishop of Llandaff" in *Prose Works* I, pp. 50–66.

which is unlikely to have taken place in their talks. This illustrates what I have implied in my Introduction, namely that *The Prelude* is not a factual record.

The political facts he learnt from Beaupuy, an "upright Man and tolerant" (IX.337)—whose "famille entière s'était distinguée par son esprit libéral dès le début de la Révolution"[24]—must have appeared particularly valuable to Wordsworth since coming from a man endowed with such fine qualities. Beaupuy and Wordsworth discussed "dearest themes, / Man and his noble nature" (IX.362-63), "noble nature" suggesting man's original goodness in a state of Nature. The importance of man being born good is further emphasized by the superlative of an adjective that expresses high esteem and affection, "dearest". We recall the strong belief in man's natural goodness (e.g., his originally absolute equality) from *Descriptive Sketches*, most of which was composed during the period which these lines of *The Prelude* depict.

Remarking on Wordsworth's ponderings over "tyrannic Power", "natural right", "equity and reason" (X.167-73), Havens comments "how literary and theoretical in its origin Wordsworth's idealism was and how little it rested upon observation of men and conditions about him".[25] This is misleading, for the present pages have borne out that Wordsworth's "first human love" for the simple country people had deepened by observation and reflection during his summer vacation from Cambridge. The base of equality and brotherhood had been established by experience; the politicized circumstances that surrounded his year in France, however, explain why he subsequently put his experiences in a theoretical framework.

Recollecting the period at Racedown and Alfoxden (1796-98), Wordsworth finds that Nature, so long

>   Foremost in my affections, had fallen back
>   Into a second place, well pleas'd to be
>   A handmaid to a nobler than herself,
>   When every day brought with it some new sense
> 235   Of *exquisite* regard for *common things,*
>   And all the earth was budding with these gifts
>   Of *more refined humanity,* thy breath,
>   Dear Sister [Dorothy], was a kind of gentler spring
>   That went before my steps.

---

[24] Emile Legouis, *La Jeunesse de William Wordsworth: Étude sur le "Prélude"* (Paris, 1896), p. 206. [The English translation of this book was not available to me.]

[25] Havens, *The Mind of a Poet,* p. 520. However, elsewhere Havens acknowledges that Wordsworth's "approach was through the concrete not the abstract, through human contacts not through reasoning" (ibid., p. 499).

>   With such a theme,
> 240   Coleridge! with this my argument, of thee
>   Shall I be silent? O most loving Soul!
>   Placed on this earth to love and understand,
>   And from thy presence shed the *light of love*,
>   Shall I be mute ere thou be spoken of?
>   (XIII.231–44; my italics)

This excerpt from the last book (XIII) precedes Wordsworth's brief biographical summary (XIII.325 ff.) and leads to the closing part of *The Prelude*—which consists of a final tribute to Coleridge and the announcement of Wordsworth's and Coleridge's plan for reviving the hopes of mankind—thus adding weight to the climactic conclusion of the poem. From his childhood until now, 1796–98, man in general and Nature had exerted their greatest influence on Wordsworth. So far, Wordsworth had acknowledged a major influence on him from only one individual, Beaupuy, and this influence centred on the social and political spheres.[26] Dorothy and Coleridge on the other hand influenced Wordsworth's development towards an extended brotherhood that acknowledges the interrelatedness of all life. Now that Nature has relapsed into second place, Dorothy's "gentler spring" (238) helps to direct Wordsworth to an "exquisite regard for common things", to a "more refined humanity" (235, 237). "Common things" testifies to the democratic subject matter of the *Lyrical Ballads* and the small natural objects Dorothy taught William to see and appreciate. Very likely Dorothy's impact prevented Wordsworth's democratic poetic vein from becoming too rustic; she added the "exquisite" element. Her brother's carefully selected "language of men" and the tender thoughts of brotherhood to which some of his poems of 1796–98 witness may to some degree reflect her moderating influence. "Refined" implies the restraining forces on Wordsworth's natural inclination for the wild, thus reinforcing the significance of "exquisite".

Last but not least come the eulogistic lines on Coleridge (240 ff.). Here the stress is not on the political Coleridge but on the man who "shed the

---

[26] Drawing on *Prelude* XII.15–312 and *The Ruined Cottage*, M. H. Abrams traces Wordsworth's development from the theories of "naive millennialists or the abstractions of the philosophers" to the democratic impact of the Bible on him and "especially the New Testament, which is grounded on the radical paradox that 'the last shall be first', and dramatizes that fact in the central mystery of God incarnate as a lowly carpenter's son who takes fishermen for his disciples, consorts with beggars, publicans, and fallen women, and dies ignominiously, crucified with thieves". (M. H. Abrams, "English Romanticism: The Spirit of the Age", in Northrop Frye, ed., *Romanticism Reconsidered: Selected Papers from the English Institute*, New York: Columbia U.P., 1963, pp. 63–66.)

light of love" (243). Dorothy's "gentler spring" is paralleled by Coleridge's love of man, his "gentle Spirit" (XIII.245) that finds its way to Wordsworth's "heart of hearts" (245). The emotive "heart of hearts" indicates how strongly Wordsworth feels that Coleridge's love of man has moulded his own, and in other words, it has engendered Wordsworth's fraternal affections for the "life / Of all things" (XIII.246-47), those feelings of brotherhood that transcend all class barriers and prepare the way for harmony among men and between man and his natural environment.

Wordsworth in France (1790, 1791-92)

Let us now turn to the French Revolution, the time in Wordsworth's life that was most conducive to the development of his systematic political thought, and the traumatic experience of which enhanced his creative imagination considerably. Liberty, equality, and fraternity in Wordsworth are closest to their original political meanings in his writings of 1792 and 1793. The same applies to the lines of the 1805 *Prelude* dealing with the summer of 1790, his one-year stay in France (1791-92), and his subsequent period of disenchantment with the Revolution. It is rewarding to concentrate on this time span, but especially on 1792, which is of particular interest, since Wordsworth then composed most of *Descriptive Sketches,* a poem of major socio-political significance. Thus we close the circle of this study with poetic subject matter similar to that of the opening pages of this thesis.

Herbert Lindenberger entitles a subsection of his study on *The Prelude* "The Unpolitical Poet"[27] in which he asserts that although "Wordsworth purports to treat a political and historical theme, his picture of England and France in the early 1790's is essentially a metaphor he employs to motivate a private struggle within himself".[28] This statement and the label "unpolitical poet" give a wrong impression of Wordsworth. Richard Onorato is closer to the point when he says that in *The Prelude* "Wordsworth had wished to see the revolution as an event in the 'certain course' of Nature and wished especially to find the principles proclaimed by the revolution true: liberty, equality, and *fraternity*".[29] However, the radical political nature of *The Prelude* is

---

[27] Herbert Lindenberger, *On Wordsworth's* Prelude (Princeton, N.J.: Princeton U.P., 1963), pp. 262-70.
[28] Ibid., p. 268.
[29] Richard J. Onorato, *The Character of the Poet: Wordsworth in* The Prelude (Princeton, N.J.: Princeton U.P., 1971), pp. 340-41; Onorato's italics.

evident in Lindenberger's article on the contemporary reception of *The Prelude*; and here we have to remember that this applies to the 1850 *Prelude*,[30] the political tone of which had been muted. Harper II (p. 144) acknowledges the "levelling tendency" of the poem as well. Havens, commenting on Wordsworth's and Jones's trip to France in the summer of 1790, observes that *The Prelude* when referring to this period reveals a "considerable interest in the brotherhood of man as well as in the life of the French people and especially in [the] enthusiasm for the new order" (*The Mind of a Poet*, p. 420).

For Wordsworth that summer "brought its liberty" from "College cares and study" (VI.338, 343). He and his friend Jones set foot in France on the eve of the first anniversary of the new era of political liberty and human brotherhood. They landed at Calais on the eve of "that great federal Day" [14 July] (VI.357) which coincided with the revolutionary festivities:

> . . .'twas a time when Europe was rejoiced,
> France standing on the top of golden hours,[31]
> And human nature seeming born again.
> (VI.352–54)

The jubilant language and thought of these lines are similar to some other climactic passages (e.g., VI.367–77, 391–413, 680–87) dealing with Wordsworth's first visit to France; the tone of Books IX and X describing Wordsworth's second visit is not so uniformly happy. The passages on the trip of 1791–92 focus more on liberty whereas those on 1790 express more the euphoria of directly felt brotherhood. Wordsworth experienced one of those rare moments in human history when a feeling of brotherhood for some days unites men and when this universal emotion manifests itself outwardly: "How bright a face is worn when joy of one / Is joy of tens of millions . . ." (VI.359–60).

---

[30] "The *British Quarterly Review* and the *Athenæum* both assumed that Wordsworth withheld publication of the poem because of his revolutionary opinions, and the former periodical even conjectured that he secretly held on to these opinions all his life. Macaulay, writing in his journal, stated the case bluntly: 'The poem is to the last degree Jacobinical, indeed Socialist. I understand perfectly why Wordsworth did not choose to publish it in his lifetime.' *Tait's Magazine* went so far as to condemn the poet for having rejoiced at English losses during the early phases of the war. But the most politically minded review of all was that of the liberal *Examiner*, which proclaimed proudly that 'Wordsworth (as has been said of Napoleon) is the child and champion of Jacobinism' . . .". (H. Lindenberger, "The Reception of *The Prelude*", BNYPL, 64 (1960), 196–208 (198).)

[31] According to de Selincourt an echo from Shakespeare, Sonnet xviii: "Now stand you on the top of happy hours." (1805 *Prelude*, p. 275.)

On their way through elated France the two young Englishmen witnessed "Dances of Liberty" (VI.381) and they

> found benevolence and blessedness
> Spread like a *fragrance* everywhere, like Spring
> That leaves no corner of the Land untouch'd.
> Where Elms, for many and many a league, in files,
> With their thin umbrage, on the stately roads
> Of that great Kingdom, *rustled* o'er our heads,
> For ever near us as we paced along[.]
> (VI.368–74; my italics)

Human kindness pervades a whole country. The human endeavour of brotherhood is linked and enhanced by the image of "Spring" that announces the freshness and birth of a new age. Unlike Keats, Wordsworth does not often evoke the sense of smell, but the overpowering dawn of a new era makes him use "fragrance". Smell, sound (the "rustling" elms) and sight are pleasant in the new era. The freshness of Nature reflects the healthy state of human affairs, in a way similar to the earlier *Descriptive Sketches* (*PW* I, p. 84, ll. 726 ff.) where political liberty is described as having effected a positive change in the environment. A glance at these lines in *Descriptive Sketches* reveals how mature Wordsworth's poetic technique has become since their composition in 1792: now man's achievement subtly fuses with the beauty of Nature whereas *Descriptive Sketches* enumerates the improvements in the environment in the form of a list.

The onomatopoeia, imagery, and alliteration of a subsequent passage, "Like bees they swarm'd, gaudy and gay as bees" (VI.398), depict the excitement of the revolutionaries into whose circle Wordsworth and Jones are

> ... welcome almost as the Angels were
> To Abraham of old. The Supper done,
> With flowing cups elate, and happy thoughts,
> We rose at signal given, and form'd a *ring*
> And, *hand in hand,* danced round and round the Board;
> All hearts were open, every tongue was loud
> With amity and glee; we bore a name
> Honour'd in France, the name of Englishmen,
> And *hospitably* did they give us Hail
> As their forerunners in a glorious course[.]
> (VI.403–12; my italics)

As in VI.359–60, once more brotherhood manifests itself ("ring", "hand in hand") and it is general ("All hearts", "every tongue") and international, since it "hospitably" includes among the French revolutionaries the young Englishmen whose forbears had restricted the power of the monarchy and extended the liberties of Englishmen in their "glorious course" a century earlier. Significantly, no reference to French political thinkers appears in the passage and the English republicans remain unspecified. Havens's (p. 425) comment on VI.469 ff. (ll. 541 ff. in 1850 text) could also be applied to this excerpt: Jones and Wordsworth "encountered nothing sophisticated or complex, only what appealed to their feelings or evidence of the brotherhood of man and other fundamental truths which were supposed, in the eighteenth century, to be self-evident to 'young and old' . . ." Thus the "two brother Pilgrims" (VI.478)

> could not chuse but read
> A frequent lesson of sound tenderness,
> The universal reason of mankind,
> The truth of Young and Old. . . .
>   (VI.474–77)

The "universal reason", supplying the rational basis for equality, brotherhood, and natural law, is reminiscent of the "eternal nature of man" in "A Letter to the Bishop of Llandaff" (see above, p. 36), and the "truth of Young and Old" recalls the American Declaration of Independence (1776): "We hold these truths to be self-evident".

The concluding verse stanza of Book VI—similar to the final lines of *Descriptive Sketches*—is a eulogy of the principles of the Revolution and the "battle in the cause of Liberty" (VI.692). "[T]riumphant looks" were "then the common language of all eyes" (VI.682–83). What cannot be expressed in words is here written on the faces of *all*, in the manner of a painting of socialist realism; the promise of a better future is first realized by one nation before becoming a universal movement, for as if roused "from sleep, the Nations [now] hail'd / Their great expectancy" (VI.684–85), that is to say *liberté, égalité, fraternité*.

Before Wordsworth began his one-year stay in France in the late autumn of 1791, he spent a few months in London, as "Free as a colt at pasture on the hill" (IX.18). In London we encounter a democratic Wordsworth, "Not courting the society of Men / By literature, or elegance, or rank / Distinguish'd . . ." (IX.21–23). In Paris, on the other hand, he experiments with a different mode of life. He visits the "formal haunts of Men, / Whom in the City privilege of birth / Sequester'd from the rest . . ." (IX.116–18). The Latinate "sequester'd"—apparently a somewhat old-fashioned word in Wordsworth's time—indicates his disapproval of that kind of separation from ordinary human society. Soon, however, he embraces equality and brotherhood in becoming "a Patriot

[Republican], and my heart was all / Given to the People, and my love was theirs" (IX.125–26).

In his retrospective view Wordsworth finds it strange that he was not more perturbed by the "concussions" (IX.87) of the Revolution. He reasons that he was "unprepared / With needful knowledge" (IX.92–93) and that events in the France of turmoil were for him "[l]oose and disjointed" (IX.107). Wordsworth's "indifference" (IX.91) on his second arrival in France is not, however, an immoral attitude but the sign of a maturing man who does not become blindly involved in the politics of another country (see also X.192–93).

The discussion of the development of liberty, equality, and fraternity in Wordsworth has shown that his political consciousness evolved gradually. When he felt sure that he was equipped to assess the political situation correctly, Wordsworth did take a stand, as evidenced in "A Letter to the Bishop of Llandaff" and the letters to Mathews. On his summer vacation (1790) with Jones, Wordsworth seems to have been satisfied with immediate impressions. Now, in December 1791, the young man is somewhat detached, gathering a little "needful knowledge" (IX.93) in Paris; but before long, at Orleans and Blois, his youthful idealism causes him to burst out that the French Revolution is

> a cause
> Good, and which no one could stand up against
> Who was not lost, abandon'd, selfish, proud,
> Mean, miserable, wilfully deprav'd,
> Hater perverse of equity and truth.[32]
>   (IX.289–93)

"Equity and truth" call to mind justice and equality. Wordsworth welcomes as best that "government of equal rights / And individual worth" (IX.248–49), namely a government which is most likely to become the guarantor of justice and equality.[33]

---

[32] Havens comments: "There is no apparent reason for the vehemence of these lines, in which adjective is piled on adjective as if the poet wished to pour out upon the opponents of the Revolution his entire vocabulary of condemnation. Yet even this was not enough, for about 1817 he added a line and a half more in the same strain . . . It will be remembered that Annette's family were Royalists; Wordsworth may have quarreled with them on both political and personal grounds and may be here expressing the opinion he held of them as typical Royalists. Such a quarrel would explain many things: his failure to marry Annette, his leaving her before their child was born, and his not returning to see her and the child during the two or three months he spent in Paris. Since the other officers spurned Beaupuy with an oriental loathing because he was a 'patriot', they probably treated Wordsworth in much the same way when he went over to the people." (*The Mind of a Poet*, p. 502).

[33] David Ferry observes that the "ideal of political equality is always honored by the [*Prelude*]; it is only later that the poem discovers how impossible it is to realize such an ideal, the nature of man being what it is" (*The Limits of Mortality*, pp. 145–46).

Although Wordsworth had not yet acquainted himself with the theories of "natural rights and civil" (IX.204), and although the Royalists with whom he was associating tried to win him over to their side (IX.200), his life experience served as a cornerstone for democracy, and thus the revolutionary events "Seem'd nothing out of nature's certain course, / A gift that rather was come late than soon"[34] (IX.253–54). The splendour and artificial inequality which sets off monarchy from the rest of mankind had disturbed Wordsworth before he became acquainted with republican political theory:[35]

> in the regal Sceptre, and the pomp
> Of Orders and Degrees, I nothing found
> Then, or had ever, even in crudest youth,
> That dazzled me; but rather what my soul
> Mourn'd for, or loath'd, beholding that the best
> Rul'd not, and feeling that they ought to rule.
> (IX.212–17)

His dream of the rule of the people came true: royalty was abolished in September 1792, but much as in Yeats's "Second Coming" ("The best lack all conviction, while the worst / Are full of passionate intensity"), extremists gained the upper hand and "Liberty" became an empty word under the Jacobins. The young French Republic—as in our century the democratic Weimar Republic—collapsed through

> The indecision on their part whose aim
> Seem'd best, and the straightforward path of those
> Who in attack or in defence alike
> Were strong through their impiety . . .
> (X.113–16)

Wordsworth's compositions up to *The Borderers* (comp. 1796–97) reveal that, despite the excesses of the Revolution, he held on to his belief in the eventual success of a democratic French Republic. "A Letter to the Bishop of Llandaff" (GCL I:42) best illustrates Wordsworth's study of the kind of political theory that is bound to have contributed to his belief in human progress. His hope for the ultimate victory of the democratic experiment was further strengthened by the shining example of the officer Beaupuy who

---

[34] On "Nature" and "natural law" as sources of liberty, see Hartman, *Wordsworth's Poetry, 1787–1814*, pp. 242–47, 249. See also "Matthew" (GCL I:79a) and "Three Years She Grew in Sun and Shower" (GCL I:86).

[35] On the isolation of the monarchy, see above, "A Letter to the Bishop of Llandaff" (GCL I:42).

> [b]y birth . . . rank'd
> With the most noble, but unto the poor
> Among mankind he was in service *bound*
> As by some *tie invisible,* oaths profess'd
> To a religious Order. Man he lov'd
> As Man; and to the *mean* and the *obscure*
> And all the *homely* in their homely works
> Transferr'd a courtesy which had no air
> Of condescension . . .
>   (IX.309–17; my italics)

These lines evoke a genuine brotherhood based on the fundamental equality of men. Beaupuy's brotherly bond with humanity is stressed by a vocabulary that strengthens the element of fraternity and democratic simplicity. Furthermore, "homely", "mean", "obscure" are the qualities that Wordsworth elevates through his choice of poetic subject matter in most of the *Lyrical Ballads,* and, in the manner of Beaupuy, he does it without any "condescension", even in the often misunderstood "Old Cumberland Beggar" (above, GCL I:53b,c). Finally, witnessing the idealism of a newly emancipated people certainly affirmed his conviction that the ideals of the Revolution would eventually materialize. Wordsworth's confidence is implied in his eulogy of

> a People risen up
> Fresh as the morning Star: elate we look'd
> Upon their virtues, saw in *rudest* men
> *Self-sacrifice* the firmest, generous love
> And *continence* of mind, and sense of right
> Uppermost in the midst of fiercest strife.[36]
>   (IX.391–96; my italics)

The elements that usually cancel each other concur here in the ordinary people: the "rudest" prove most cultured and civilized. This is comparable to the democratic poetics of *The Ruined Cottage* (GCL I:57e; MS. B, comp. 1798), illustrated in the pedlar who, although untaught, is capable of deep emotions and endowed with the gift of creative imagination. In IX.391–96 poetic and political democracy fuse, for here the ordinary people are possessed of the superior qualities that ought to characterize a ruling aristocracy.

---

[36] "Miss Worthington has pointed out [that] *The Prelude* also contains an emphatic restatement of the idea that states perish when peoples become corrupt and that a virtuous people is the first condition of a flourishing government. In the account of the conversations with Beaupuy, [Wordsworth] tells us that they founded their optimism for the Revolution on a sense of the moral regeneration of the French people." (Fink, "Wordsworth and the English Republican Tradition", *JEGP,* 47 (1948), 107–26 (123).)

The well-known passage of the "hunger-bitten Girl" (IX.512) portrays feelings of a natural, immediately felt brotherhood. In the new era, "poverty[,] / At least like this, would in a little time / Be found no more . . ." (IX.522–24). Moorman comments that Beaupuy and Wordsworth hoped for a "golden age in which poverty and 'cruel power' would be abolished and a healthy and responsible democracy would bring in 'better days to all mankind' " (Moorman I, p. 194). This is not quite true, for the interpolation ("At least like this")[37] points to the abolishment of utter destitution, but not poverty as such. Even the *Déclaration des droits de l'homme* (1789) did not promise to remove poverty. From the implied appeal to spontaneous brotherhood engendered by the hunger-bitten girl, Wordsworth goes on to attack that kind of inequality which is responsible for extreme want. He wishes to see

> All institutes for ever blotted out
> That legalised exclusion, empty pomp
> Abolish'd, sensual state and cruel power
> Whether by edict of the one or few[.]
> (IX.527–30)

As in "A Letter to the Bishop of Llandaff" (*Prose Works* I.37.219–29) he wants democratic rule; he wants to "see the People having a strong hand / In making their own Laws, whence better days / To all mankind" (IX.532–34). "All" connotes that democratic legislation should become universal, recalling thus the hoped-for universal appeal of the contemporary *Déclaration des droits de l'homme*.

The stress in the *Déclaration* of 1789 is on liberty; liberty dominates in Wordsworth's account of 1792 as well. The optimism of the *Déclaration* is reflected in Wordsworth's belief in man as the creature who is

> Capable of clear truth, the one to break
> Bondage, the other to build liberty
> On firm foundations, making social life,
> Through knowledge spreading and imperishable[.]
> (IX.366–69)

"Break bondage" points to liberty, hence reinforcing the ensuing "build liberty". Education ("knowledge") according to the principle of natural law will cement the basis of liberty. Man's "noble nature, as it is / The gift of God" (IX.363–64) makes him capable of perceiving "clear truth", i.e. able to discern the self-evident truths inherent in the natural law. Thus Wordsworth's belief in human progress is justified.

---

[37] 1850 *Prelude:* "poverty / Abject as this would . . ." (IX.520–21).

An address to Coleridge in the next verse paragraph (IX.397 ff.) interrupts the narrative about France, but lines 402–03—dealing with the discussions between Wordsworth and Coleridge on "rational liberty, and hope in man, / Justice and peace"—establish the link with the earlier account of political liberty. Lines 415 ff. in the same verse paragraph illustrate political liberty with an example from ancient history, Dion's overthrow of the tyrant Dionysius.[38] Wordsworth draws a parallel between Dion, the deliverer of Sicily, and Beaupuy who

> perish'd fighting[39] in supreme command
> Upon the Borders of the unhappy Loire
> For Liberty against deluded Men,
> His Fellow-countrymen . . .
> (IX.431–34)

The analogy between Dion and Beaupuy testifies to how strong Wordsworth's admiration for Beaupuy was. "Deluded" suggests that only men whose reasoning power was suspended could fight against liberty. Harmodius and Aristogiton[40] and Brutus supply more historical examples of man's struggle for liberty. They prove that

> tyrannic Power is weak,
> Hath *neither* gratitude, *nor* faith, *nor* love,
> *Nor* the support of good *or* evil men
> To trust in, that the Godhead which is ours
> Can never utterly be charm'd or still'd,
> That nothing hath a natural right to last
> But equity and reason,[41] that all else
> Meets foes irreconcilable, and at best
> Doth live but by variety of disease.
> (X.167–75; my italics)

The rhetorical enumerations, "neither–nor–or", hammer home the flaws of dictatorship before pointing to the chief reason of tyranny's deficiency: the lack of trust (X.170). In IX.363–64 Wordsworth had referred to man's "noble nature, as it is / The gift of God". Here this becomes man's divine nature: the "Godhead which is ours" (X.170). These forces

---

[38] On Wordsworth's reading of ancient history, see de Selincourt's note, 1805 *Prelude*, p. 248 (ll. 186–95); on the story of Dion and Dionysius, 1805 *Prelude*, p. 293 (ll. 415–24). For a general survey, see Worthington, *Wordsworth's Reading of Roman Prose*.

[39] "In this statement Wordsworth was mistaken. Beaupuy was dangerously wounded in Vendée, but recovered, and served the republican cause with distinction and unswerving loyalty till 1796, when he fell at the battle of the Elz, on 19 November . . ." (1805 *Prelude*, p. 293).

[40] See ch. 1, n. 1.

[41] See also above, p. 156.

in man, since godlike, can "never utterly be charm'd or still'd" (X.171). Man's innate love of liberty, as the references to history have made clear, will oust tyranny; man's longing for liberty cannot be withstood. The appeal to "natural right", "equity and reason"—suggesting man's equality—finally, reinforces the moral justification for destroying a dictatorship. The passage is full of political wisdom; as in many other instances in his poetry, Wordsworth's demand for morality in politics is apparent.

To what extent the "Vaudracour and Julia story" (IX.556 ff.) is hidden biography is debatable.[42] It is certain, however, that the tale of Vaudracour and Julia's unhappy love is an attack on the old social and political order of France or, as Havens puts it, an "attack on class privilege and class prejudice".[43] The anecdote of the young lovers is preceded by a censure on mock justice:

> Captivity by mandate without law[44]
> Should cease, and *open accusation* lead
> To sentence in the hearing of the world
> And *open punishment,* if not the air
> Be free to breathe in, and the heart of Man
> Dread nothing . . .
> (IX.538–43; my italics)

Wordsworth's general attack on imprisonment without trial (538), a gross infringement of human rights, is later individualized in Vaudracour who becomes the victim of a "mandate / Bearing the private signet of the State" (IX.666–67). The private injustice caused by the inequality of a society torn by a rigid hierarchical order prevents the marriage between Vaudracour and Julia; Julia's family, "with rights / Unhonour'd of Nobility" (IX.566–67), was below the rank of Vaudracour's family. The public injustice of a pseudojudiciary system causes Vaudracour to commit unpremeditated murder. This is similar to the sailor-murderer's unpremeditated killing in *Adventures on Salisbury Plain*; inequality before the law had deprived him of the means to support his family, with the consequent result of murder. In *Adventures on Salisbury Plain* wife and children suffer. In the Vaudracour and Julia story the formation of a

---

[42] On this problem, see de Selincourt's and Helen Darbishire's comments, 1805 *Prelude*, pp. 295–96 (ll. 554–55).

[43] *The Mind of a Poet*, p. 512.

[44] E.g., lettres de cachet, important instruments of administration under the *ancien régime*, used primarily to authorize someone's imprisonment. In the law of the *ancien régime* the *lettre de cachet* was an expression of that exercise of justice that the king reserved to himself, independently of the law courts and their processes. (Adapted from *Encyclopædia Britannica: Micropædia* (1974 ed).)

family is prevented. As the misery of the female vagrant in *Salisbury Plain* had thrown light on the social and political condition of England, so the lot of Vaudracour and Julia reflects the inequality and infringement of personal liberty under the old order in France.

The interpolation of the Vaudracour and Julia story into Wordsworth's description of his experiences of 1792 intrudes into his account of the Revolution; but seen in the context of the theme of liberty, the story is an effective means for concretizing and particularizing abstract liberty: there are, for instance, three overt references to personal liberty in one verse paragraph (IX.698, 756, 763). The final lines of the tale —concluding Book IX—show us Vaudracour as crazed. Private grief has made him completely oblivious of the great public events:

> Nor could the voice of Freedom, which through France
> Soon afterwards resounded, public hope,
> Or personal memory of his own deep wrongs,
> Rouze him . . .
> His days he wasted, an imbecile mind.
>
> (IX.931–35)

Let us now turn to the remainder of Wordsworth's reminiscences of the France of 1792, mostly dealt with in the first two hundred lines of Book X (the rest of Book X covers primarily the period 1793–95). Wordsworth's friend Beaupuy left Blois for active service with his regiment in late July 1792; in September or October Wordsworth departed for Orleans where he spent a couple of weeks before he continued on to Paris in late October (Reed I, pp. 135–37). In the meantime (August 1792) from "his Throne / The King had fallen" (X.8–9) and the Royalist armies, "the congregated Host, / *Dire cloud* upon the front of which was written / The tender mercies of the *dismal wind* / That bore it, on the Plains of Liberty / Had burst innocuously . . ." (X.9–13; my italics). "Dire" is a strong word foreboding evil. "Dire cloud" and "dismal wind" reinforce each other, and placed as they are, at the beginning of Book X, they create the atmosphere for the ensuing sombre matter of this book. The onslaught on the "Plains of Liberty" remains unsuccessful; "innocuously" implies that the Royalist armies cannot do any harm. They were actually defeated at Valmy on 20 September; and on 22 September France took on

> The body and the venerable name
> Of a Republic: lamentable crimes [September massacres]
> 'Tis true had gone before this hour, the work
> Of massacre, in which the senseless sword
> Was pray'd to as a judge; but these were past,

35 Earth free from them for ever, as was thought,
   Ephemeral monsters, to be seen but once;
   Things that could only shew themselves and die.
         (X.30–37)

Bearing in mind that this was written about twelve years after these occurrences, it is remarkable how meticulously Wordsworth tries to render his feelings as a twenty-two-year-old. He reveres the new Republic, and although the concession of "lamentable crimes" is strengthened by " 'Tis true" (32), the "but" in line 34—limiting what has gone before—introduces the rationalizations of young Wordsworth: the crimes are "ephemeral monsters", never to return. The cruelty of the times is much underlined in combining "senseless" and "sword" and yet more by linking this combination with "judge" (33–34); the elevation of a senseless weapon to the position of a judge (implying a man of integrity) brings out Wordsworth's deep concern. The September massacres make Wordsworth sleepless (X.61 ff.); even if he is a revolutionary, he is not a heartless fanatic.

An extremist minority, the Jacobins, rules over "Liberty, and Life, and Death" (X.108), but Wordsworth's strong belief in the ultimate victory[45] of simple democratic men makes him pray that

   throughout earth upon all souls
  Worthy of liberty, upon every soul
  Matured to live in *plainness* and in *truth*
  The gift of tongues might fall . . .
      (X.118–21; my italics)

Wordsworth has portrayed the excesses of the Revolution. He now points the way to stability. His political insight tells him that "plainness" and "truth" in the emancipated citizens do not suffice to make the Republic function; for the "gift of tongues" is needed as well if the democratic process of mutual persuasion is to succeed. The mastery of persuasive language in turn depends on education, and thus we are once more reminded of the Swiss "herdsman with the staff in one hand and the book in the other" (above, p. 42). A few lines further down Wordsworth reiterates his demand for the republican virtues of "self-restraint" and "simplicity" (X.153, 154) implying a dislike of the pomp of the monarchy and a championship of equality.

At the end of his account of 1792 Wordsworth has become aware that

---

[45] "Wordsworth had no doubts as to the ultimate success of the Revolution . . . although he feared that its triumph might be unduly delayed and that in the meantime much harm might be done by extremists" (Havens, *The Mind of a Poet*, p. 519).

although hereditary leadership had been abolished, the "destiny of man had still / Hung upon single persons" (X.137–38). His belief in the historic mission of a natural (perhaps charismatic) leader who is capable of saving the young democratic Republic explains his optimism in the eventual success of the Revolution:

> the virtue of one paramount mind
> Would have abash'd those impious crests, have quell'd
> Outrage and bloody power, and in despite
> Of what the People were through ignorance
> And immaturity, and, in the teeth
> Of desperate opposition from without,
> Have clear'd a passage for just government,
> And left a solid birthright to the State,
> Redeem'd according to example given
> By ancient Lawgivers.
>
> (X.179–88)

It is interesting to note that Wordsworth does not refer to the desirability of a "paramount mind" in his piece of political theory, "A Letter to the Bishop of Llandaff", which he wrote a few months after his 1791–92 stay in France. Although he may have "inly revolved" (X.136) about a natural leader, the more democratic and systematic "Letter" was probably not the right place to advocate these ideas, or, alternatively, Wordsworth had forgotten what he had felt in that autumn of 1792. Be this as it may, in *The Prelude* the stress on "virtue" (X.179) in a statesman corresponds to the emphasis on virtue in the democratically elected representatives in the "Letter".[46] The implied charisma of Wordsworth's ideal leader, who consequently enjoys the voluntary support of the majority of the people, makes it likely that his guidance will lead the disagreeing factions to consensus on the principles of state legitimacy (185–86). The constitutional legality of the new France in turn will guarantee that the principle of liberty will be honoured, or, as Wordsworth had put it earlier: "a republic legitimately constructed contains less of an oppressive principle than any other form of government" ("A Letter to the Bishop of Llandaff", *Prose Works* I.36.213–14).

A few weeks after Wordsworth's return to England hostilities broke out between France and Britain (February 1793). Wordsworth was still pondering his experiences in France when the chaos of war made it impossible for him to see his love-child Anne-Caroline who was born on

---

[46] On the importance of "virtue" in leaders, see "A Letter to the Bishop of Llandaff" (*Prose Works* I, ll. 245, 286); see also "1801" ["I grieved for Buonaparte"] (GCL II:71) and "The Character of the Happy Warrior" (GCL II:147).

15 December 1792 in Orleans; not until the Peace of Amiens in 1802 was he to see her for the first time. Thus the world of politics had cut into Wordsworth's private life. Both the political situation and his personal problems are bound to have transformed him into a man looking for certainties. He had begun to think

> with *fervour* upon management
> Of Nations, what it is and ought to be,
> And how their worth depended on their Laws
> And on the Constitution of the State.
> (X.685–88; my italics)

Wordsworth's political studies enabled him to take a long-term view of socio-political events. He therefore does not become unduly excited over the slave-trade debate[47] on his return to England but implies that when the liberty of France becomes universal, the abolition of the slave trade, "this most rotten branch of human shame" (X.224), will ensue as a natural consequence (X.202–26).

Wordsworth is incensed by the excesses of the revolutionary Terror (X.307–45); however, he sees the outer threat to the Republic as a source of inner oppression:

> In France, the Men who for their desperate ends
> Had pluck'd up mercy by the roots were glad
> Of this new enemy. Tyrants, strong before
> In devilish pleas were ten times stronger now[.][48]
> (X.307–10)

Demagoguery exploits the natural solidarity of a nation under attack. Viscount Grey comments on these lines: "[Wordsworth] pronounced a wise political judgement upon the un-wisdom of interfering with the Revolution from outside. In the whole of Wordsworth's account of the Revolution, there is nothing with more insight than this wise political judgement".[49] Political wisdom is also apparent in X.429–39 where Wordsworth refutes the notion that disorder derives from "popular Government and Equality" (432).[50] Book X.745–47, exactly like "A Letter to the Bishop of Llandaff" (*Prose Works* I.33.100–01), implies that a revolution is not the season of true liberty. Indeed, carried away

---

[47] Cf. 1805 *Prelude*, p. 300 (note to l. 205).
[48] "*Tyrants . . . pleas:* Cf. Milton, *Paradise Lost*, iv.394–95: 'So spake the Fiend, and with necessitie, / The Tyrant's plea, excus'd his devilish deeds'" (1805 *Prelude*, p. 301).
[49] Viscount Grey of Fallodon, "Wordsworth's 'Prelude'", The English Association, pamphlet 57 (1923), 13.
[50] Cf. Wordsworth's refutation of Bishop Watson's attack on the "tyranny of equals" (above, p. 41).

by the tide of events, "even thinking minds / . . . / Forgot that such a sound was ever heard / As Liberty upon earth . . ." (X.346–49). To illustrate his point Wordsworth instances the fate of Madame Roland (X.352), a leading Girondist, who was executed in November 1793 and whose last words were: "Ô Liberté, que de crimes l'on commet en ton nom!" (1805 *Prelude*, p. 302).

At home in Britain, in 1793, the Government also took steps to "undermine / Justice, and make an end of Liberty" (X.655–56).[51] Irrespective of internal political oppression and revolutionary confusion abroad, Wordsworth's thoughts turn to that happy time of July 1790 when he and Jones had passed through

> an Arch that spann'd the street,
> A rainbow made of garish ornaments,
> Triumphal pomp for Liberty confirm'd,
> (X.451–53)

that arch of liberty decorated Arras, Robespierre's native town. Four years later the world was to be liberated from him and his "foul Tribe of Moloch" (X.468).[52] Wordsworth celebrates Robespierre's downfall (July 1794) in elated terms, intensified by alliteration (539):

> Great was my glee of spirit, great my joy
> In vengeance, and eternal justice, thus
> Made manifest. . . .
> (X.539–41)

The hope for genuine liberty is emphasized by "glee", a word that at the end of the eighteenth century carried the strength and freshness of a new word.[53]

Despite all upheavals Wordsworth continues to be optimistic:

> in the People was my trust
> And in the vertues which mine eyes had seen,
> And to the ultimate repose of things
> I look'd with unabated confidence;
> (X.577–80)

This democratic faith in simple men is developed through much of Book XII, for example XII.181–84. In the same book we encounter the angry tone of the younger egalitarian William who implies that intellectual

---

[51] For the detailed social and political background referring to these lines, see 1805 *Prelude*, pp. 304–05. See also Wordsworth's writings of 1793, above, ch. 1.

[52] Cf. *Paradise Lost* i.392–95 (1805 *Prelude*, p. 302).

[53] Phillips (1706) marks "glee" as obsolete, and Johnson (1755) "considered it a merely comic word. It again became common towards the end of the 18th c." (*OED*).

truth is distorted by a rich minority (XII.205 ff.) and who lashes out against theories of inequality

> that ambitiously set forth
> The differences, the outside marks by which
> Society has parted man from man,
> Neglectful of the universal heart.
> (XII.216–19)

On the whole, Book XII is democratic in tone (see especially ll. 223–77[54]), and, as most of *The Prelude,* it inspires man with optimism. Wordsworth's self-defined task is to fill us with "rapture, tenderness, and hope" (XII.239); his theme is "No other than the very heart of man" (XII.240). Through the account of his own and a wider socio-political life in *The Prelude* Wordsworth, the poet-redeemer, makes us sense the universal brotherhood of man, for the "very heart of man" refers to us all. The optimism of the first major European revolution may return one day and inspire men and women once more to exclaim:

> Bliss was it in that dawn to be alive,
> But to be young was very heaven . . .
> (X.692–93)

---

[54] First printed in "Postscript. 1835", *Poetical Works,* vol. V (1837), pp. 372–73.

SUMMARY AND CONCLUSION

This study has traced Wordsworth's ideas of liberty, equality, and fraternity/brotherhood from the time of his overt political commitment (1791-94) through the period when his interest in politics diminished (1795-98) to his apparently unpolitical period (autumn 1798 to 1800) and established that his compositions continue to have important social and political implications even after 1794. I have substantiated in detail from within Wordsworth's poetry, prose, and letters that there is a strong element of liberty, equality, and fraternity in Wordsworth's writings. The chronological juxtaposition in this thesis of social and political events with Wordsworth's biography and his works—with particular attention to the earliest available texts—has supplied some of the hard evidence needed to throw a clearer light on Wordsworth's formative years. So far, Wordsworth's development during the 1790s has mostly been explained on the basis of *The Prelude,* much of which was written a decade and longer after the events it depicts. Let us consider the chief results:

1791-94 (ch. 1).—Between 1791 and 1794 political liberty was paramount in Wordsworth. He also implied freedom of religion as early as *Descriptive Sketches* (comp. 1791-92, ll. 654-55) in his sympathetic treatment of Roman Catholics. In addition to his ardent love for political liberty *Descriptive Sketches* reveals his advocacy of national liberty, mainly exemplified by the struggle of the Swiss for national independence. He again takes up the subject of national liberty in a letter to Mathews of June 1794 (*E.Y.*, p. 128) and in the "Imitation of Juvenal" (comp. 1796), in both cases with reference to Poland.[1]

In "A Letter to the Bishop of Llandaff" (comp. 1793) we have met Wordsworth as a radical republican propagandist. Some of his rhetorical devices in the "Letter" are superb; for example, when he attacks hereditary nobility, he continually uses the singular form of pronouns (see above, p. 37), reserving the plural for his references to the

---

[1] Wordsworth's championship of national self-determination continued throughout his life. On his political insight and premonition about the rising forces of nationalism, see especially A. V. Dicey, *The Statesmanship of Wordsworth: An Essay* (Oxford: Clarendon Press, 1917), pp. 76-77 and 82-83.

brotherhood of man. "A Letter to the Bishop of Llandaff" is Wordsworth's nod to *realpolitik*. His keenness to see the political emancipation of the common man realized makes him assert that the contradiction between the ideals of freedom and the bloody Revolution is not real but seeming: therefore a "revolution is not the season of true Liberty" (*Prose Works* I.33). The "Letter" is extremist in the context of the 1790s, but anticipates much of what is being debated in modern twentieth-century democratic states: political equality, the importance of education for democracy, rotation in political office, redistribution of excessive wealth. In the 1802 addition to the Preface to the *Lyrical Ballads* Wordsworth wanted the poet to "descend from [his] supposed height, and . . . express himself as other men express themselves" (Brett & Jones, p. 261). The same democratic sentiment is expressed in the "Letter": "the person in whom authority has been lodged should occasionally descend to the level of private citizen" (*Prose Works* I.42.417–18). Wordsworth saw the connection between economic and political power when he pointed to the "oppressive principle" of wealth (*Prose Works* I.43.435–36) long before Karl Marx. In *Descriptive Sketches* Wordsworth had praised the virtually absolute liberty of primeval man; a few months later, in the politically more mature "Letter to the Bishop of Llandaff", there is no reference to that kind of liberty, nor to the natural rights of primeval man. My close attention to Wordsworth's language has shown that by 1793 he had mastered the techniques of political rhetoric better than the techniques of poetry, as can easily be seen from the social-protest poem *Salisbury Plain* (MS. 1).

In *Descriptive Sketches* (comp. 1791–92) the liberty and equality of prelapsarian man were pointed to as signs of a golden age. In *Salisbury Plain* (comp. 1793) the tradition of portraying prehistoric man in a state of bliss is reversed: the universal equality of prelapsarian man in *Salisbury Plain* entails an equal sharing by all people in the hardships and deprivations of existence. In *Salisbury Plain* Wordsworth has acquired the technique of individualization. He delineates the fate of the wanderer and the female vagrant and in doing so attacks the inequality and lack of brotherhood in a whole nation. He still uses the Gothic phraseology of *An Evening Walk* and *Descriptive Sketches* but in a manner that engenders pity instead of sensation.

1794 saw Wordsworth's most rapid—and well documented—political change; we have followed this development step by step in the pages on the letters to William Mathews. In May he calls himself a "democrat", that is to say a leftist radical. In June he criticizes the British Constitution, and his notion of equality excludes monarchy and aristocracy from any kind of government; but the tone of the June letter is not so inflammatory as that of "A Letter to the Bishop of Llandaff". By now, approximately a year after "A Letter to the Bishop of Llandaff", a revolution is a "dreadful event" and is only desirable when all other means fail. The *realpolitik* of restricting liberty is being replaced by Wordsworth's uncompromising insistence on a free press: "rather than restrain the liberty of the press I would suffer the most atrocious doctrines to be recommended: let the field be open and unencumbered, and truth must be victorious" (*E.Y.*, p. 125). If we reflect for a moment on the fact that most countries in the world do not enjoy a free press nearly two centuries after this was written by the revolutionary Wordsworth, we cannot help but note his relevance for our time. The style of the November letter to Mathews is yet more moderate, and in December 1794 Wordsworth admits for the first time that the British Constitution protects political dissenters from persecution. Roughly one-and-a-half years after approving of regicide, Wordsworth has moved towards advocating political evolution.

However, Wordsworth persisted as a supporter of the French Revolution throughout 1794, although the French Army had begun to wage a war of aggression. Not until his trip to Germany in the autumn of 1798 did Wordsworth openly renounce his sympathy for the French cause. Wordsworth's was a modern mind in that he did not ally himself with his country's war but with an ideology.

1795–97 (ch. 2).—In *Adventures on Salisbury Plain* (MS. 2; comp. 1795–96) Wordsworth's socio-political criticism is more indirect than in the earlier *Salisbury Plain* (MS. 1), and he is no longer committed to international issues. *Adventures on Salisbury Plain* documents poetically a part of English social history: inequality in the administration of justice, the press-gang, poverty as a result of war. Implicit in the poem is Wordsworth's advocacy of racial equality in his sympathetic description of gipsies. The comparison between *Salisbury Plain* and *Adventures on Salisbury Plain* has demonstrated the poetic improvement in the later poem. For the most part its diction is not accusatory; it is free from the terror-invoking Gothic convention and engenders instead anger and occasionally sadness. Throughout *Adventures on Salisbury Plain* there is an implicit appeal to brotherhood and equality.

With the "Imitation of Juvenal—Satire VIII" (comp. in spring 1796) Wordsworth reverted to his socio-political wrath in his support of liberty and equality, and to a minor degree, of brotherhood. Also in 1796 he wrote "The Convict", an anti-monarchical sentimental piece in which a prison visitor extends the hand of brotherhood to an idealized prisoner.

Summary and Conclusion 177

The republican propaganda and reformist didacticism in "Imitation of Juvenal" and "The Convict" go hand in hand with a deterioration of Wordsworth's verse. In the early version of *The Borderers* (MS. 15), however, there is no trace of reformist optimism. In this sombre play Wordsworth uses Rivers [Oswald] as a negative example whose black arguments support the cause of justice, liberty, equality, and brotherhood.

My close attention to vocabulary in *The Borderers* has pointed to a link between the perversion of language and dehumanization. I have shown that "monster"—designating "man"—occurs far more often in *The Borderers* than in any other of Wordsworth's major compositions; and it occurs more frequently in the manuscript version of about 1796–97 than in the published play of 1842. By the period of *The Borderers* Wordsworth had learnt that even an oppressive class includes individuals who are the embodiment of brotherhood: for the first time in his opus he sympathetically depicts a member of the nobility, the Baron Herbert.

From 1797 onward Wordsworth's ideas of brotherhood and implied equality are hardly abstract and political. They have become deep and permanent, and escape the redefinitions of the political ideologue to fit ever new circumstances. In "The Old Cumberland Beggar" Wordsworth has regained his confidence. He fights for the beggar's personal liberty and indirectly for the cohesive force of brotherhood of local communities.

1798–99 (ch. 3).—*The Ruined Cottage* (MS. B; comp. probably between Jan. and Mar. 1798) strikes a quiet sad note and the social protest is yet more implied than in *Adventures on Salisbury Plain*. Again the poetry seems to benefit from the unobtrusive social and political protest. There is a parallel between the choice of simple country people as hero and heroine of *The Ruined Cottage* and Wordsworth's democratic sentiment in selecting in the *Lyrical Ballads* (1798) an insane mother, an idiot boy, and the weak old Simon Lee as important characters. I have pointed out that the pedlar in *The Ruined Cottage* combines characteristics that would exclude each other in the poetry of Wordsworth's predecessors: poor occupation + no vulgar mind; untaught + deep feelings; outwardly poor + rich with creative imagination. The pedlar has learnt that passions and feelings are more genuine and "speak a plainer language" (*R.C.*, Cornell Wordsworth, p. 46) among simple country people than in the upper layers of society. This elevation of ordinary people looks forward to the democratic implications of the Preface to the *Lyrical Ballads*. In its questioning of class characteristics, in other words in casting doubt on the social order, both *The Ruined Cottage* and the *Lyrical Ballads* are political.

The serene mood of *The Ruined Cottage* engenders more thoughtfulness than anger and thus may have a greater long-term impact in bringing about social change. As in the *Lyrical Ballads* the appeal in *The Ruined Cottage* is more to equality and brotherhood than to liberty.

Not all of the spring 1798 poetry, however, is as quiet as *The Ruined Cottage*. "Goody Blake and Harry Gill" strongly condemns social injustice and begs for a world of brotherhood and equality: "And kneeling on the sticks, [Goody Blake] pray'd / To God that is the judge of all". The naturalistic "Last of the Flock" of the same period is a violent indictment of the poor law as administered by the parish bureaucracy. In "The Last of the Flock" Wordsworth is conscious of how economic insecurity destroys family affections. We recall that metaphoric references to the human body have been used in "The Last of the Flock" to stress the close connection between the smallholder and his little property. In *The Ruined Cottage* too Wordsworth had portrayed a remarkable insight into the social evil of long-term unemployment.

Whether Wordsworth's poems are overtly socio-critical as "The Last of the Flock" or "Goody Blake and Harry Gill" or reflective in tone as "Tintern Abbey", we have seen his interest in the human and the social; when Nature makes the mature man hear the "still, sad music of humanity", one may hope that the perception of this human condition makes man also consider the importance of liberty, equality, and fraternity. By the summer of 1798 Wordsworth had learnt the principle of selecting from the multitude of life impressions those that are lasting and important for the good life, as opposed to those that are trivial and impermanent.

Our look at the "Advertisement to *Lyrical Ballads*" has shown that the "Advertisement" sums up the democratic subject matter of the 1798 volume and that it is a forerunner to the Preface to the *Lyrical Ballads* (1800 and 1802) through its implicit linguistic democracy suggested in adopting the "language of conversation in the middle and lower classes of society" as poetic language. Wordsworth's unfinished "Essay on Morals" (comp. ca. Sept. 1798 to 1799) suggests that philosophy too should be written in a language which the common man understands.

By the time Wordsworth had arrived in Germany (autumn 1798) French military despotism was beyond doubt. The German Anglophiles, who regarded England as a bastion against French expansionism—and his isolation in Germany—made Wordsworth see the good points of England. Slowly but surely Wordsworth was to turn into an ardent

English patriot. While in Germany, Wordsworth wrote a series of poems (e.g. the "Matthew" poems and "A Poet's Epitaph") that reflect the unpretentious brotherhood and equality of his native Lake District. In early 1799 Wordsworth added the element of restraint to his notion of liberty. In "Three Years She Grew in Sun and Shower" Nature is law and impulse and she kindles and restrains. This is a far cry from *Descriptive Sketches* where man was "entirely free, alone and wild, / Was bless'd as free—for he was Nature's child" (520–21).

In the fragment "There is an Active Principle Alive in All Things", perhaps written during his stay in Germany, Wordsworth defines for the first time what he actually means by liberty. At that time, 1798–99, this was principally the liberty of "beneficence" and "doing good". Another fragment of the same period, "There is a Law Severe of Penury", resumes to some degree the tone of Wordsworth's early social-protest poetry. This fragment is directed against child labour which may destroy man's potentiality of developing an appreciation of liberty in adult life: "The limbs increase but liberty of mind / Is gone for ever . . ." (MS. 18A).

Wordsworth's welcome gift to the nineteenth century was "The Brothers" (comp. 1799–1800), in which two lower-class boys could write and speak as well as those above them in rank and station. We had found references to lower-class literacy, a precondition of democracy, in Wordsworth's earlier period, for example, in *Descriptive Sketches* and *Adventures on Salisbury Plain*.

The discussion on the two-part *Prelude* has concluded the period 1798–99; and although the 1798–99 *Prelude* is devoid of direct political thought, it has shown us through Wordsworth's eyes those episodes in his childhood that may have led to a commitment to liberty, equality, and fraternity in later life. We may infer from the early *Prelude* that the adults in Wordsworth's childhood were what Nature was for Lucy: both "law and impulse . . . / To kindle or restrain". Indeed, this seems to me the right kind of ground to foster feelings of liberty and democracy.

1800 (ch. 4).—Most of the verse written in 1800 is not as directly concerned with human relationships as that of 1797/8–99. Still, we derive moral lessons from such poems as "The Oak and the Broom" and "Hart-Leap Well" (GCL II:21). The strong oak (implying power) succumbs to the wind of change in "The Oak and the Broom", whereas the little broom (suggesting lack of power) re-emerges after the revolutionary storm. This little piece is representative of the implicit radicalism in Wordsworth's subtle poetics. We have seen the similarity between "Hart-Leap Well" and Coleridge's *Ancient Mariner*. Both poems extend the idea of brotherhood to the animal kingdom; in addition, "Hart-Leap Well" is an attack on social pride. Just as in earlier years, Wordsworth furthers racial equality in his thoughtful "Song for the Wandering Jew"; and his love of children makes him continue to champion the spirit of equality between adult and child: in "Michael" the father and his son Luke "Were as companions", in them "the old and young / Have play'd together". We recall that Wordsworth is against restricting the liberty of children unduly, and where he sees the need for correction he reprimands in a gentle manner, as in "The Idle Shepherd-Boys".

"Michael" carries on Wordsworth's social criticism. The poem illustrates the personal liberty and independence of the shepherd and substantiates that Michael's contentment is inextricably linked with the freedom of the patrimonial fields. This is important if we bear in mind the land enclosures of the time. "Michael" takes place entirely in the present, as most of Wordsworth's verse between 1797 and 1800. Like the pedlar's sensitivity in *The Ruined Cottage* Michael's fine appreciation of the natural scenery is radically democratic in its invading of the middle- and upper-class territory of elevated thoughts: "And grossly that man errs, who should suppose / That the green Valleys, and the Streams and Rocks / Were things indifferent to the Shepherd's thoughts".

We have noted that Wordsworth's hero in 1800 is still drawn from simple people, but we can discern an important development in the response of the plain man to the frustrations of life and social injustice: The sailor-father in *Adventures on Salisbury Plain* (comp. 1795–96) reacted violently against iniquity and he committed murder. In "The Last of the Flock" of 1798 the shepherd's rage was internalized ("To wicked deeds I was inclined"). "Michael's" shepherd-hero, finally, does not show any signs of anger.

Wordsworth makes clear in the Preface to the *Lyrical Ballads* (1800) that every one of his poems "has a worthy *purpose*" (Brett & Jones, p. 246). He believed in the power of literature. Immediately upon the publication of the *Lyrical Ballads* (1800) Wordsworth sent a copy of them to Charles James Fox in which he pointed out the social implications of his poems, in particular of "The Brothers" and "Michael". The "primary passions" of man, which link men into one brotherhood, are in evidence throughout the *Lyrical Ballads*.

My work on the Preface to the *Lyrical Ballads* is the first detailed attempt to bring out the political implications of the Preface; I have demonstrated that the concepts of brotherhood and equality form an important part of Wordsworth's thought in it as do his references to the democratic idea in general. Wordsworth suggests that poetry and the idea of human brotherhood are interconnected: "Poetry sheds no tears 'such as Angels weep', but natural and human tears"; his implicitly democratic topics are the "subjects from common life" and the "ordinary things" exactly as in the "Prospectus to *The Recluse*", where he derives his subject matter from the "growth of common day". The poet's unifying role as expressed in Wordsworth's poetry since 1797 (and somewhat earlier in *The Borderers*) is summed up in the Preface: "the Poet binds together . . . the vast empire of human society", whereas the "Man of Science seeks truth as a remote and unknown benefactor" (Brett & Jones, p. 259); the first part also suggests the basic equality between men. Wordsworth reinforces the idea of the brotherhood of man by the frequent generic use of "man/men" in the Preface. The accumulation of "man/men" in it corresponds to that in the poetry: "man/men" is probably the third-most-often-used noun in Wordsworth's verse.

My attention to Wordsworth's vocabulary has produced an important by-result. I have established the fact that Wordsworth kept out of his poetry the many specialist terms with a socio-political meaning that came into English between 1789 and 1805 (see Appendix). Thus Wordsworth adheres to his principles of generality and the language of men as laid down in the Preface.

We have discerned a new impulse in Wordsworth's notion of liberty in the "Prospectus to *The Recluse*" where he implies that there is an indestructible kind of liberty inherent in the individual mind; he ends the "Prospectus" with a passionate prayer to God to nurse him "in genuine freedom". In the course of about ten years Wordsworth has developed from a praise of primeval man's outer "absolute" liberty (*Descriptive Sketches*) to an insistence on inner freedom. My interest in the concept of liberty and Wordsworth's vocabulary has produced yet another important by-result. I have shown that the collocation "genuine freedom" in Wordsworth is unlikely before 1802; this finding may be another step in solving the dating problem of the "Prospectus to *The Recluse*".

The Prelude (ch. 5).—The first section of the chapter on *The Prelude* has dealt with some critics' views on the origin of liberty, equality, and fraternity in Wordsworth, but my emphasis has been on Wordsworth's own reflections on the origin and development of these concepts. In his childhood the "lowly Cottages" of Hawkshead that dealt out with "plain and seemly countenance" their "plain comforts" (1805 *Prelude* 1.525, 531–32), strengthened by the liberal educational policies of Hawkshead Grammar School, very likely fostered a spirit of equality and democracy. His love for liberty was also kindled in both childhood and adolescence by observing the shepherds and peasants of his native Lake District where "Man [was] free, man working for himself, with choice / Of time, and place, and object" (1805 *Prelude* VIII.152-53); and the account of the conversations with Beaupuy in 1792 has portrayed how Wordsworth's political ideas thenceforth became more philosophical. Nature as well taught Wordsworth "High thoughts of God and Man" (1805 *Prelude* VIII.64). Finally Wordsworth acknowledges Dorothy's and Coleridge's influence in his extending the idea of brotherhood to all that lives.

The second section of the chapter has discussed those parts of *The Prelude* that deal with Wordsworth's stays in France in 1790 and 1791-92, and with his experience of England in 1793. I have compared these passages with Wordsworth's writings of 1791-93 in order to obtain Wordsworth's retrospective views of the same time-span that has introduced this dissertation (chapter 1). Wordsworth's first visit to France (1790, Book VI) reflects throughout the joy of a soul-stirring universal brotherhood. Except for a reference to the "universal reason of mankind"—implying the fundamental equality of man—we discern no sign of political sophistication in the young university student, although he was undoubtedly acquainted with some political theory at the time. Fraternal emotions are predominant, and they are put into action: Englishmen and Frenchmen "rose at signal given, and form'd a ring / And, hand in hand, danced round and round . . .".

As in *Descriptive Sketches* and "A Letter to the Bishop of Llandaff" Wordsworth's descriptions of 1791-93 are interspersed with the theories of natural right and natural law, and in consequence he advocates a revolt against "tyrannic Power", since "nothing hath a natural right to last / But equity and reason" (VI.172-73). Throughout *The Prelude* Wordsworth illustrates from history that man's inherent love for liberty is victorious. We have seen how even the structurally intrusive Vaudracour and Julia story advances the cause of liberty and equality in its attack on class prejudice.

We remember from "A Letter to the Bishop of Llandaff" how skilfully Wordsworth had used language to indicate the separateness of the nobility from the human brotherhood. Wordsworth's use of language is equally effective in *The Prelude,* where, for example, aristocracy is by "privilege of birth / Sequester'd from the rest" (IX.117-18). The Latinate "sequester'd" (a term somewhat old-fashioned in the 1790s) reinforces the inequality. Nearly all of *The Prelude* witnesses to Wordsworth's first-hand experience and realism. He realizes that the ordinary citizens' "plainness" and "truth" are not sufficient to make the Republic work—simple men have to acquire the "gift of tongues" in order to persuade their fellow citizens of their democratic rights and duties. Wordsworth's belief in the realization of the revolutionary slogan *liberté, égalité, fraternité* is convincing, for he had watched "a People risen up / Fresh as the morning Star . . ." and he "saw in rudest men / Self-sacrifice the firmest, generous love / And continence of mind", etc. (IX.391–95). His trust was in the people (X.577) in whom he had seen the very same qualities of which a ruling aristocracy ought to be possessed. However, elsewhere Wordsworth's usual attention to fact makes him propagate for a great leader—"the virtue of one paramount mind" (X.179)—to restore order after the revolutionary terror.

The tone of Books IX and X is not as joyous as that of Book VI. We have noted how Wordsworth's language reflects his development: the euphoric fraternal vocabulary relating to 1790, his cautious observation of France on his second arrival in 1791, and a notably greater stress on liberty and systematic political thought in 1792[–93]. My treatment of *The Prelude* has only hinted at the volumes of political wisdom this poem on the "Growth of a Poet's Mind" contains. If Wordsworth indeed gave "twelve hours thought" to social and political questions "for one to poetry" (see above, Introduction), we ought to ask ourselves what we can learn from that seminal mind which had helped to inaugurate our modern age of popular revolutions and romantic brotherhood.

The chronological arrangement of this thesis has shown that Wordsworth does not exactly reflect the social and political events of his time, except during 1792. The timelessness that Wordsworth reveals in his post-1797 work is something he would like to see in the art of others, as he implies in a letter to Sir George Beaumont in 1804: "The industry and love of truth which distinguish Sir Joshua's mind are most admirable, but he appears to me to have lived too much for the age in which he lived and the people among whom he lived, though this in an infinitely less degree than his friend Burke . . ." (*E.Y.*, p. 491). The development of the ideas of liberty, equality, and fraternity in Wordsworth is linear, but not strictly so. Just as most artists in our era side with revolutions that promise greater liberty, Wordsworth had sided with his Revolution—and one may hope and speculate that the disappointment in several revolutions of our age will engender in our contemporary poets a similar kind of confident calm and concern with permanence as the disappointment in the French Revolution did in Wordsworth. Some of the intelligentsia of the European and American left have become uncertain of the western liberal tradition. For Wordsworth, however, liberty and freedom are no illusion; in this respect he is closer to the plain uneducated man of today than many an academic apologist of repressive regimes. There is little scope for moral relativism in the Wordsworth of 1791–94 and none at all by 1800. Wordsworth is a constructive intellect who insists on a moral direction in politics and science. We have seen Wordsworth develop from a poet of class struggle into a humanist who is an advocate of small communities, a subject covered in detail by Michael Friedman in his recent study *The Making of a Tory Humanist: William Wordsworth and the Idea of Community* (1979).

Wordsworth's poetry, prose, and letters show sometimes a social, political, and humanitarian awareness that, one and a half centuries later, finds systematic expression in the Universal Declaration of Human Rights (1948). Although he does not erect a theoretical framework for democracy, liberty, equality, and brotherhood, his art and its implicit advocacy of the fundamental equality of man has strongly influenced scholars, statesmen, and philosophers of the English-speaking world (see above, Introduction). For example, it is held that Alfred North Whitehead was probably influenced by Wordsworth more than by any other man.[2] And I am certain that the revaluation of Wordsworth's early poetry will gain momentum now that we are beginning to see the social havoc of a fully industrialized and urbanized society. Wordsworth's work questions any social, political, scientific, or technological "achievement" that impairs human relationships. The laissez-faire attitude of unrestricted economic activity is as objectionable to Wordsworth as the suppression of the freedom of the press, and his life-long insistence on national self-determination makes him indeed our contemporary.

Robert Penn Warren in his *Democracy and Poetry* (1975), p. 51, quotes A. N. Whitehead as saying that "if civilization is to survive, the expansion of understanding is a prime necessity". It seems that Wordsworth's "bottomless social understanding", as J. P. Ward calls it,[3] has come a long way in this direction. I have attempted to present Wordsworth within the historical context of the 1790s, and I have indicated that Wordsworth's fundamental, timeless kinds of brotherhood and equality are important for our own period of history. Finally I hope I have

---

[2] Paul Arthur Schilpp, ed., *The Philosophy of Alfred North Whitehead*, The Library of Living Philosophers, vol. 3 (Evanston and Chicago, 1941), p. 118.
[3] Ward, "Wordsworth and the Sociological Idea", *CritQ*, 16 (1974), 331–55 (348).

succeeded in illustrating from within Wordsworth's writings what Carl Woodring expressed so well in the 1950s: "No poet has communicated better than Wordsworth the relaxed experience of a free member of a sovereign state . . ."[4]

Note added in proof

In this dissertation I have touched on Wordsworth's interest in democratic principles of education. It is hoped that my present co-operation with Dr. Thor Nordin of the Department of Education in the University of Uppsala will result in a publication dealing with the democratic educational ideas of the Romantic writers. The Department of Education (*Pedagogiska Institutionen*) at Uppsala is responsible for a comprehensive project entitled "Freedom and Equality as Fundamental Educational Principles in Western Democracy" (leader of the project: Professor W. Sjöstrand). One major work from this research programme is available in English: W. Sjöstrand, *Freedom and Equality as Fundamental Educational Principles in Western Democracy: From John Locke to Edmund Burke*. In: Studia Scientiae Paedagogicae Upsaliensia, XII (1973). To date, Nordin's results are in Swedish only (with summaries in English).

---

[4] Woodring, "On Liberty in the Poetry of Wordsworth", *PMLA*, 70 (1955), 1033–48 (1039).

WORKS CITED

Primary Sources (W. Wordsworth)

Brett, R. L., and A. R. Jones, eds. *Lyrical Ballads* (1798 and 1800). 1963; rpt. London: Methuen, 1975.

Butler, James, ed. *The Ruined Cottage* and *The Pedlar*. The Cornell Wordsworth (gen. ed. Stephen Parrish). Ithaca, N.Y.: Cornell U.P., 1979.

Darbishire, Helen, ed. *Poems in Two Volumes, 1807*. 2nd ed. Oxford: Clarendon Press, 1952.

Darlington, Beth, ed. *Home at Grasmere:* Part First, Book First, of *The Recluse*. The Cornell Wordsworth (gen. ed. Stephen Parrish). Ithaca, N.Y.: Cornell U.P., 1977.

Gill, Stephen, ed. *The Salisbury Plain Poems of William Wordsworth*. The Cornell Wordsworth (gen. ed. Stephen Parrish). Ithaca, N.Y.: Cornell U.P., 1975.

Grosart, Alexander B., ed. *The Prose Works of William Wordsworth*. Vol. I. London: Edward Moxon, 1876.

Hutchinson, Thomas, ed. *Wordsworth: Poetical Works*. Revised by E. de Selincourt. 1904; rev. rpt. London: Oxford U.P., 1969.

Maxwell, J. C., ed. *The Prelude: A Parallel Text*. Harmondsworth: Penguin, 1976.

Osborn, Robert, ed. *The Borderers*. The Cornell Wordsworth (gen. ed. Stephen Parrish). Ithaca, N.Y.: Cornell U.P. (in press).

Owen, W. J. B., ed. *Wordsworth's Preface to Lyrical Ballads*. Copenhagen: Rosenkilde & Bagger, 1957. Vol. IX of *Anglistica*.

—, and Jane Worthington Smyser, eds. *The Prose Works of William Wordsworth*. Vol. I. Oxford: Clarendon Press, 1974.

Parrish, Stephen, ed. *The Prelude, 1798–1799*. The Cornell Wordsworth. Ithaca, N.Y.: Cornell U.P., 1977.

Selincourt, Ernest de, ed. *The Letters of William and Dorothy Wordsworth*. I. *The Early Years 1787–1805*. 2nd ed., rev. by Chester L. Shaver. Oxford: Clarendon Press, 1967.

—, ed. *The Letters of William and Dorothy Wordsworth*. II. *The Middle Years 1806–1811*. 2nd ed., rev. by Mary Moorman. Oxford: Clarendon Press, 1969.

—, ed. *The Prelude or Growth of a Poet's Mind* [1805 and 1850 texts]. 2nd ed., rev. by Helen Darbishire. Oxford: Clarendon Press, 1959.

—, ed. *The Prelude or Growth of a Poet's Mind* [1805 text]. 2nd ed., corrected by Stephen Gill. Oxford: Oxford U.P., 1970.

—, and Helen Darbishire, eds. *The Poetical Works of William Wordsworth*. 5 vols. 2nd ed. and revised issues. Oxford: Clarendon Press, 1952–59.

Wordsworth, Jonathan, M. H. Abrams, and Stephen Gill, eds. *The Prelude: 1799, 1805, 1850*. New York: Norton, 1979.

[Wordsworth, W.,] *Poetical Works*. Vol. V (1837).

MS. 18A: (*a*) fragments "There is an Active Principle Alive in All Things", "There is a Law Severe of Penury"; (*b*) elegies on Matthew. (Transcripts by Stephen Gill, Lincoln College, Oxford.)
MS. Verse 56 ("Nutting", transcript by Stephen Gill).

Secondary Sources

Abrams, M. H. *The Mirror and the Lamp: Romantic Theory and the Critical Tradition.* 1953; reissued Oxford: Oxford U.P., 1971.
—. "English Romanticism: The Spirit of the Age." In *Romanticism Reconsidered: Selected Papers from the English Institute.* Ed. Northrop Frye. New York: Columbia U.P., 1963.
—. *Natural Supernaturalism: Tradition and Revolution in Romantic Literature.* London: Oxford U.P.; New York: Norton, 1971.
—, ed. *Wordsworth: A Collection of Critical Essays.* Englewood Cliffs, N.J.: Prentice-Hall, 1972.
Allen, B. S. "Minor Disciples of Radicalism in the Revolutionary Era." *MP,* 21 (1923–24), 277–301.
Arnold, Matthew. *Essays in Criticism,* second series. 1888; rpt. London: Macmillan, 1900.
Bateson, F. W. *Wordsworth: A Re-interpretation.* 2nd ed. 1956; rpt. London: Longman, 1971.
Beach, Joseph Warren. "Reason and Nature in Wordsworth." *JHI,* 1 (1940), 335–51.
Beer, John. *Wordsworth and the Human Heart.* London: Macmillan, 1978.
—. *Wordsworth in Time.* London: Faber, 1979.
Benn, S. I., and R. S. Peters. *Social Principles and the Democratic State.* London: George Allen & Unwin, 1959.
Bernbaum, Ernest. *Guide through the Romantic Movement.* 2nd ed. New York: Ronald Press, 1949.
—, James V. Logan, and Ford T. Swetnam. "Wordsworth." In *The English Romantic Poets: A Review of Research and Criticism.* Ed. Frank Jordan. 3rd ed. New York: MLA, 1972.
Bloom, Harold. "To Reason with a Later Reason: Romanticism and the Rational." *Midway,* 11, No. 1 (1970), 97–112.
Bode, Christoph. *William Wordsworth und die Französische Revolution.* Abhandlungen zur Kunst-, Musik- und Literaturwissenschaft, Bd. 219. Bonn: Bouvier, 1977.
Bostetter, Edward E. *The Romantic Ventriloquists: Wordsworth, Coleridge, Keats, Shelley, Byron.* Seattle: Univ. of Washington Press, 1963.
Boulton, James T. *The Language of Politics in the Age of Wilkes and Burke.* London: Routledge & Kegan Paul, 1963; Toronto: Univ. of Toronto Press, 1963.
Bradbury, Malcolm. "Literature and Sociology." *Essays and Studies,* N.S., 23 (1970), 87–100.
Brinton, Crane. *The Political Ideas of the English Romanticists.* London: Oxford U.P., 1926. [Reissued by the Univ. of Michigan Press in 1966.]
Brooks, Cleanth. "Wordsworth and Human Suffering: Notes on Two Early

Poems." In *From Sensibility to Romanticism: Essays Presented to Frederick A. Pottle.* Eds. F. W. Hilles and H. Bloom. New York: Oxford U.P., 1965, pp. 373–87.

Brown, Philip Anthony. *The French Revolution in English History.* 1918; rpt. London: Frank Cass, 1965.

Burke, Edmund. *Works* (Bohn edition, 1854–89). Vol. II.

—. "Thoughts and Details on Scarcity [1795]." In *The Works of the Right Honourable Edmund Burke.* Vol. V. London: John C. Nimmo, 1899.

Butler, Marilyn. *Jane Austen and the War of Ideas.* Oxford: Clarendon Press, 1975.

Caudwell, Christopher. "The Bourgeois Illusion and English Romantic Poetry." [First publ. 1936.] In *Romanticism: Points of View.* Eds. Robert F. Gleckner and Gerald E. Enscoe. Englewood Cliffs, N.J.: Prentice-Hall, 1962, pp. 117–29.

Cestre, Charles. *La Révolution française et les poètes anglais (1789–1809).* Dijon, 1905.

Chard, Leslie F. *Dissenting Republican: Wordsworth's Early Life and Thought in Their Political Context.* Studies in English Literature, vol. 66. The Hague: Mouton, 1972.

Cobban, Alfred. *Edmund Burke and the Revolt Against the Eighteenth Century: A Study of the Political and Social Thinking of Burke, Wordsworth, Coleridge and Southey.* London: George Allen & Unwin, 1929.

Coleridge, S. T. *Lectures 1795 on Politics and Religion.* Eds. Lewis Patton and Peter Mann. The Collected Works of Samuel Taylor Coleridge, vol. I. London: Routledge & Kegan Paul; Princeton, N.J.: Princeton U.P., 1971.

—. *Biographia Literaria.* Ed. J. Shawcross. 2 vols. Oxford: Clarendon Press, 1907 [1st ed. 1817].

—. *Poetical Works.* 3rd impr. Ed. Ernest Hartley Coleridge. 1912; rpt. O.U.P. paperback, Oxford U.P., 1974.

—. *Collected Letters of Samuel Taylor Coleridge.* Ed. Griggs. Vol. I. Oxford: Clarendon Press, 1956.

—. *Essays on His Times, in The Morning Post and The Courier* (I and III). Ed. David V. Erdman. The Collected Works of Samuel Taylor Coleridge. London: Routledge & Kegan Paul; Princeton, N.J.: Princeton U.P., 1978.

Cone, Carl B. *The English Jacobins: Reformers in Late 18th Century England.* New York: Charles Scribner's, 1968.

Cooper, Lane. *A Concordance to the Poems of William Wordsworth.* London: Smith, Elder, 1911.

Davis, David Brion. *The Problem of Slavery in the Age of Revolution, 1770–1823.* Ithaca, N.Y.: Cornell U.P., 1975.

"Déclaration des droits de l'homme (1789)." *Grand Larousse encyclopédique.* 1969 ed.

Dicey, A. V. *The Statesmanship of Wordsworth: An Essay.* Oxford: Clarendon Press, 1917.

Edinburgh Review. [Review of R. Southey's *Thalaba.*] Oct. 1802, No. 1, pp. 63–83. Constable & Longman, 1814.

Eisold, Kenneth. *Loneliness and Communion: A Study of Wordsworth's Thought and Experience.* Salzburg Studies in English Literature. Romantic Reassessment, No. 13. Salzburg: Universität Salzburg, 1973.

Encyclopædia Britannica. 1797 ed.

Encyclopædia Britannica: Micropædia. 1974 ed.
Ferry, David. *The Limits of Mortality: An Essay on Wordsworth's Major Poems.* Middleton, Conn.: Wesleyan U.P., 1959.
Fink, Zera S. "Wordsworth and the English Republican Tradition." *JEGP,* 47 (1948), 107–26.
—. "'Dion' and Wordsworth's Political Thought." *SP,* 50 (1953), 510–14.
—, ed. *The Early Wordsworthian Milieu: A Notebook of Christopher Wordsworth, with a Few Entries by William Wordsworth.* Oxford: Clarendon Press, 1958.
Finkenstaedt, T., E. Leisi, and D. Wolff, eds. *A Chronological English Dictionary.* Heidelberg: Carl Winter, 1970.
Fischer, Ernst. *Zeitgeist und Literatur: Gebundenheit und Freiheit der Kunst.* Wien: Europa Verlag, 1964.
Friedman, Michael H. *The Making of a Tory Humanist: William Wordsworth and the Idea of Community.* New York: Columbia U.P., 1979.
Fruman, Norman. *Coleridge, the Damaged Archangel.* London: George Allen & Unwin, 1972.
Gates, Barbara T. "Wordsworth's Lessons from the Past." *WC,* 7 (1976), 133–41.
Gill, Stephen. "Wordsworth's Breeches Pocket: Attitudes to the Didactic Poet." *EIC,* 19 (1969), 385–401.
—. "'Adventures on Salisbury Plain' and Wordsworth's Poetry of Protest 1795–97." *SIR,* 11 (1972), 48–65.
Godwin, William. *An Enquiry Concerning Political Justice.* Vol. I. 1793.
Goodwin, Albert. *The Friends of Liberty: The English Democratic Movement in the Age of the French Revolution.* London: Hutchinson, 1979.
Graham, W. "The Politics of the Greater Romantic Poets." *PMLA,* 36 (1921), 60–78.
Grey [Viscount Grey of Fallodon]. "Wordsworth's 'Prelude'." The English Association, pamphlet 57 (1923).
Grierson, H. J. C. *Milton and Wordsworth, Poets and Prophets.* Cambridge: Cambridge U.P., 1937.
Grob, Alan. "Wordsworth and Godwin: A Reassessment." *SIR,* 6 (1967), 98–119.
—. *The Philosophic Mind: A Study of Wordsworth's Poetry and Thought, 1797–1805.* Columbus: Ohio State U.P., 1973.
Güttler, Felix. *Wordsworth's politische Entwicklung.* Diss. Breslau, 1914.
Hamill, Paul. "Other People's Faces: The English Romantics and the Paradox of Fraternity." *SIR,* 17 (1978), 465–82.
Harper, George McLean. *William Wordsworth: His Life, Works, and Influence.* 2 vols. London: John Murray, 1916.
—. "The Crisis in Wordsworth's Life and Art." *QQ,* 40 (1933), 1–13.
Hartman, Geoffrey H. "Wordsworth, *The Borderers,* and 'Intellectual Murder'." *JEGP,* 62 (1963), 761–68.
—. *Wordsworth's Poetry, 1787–1814.* 2nd ed. 1964; rpt. New Haven and London: Yale U.P., 1971.
Havens, Raymond Dexter. *The Mind of a Poet: A Study of Wordsworth's Thought with Particular Reference to* The Prelude. Baltimore: The Johns Hopkins Press, 1941.
Hayden, John O., ed. *Romantic Bards and British Reviewers: A Selected Edition*

of the Contemporary Reviews of the Works of Wordsworth, Coleridge, Byron, Keats and Shelley. London: Routledge & Kegan Paul, 1971.
Hazlitt, William. *Lectures on the English Poets*. 1818; rpt. London: Oxford U.P., 1929.
—. *The Spirit of the Age: Or Contemporary Portraits*. 1825; rpt. from 1st edition Menston, Yorks.: Scolar Press, 1971.
Hedin, Greta. *Natur och politik i Wordsworths ungdomsverk*. [Nature and Politics in Wordsworth's Early Work.] Acta Universitatis Gotoburgensis. Göteborgs Högskolas Årsskrift, 56. Göteborg: Wettergren & Kerber, 1951.
Heffernan, James A. W. *Wordsworth's Theory of Poetry: The Transforming Imagination*. Ithaca, N.Y.: Cornell U.P., 1969.
Hodgart, Patricia, and Theodore Redpath, eds. *Romantic Perspectives: The Work of Crabbe, Blake, Wordsworth, and Coleridge as Seen by Their Contemporaries and by Themselves*. London: George G. Harrap, 1964.
Hunt, William. *The History of England*. Vol. X. London: Longman, 1930.
Jacobus, Mary. "Southey's Debt to *Lyrical Ballads (1798)*." *RES*, N.S., 22 (1971), 20–36.
—. *Tradition and Experiment in Wordsworth's* Lyrical Ballads *(1798)*. Oxford: Clarendon Press, 1976.
Jordan, J. E. *De Quincey to Wordsworth: A Biography of a Relationship*. Berkeley and Los Angeles: Univ. of California Press, 1962.
Kaufman, Paul. "Wordsworth's 'Candid and Enlightened Friend'." *N&Q*, 207, N.S., 9 (Nov. 1962), 403–08.
Kiernan, V. G. "Wordsworth and the People." In *Democracy and the Labour Movement: Essays in Honour of Dona Torr*. Ed. John Saville. London: Lawrence & Wishart, 1954.
Krüper, A. "Wordsworth als politischer Dichter." *Die Neueren Sprachen*, 45 (1937), 66–72.
Legouis, Emile. *La Jeunesse de William Wordsworth: Étude sur le "Prélude"*. Paris, 1896.
Lehman, B. H. "The Doctrine of Leadership in the Greater Romantic Poets." *PMLA*, 37 (1922), 639–61.
Lerner, Laurence. "What Did Wordsworth Mean by 'Nature'?" *CritQ*, 17, No. 4 (1975), 291–308.
Lienemann, Kurt. *Die Belesenheit von William Wordsworth*. Berlin: Mayer & Müller, 1908.
Lindenberger, Herbert. "The Reception of *The Prelude*." *BNYPL*, 64 (1960), 196–208.
—. *On Wordsworth's* Prelude. Princeton, N.J.: Princeton U.P., 1963.
Little, Geoffrey. "An Incomplete Wordsworth Essay upon Moral Habits." *A Review of English Literature*, 2 (1961), 9–20.
Maccoby, S. *English Radicalism 1786–1832: From Paine to Cobbett*. London: George Allen & Unwin, 1955.
McKillop, A. D. "The Poet as a Patriot—Shakespeare to Wordsworth." In *The Rice Institute Pamphlets* (Houston, Tex.), xxix, No. 4 (1942), 309–36.
MacLean, Kenneth. *Agrarian Age: A Background for Wordsworth*. 1950; rpt. Hamden, Conn.: Archon Books, 1970. Yale Studies in English, vol. 115.
Mayo, Robert. "The Contemporaneity of the *Lyrical Ballads*." *PMLA*, 69 (1954), 486–519.

Miles, Josephine. *The Vocabulary of Poetry: Three Studies*. [Study 1:] *Wordsworth and the Vocabulary of Emotion*. Univ. of California Publications in English, vol. 12, No. 1. Berkeley: Univ. of California Press, 1942.

—. "Wordsworth: The Mind's Excursive Power." In *The Major English Romantic Poets: A Symposium in Reappraisal*. Eds. Clarence D. Thorpe, Carlos Baker, and Bennett Weaver. Carbondale: Southern Illinois U.P., 1957.

Mill, Anna J. "John Stuart Mill's Visit to Wordsworth, 1831." *MLR*, 44 (1949), 341–50.

Moorman, Mary. *William Wordsworth, A Biography: The Early Years, 1770–1803*. 1957; corrected rpt. Oxford: Oxford U.P., 1968.

The Norton Anthology of English Literature. Vol. II. 3rd ed. New York: Norton, 1974.

Noyes, R. "Wordsworth and Burns." *PMLA*, 59 (1944), 813–32.

Onorato, Richard J. *The Character of the Poet: Wordsworth in* The Prelude. Princeton, N.J.: Princeton U.P., 1971.

Oxford English Dictionary (1933).

Parrish, Stephen. "Dramatic Technique in the *Lyrical Ballads*." *PMLA*, 74 (1959), 85–97.

—. "*Michael* and the Pastoral Ballad." In *Bicentenary Wordsworth Studies in Memory of John Alban Finch*. Ed. Jonathan Wordsworth. Ithaca, N.Y., and London: Cornell U.P., 1970, pp. 50–75.

—. *The Art of the* Lyrical Ballads. Cambridge, Mass.: Harvard U.P., 1973.

Perkins, David. *Wordsworth and the Poetry of Sincerity*. Cambridge, Mass.: The Belknap Press of Harvard U.P., 1964.

Plumb, J. H. "Political Man." In *Man Versus Society in Eighteenth-Century Britain: Six Points of View*. Ed. J. L. Clifford. Cambridge: Cambridge U.P., 1968, pp. 1–21.

Pottle, Frederick A. "Wordsworth in the Present Day." In *Romanticism: Vistas, Instances, Continuities*. Ithaca, N.Y., and London: Cornell U.P., 1973.

Reed, Mark L. *Wordsworth: The Chronology of the Early Years, 1770–1799*. Cambridge, Mass.: Harvard U.P., 1967.

—. *Wordsworth: The Chronology of the Middle Years, 1800–1815*. Cambridge, Mass.: Harvard U.P., 1975.

Roberts, Charles W. "Wordsworth, *The Philanthropist*, and *Political Justice*." *SP*, 31 (1934), 84–91.

Rodway, Allan. "Radical Romantic Poets: Wordsworth." In *The Romantic Conflict*. London: Chatto & Windus, 1963.

San Juan, E., Jr. "Wordsworth's Political Commitment." *DR*, 45 (1965), 299–306.

Schilpp, Paul Arthur, ed. *The Philosophy of Alfred North Whitehead*. The Library of Living Philosophers, vol. III. Evanston and Chicago, 1941.

Schneider, Ben Ross, Jr. *Wordsworth's Cambridge Education*. Cambridge: Cambridge U.P., 1957.

Shakespeare, William. *The Riverside Shakespeare*. Boston: Houghton Mifflin, 1974.

Sharrock, Roger. "Wordsworth and John Langhorne's 'The Country Justice'." *N&Q*, N.S., 1 (July 1954), 302–04.

—. "*The Borderers:* Wordsworth on the Moral Frontier." *Durham Univ. Jnl.,* 56, N.S., 25 (1964), 170–83.

Sheats, Paul D. *The Making of Wordsworth's Poetry, 1785–1798.* Cambridge, Mass.: Harvard U.P., 1973.

Snyder, Franklyn Bliss. "Wordsworth's Favorite Words." *JEGP,* 22 (1923), 253–56.

Somervell, D. C. *English Thought in the Nineteenth Century.* 5th ed. London: Methuen, 1947.

Stallknecht, Newton P. "Wordsworth and the Quality of Man." In *The Major English Romantic Poets: A Symposium in Reappraisal.* Eds. Clarence D. Thorpe, Carlos Baker, and Bennett Weaver. Carbondale: Southern Illinois U.P., 1957.

Sypher, Wylie. *Guinea's Captive Kings: British Anti-Slavery Literature of the XVIII Century.* Chapel Hill: Univ. of North Carolina Press, 1942.

Thompson, E. P. *The Making of the English Working Class.* Rev. ed. Harmondsworth: Penguin, 1968.

—. "Disenchantment or Default? A Lay Sermon." In *Power and Consciousness.* Eds. Conor Cruise O'Brien and William Dean Vanech. London and New York: New York University, 1969, pp. 149–81.

Todd, F. M. "Wordsworth in Germany." *MLR,* 47 (1952), 508–11.

—. *Politics and the Poet: A Study of Wordsworth.* London: Methuen, 1957.

Trilling, Lionel. "Wordsworth and the Iron Time." *Kenyon Review,* 12 (1950), 477–97.

Ward, J. P. "Wordsworth and the Sociological Idea." *CritQ,* 16 (1974), 331–55.

Warnock, Mary. *Imagination.* London: Faber, 1976.

Warren, Robert Penn. *Democracy and Poetry.* Cambridge, Mass.: Harvard U.P., 1975.

Wesker, Arnold. *Words as Definitions of Experience.* London: Writers and Readers Publishing Co-operative, 1976.

Whitney, Edward Allen. "Humanitarianism and Romanticism." *HLQ,* 2 (1938–39), 159–78.

Whitney, Lois. *Primitivism and the Idea of Progress in English Popular Literature of the Eighteenth Century.* Baltimore: The Johns Hopkins Press, 1934.

Willey, Basil. *The Eighteenth-Century Background: Studies on the Idea of Nature in the Thought of the Period.* 1940; rpt. Harmondsworth: Penguin, 1972.

Williams, Neville. *Chronology of the Modern World, 1763–1965.* 1966; rev. ed. Harmondsworth: Penguin, 1975.

Williams, Raymond. *Culture and Society: 1780–1950.* 1958; rpt. Harmondsworth: Penguin, 1968.

—. *Keywords: A Vocabulary of Culture and Society.* London: Croom Helm, 1976.

Woodring, Carl. "On Liberty in the Poetry of Wordsworth." *PMLA,* 70 (1955), 1033–48.

—. *Politics in the Poetry of Coleridge.* Madison: Univ. of Wisconsin Press, 1961.

—. *Wordsworth.* Cambridge, Mass.: Harvard U.P., 1968.

—. *Politics in English Romantic Poetry.* Cambridge, Mass.: Harvard U.P., 1970.

Wordsworth, Dorothy. *Journals of Dorothy Wordsworth: The Alfoxden Journal 1798, The Grasmere Journals 1800–1803*. Introd. Helen Darbishire. Ed. Mary Moorman. 1958, 1971; new ed. and rpt. with corrections London: Oxford U.P., 1974.
Wordsworth, Jonathan. *The Music of Humanity: A Critical Study of Wordsworth's "Ruined Cottage", incorporating texts from a manuscript of 1799–1800*. New York: Harper & Row, 1969.
—. "A Note on the Ballad Version of 'Michael'." *Ariel*, 2 (1971), 66–71.
—. "The Five-Book *Prelude* of Early Spring 1804." *JEGP*, 67 (1977), 1–25.
—. "On Man, on Nature, and on Human Life." *RES*, N.S., 31 (1980), 17–29.
Worthington [Smyser], Jane. *Wordsworth's Reading of Roman Prose*. New Haven: Yale U.P., 1946.

APPENDIX

(For commentary, see above, pp. 141–42)

1786. Idealize *v*; Seditionist *n*.
1787. Constitutionality *n* (*OED*: 1801; *SOED*: 1801; *CED*: 1787); Federalist *n*; Statistical *adj*; Statistics *n*.
1788. [No entry.]
1789. Electioneer *v*; Libertarian *n* (*OED*: def. 1. "One who holds the doctrine of the freedom of the will, as opposed to that of necessity. Opposed to *necessitarian*."); Philanthropic *adj*; Statistic *adj*.
1790. Anarchic *adj*; Democrat *n*; Electoral *adj*; Feudality *n*; Insubordination *n*; Municipality *n*; Sansculotte *n*.
1791. Capitalist *n* (*OED*: 1792); Civism *n* (*OED*: 1792); Legitimatize *v*.
1792. Commonish *adj*; Émigré *n*; Fraternization *n* (*OED*: "The action of fraternizing or uniting as brothers, the state or condition of fraternity, fraternal association." The *OED* quotes the following example: "1792 *Hist.* in *Ann. Reg.* 2. They . . . give the kiss of fraternization to negroes."); Jacobinism *n*; Monocrat *n*.
1793. Counter-revolution *n*; Democratism *n*; Demoralize *v* (*OED*: def. 1. "*trans.* To corrupt the morals or moral principles of; to deprave or pervert morally."); Federalism *n*; Guillotine *n*; Jacobinize *v*; Liberticide *n*; Provincialism *n* (*OED*: def. 3. "The manner of speech characteristic of a particular province; with *pl.*, A local word, phrase, or peculiarity of pronunciation which is not part of the standard language of a country."); Septembrize *v*; Sub-human *adj*.
1794. Boroughmonger *n*; Disorganization *n*; Dualism *n*; Guillotine *v*; Pantisocracy *n* (*OED*: "A form of social organization in which all are equal in rank and social position; a Utopian community in which all are equal and all rule."); Perfectibility *n*; Pessimism *n* (*OED*: def. 1. "†The worst condition or degree possible or conceivable; the state of greatest deterioration . . ."); Septembrizer *n*.
1795. Directoire *n*; Disarmament *n*; Moderatism *n*; Pourparler *n*; Roundsman *n*; Terrorism *n* (*OED*: def. 1. "Government by intimidation as directed and carried out by the party in power in France during the Revolution of 1789–94 . . ."); Terrorist *n* (*OED*: def. 1a. "Applied to the Jacobins and their agents and partisans in the French Revolution, esp. to those connected with the Revolutionary tribunals during the 'Reign of Terror' ").
1796. Consulting *adj*; Diplomacy *n*; Idealism *n* (referring to philosophy); Ideology *n*; Lenience *n*.
1797. Antisocial *adj* (*OED*: def. 1. "Opposed to sociality, averse to society or companionship."); Expatriation *n*; Ideological *adj*; Popularize *v* (*OED*: def. 2. "*trans.* To make popular. a. To gain popular favour for; to cause to be generally known and accepted, liked, or admired."); Profiteer *n*; Republicanize *v*; Revolutionize *v*; Usurpative *adj*.

1798. Democratize *v*; Fronde *n* (*OED*: "party which rose in rebellion against Mazarin and the Court during the minority of Louis XIV; hence, a malcontent party; also, violent political opposition".); Frondeur *n*; Ideologist *n*; Necessitarian *n*; Physiocrat *n*; Tactician *n*.

1799. Equalitarian *n*; Obscurant *n* (*OED*: def. A. "One who obscures; one who strives to prevent inquiry, enlightenment or reform."); Unionist *n*.

1800. Anarchize *v*; Autonomous *adj*; Centralize *v* (*OED*: 1801; def. 2. "*trans*. To bring to a centre . . . *esp.* to concentrate (administrative powers) . . ."); Codify *v* (*OED*: def. 1. "To reduce (laws) to a code; to digest."); Denaturalize *v* (*SOED*: def. 1. "To deprive of its original nature; to make unnatural."); Nationalize *v* (*OED*: def. 1. "*trans*. To invest with a national character; to make distinctly national.")

1801. Centralization *n*; Conventionalist *n* (*OED*: def. 1. "A member or supporter of the French Convention of 1792."); Decadary *adj*; Dualistic *adj*; Federalize *v*; Girondist *n*.

1802. Parvenu *n*; Philanthropine *n*. ("Natural system" of education for children.); Surveillance *n* (Watch or guard, esp. over a suspected person.)

1803. Autocrat *n*; Brumaire *n*; Jeffersonian *adj*; Kantian *adj*; Negrophil *n* (*OED*: "A friend of the negroes; one who favours the advancement of negro interests or rights."); Statist *n* (*OED*: def. 2. "One who deals with statistics, a statistician").

1804. Squirearchy *n* (*OED*: def. 1. "The collective body of squires, landed proprietors, or country gentry; the class to which squires belong, regarded especially in respect of its political or social influence.")

1805. Anticivic *adj*.

INDEX

Works by W. Wordsworth (WW), anonymous publications, and periodicals are indexed under their titles, other works under the names of their authors.

Abstract political theories: WW against, 115
"Address to the Scholars of the Village School of —". *See* Elegies on Matthew
Adventures on Salisbury Plain (MS. 2), 55–64, 70, 74, 94, 99, 102, 105, 112, 142, 167; anti-war, 61; brotherhood, 57, 58, 60; brotherhood practised by lower classes (and gipsies), 58, 61; democratic sentiment in choice of character, 61; economic independence, 60; endeavours to correct lower-class prejudices, 63; equality, 57; equality before the law, 63; inequality in administration of law, 60; justice and law, 58, 61; kindly treatment of gipsies, 61; lack of liberty, equality, brotherhood destroys individuals, family, 63; liberty, 57; murder rends bond of brotherhood, 59; poverty, 57; press-gang, 58; racial equality, 61; social injustice, 57, 61, 63; tyranny of landlords, 60–61; vocabulary of factual description, alliteration, 57; dark vocabulary, 59; no revolutionary vocabulary, 61; WW's love of children, 60
Advertisement to *Lyrical Ballads*, 104n., 106–07; democratic linguistic theory, d. subject matter, 107
Alfoxden House, 78, 79, 144
America: golden age of liberty, equality in new American republic, 55–56
American Revolution, 14, 27, 38, 155, 161
"Andrew Jones", 103; local brotherhood endangered, 104
"Anecdote for Fathers", 103, 114, 131; breaks hierarchical order and decorum of 18th c., 103; children's rights, 103; democratic tone, 103
Anne-Caroline (WW's French daughter), 71, 170
Anonymity of the State, 86
The Anti-Jacobin: conservative British liberty, 89; diatribes against fraternity/brotherhood, 109
Anti-Slavery. *See under* Slavery
"Argument for Suicide": social protest in, 79

Arnold, Matthew, 21, 23
Athens, 25, 29
"Away, Away, it is the Air", 102n.

Bage, R., 56n.
"The Baker's Cart", 61n.; hunger, 77
Barry, Henry (Colonel), 95
Basic needs, 46
Beattie, James, 149
Beaupuy, Michel, 153, 155; his genuine brotherhood, 164
Beccaria, Cesare, 52
Bible (N.T.): democratic impact of, 157
Bill of Rights: American, 155; English, 13, 155
Blake, William, 18, 19
The Borderers (Early Version), 67–77, 79, 80, 81; argues negatively for justice, liberty, equality, brotherhood, 70; contempt for egalitarian and democratic principles by protagonist Rivers, 71; crime against mankind, 73; denies fundamental equality, 69, 71; extreme individualism, 71, 75; frequent use of "justice", 68; general truth, 69; "Iago" and "Satan" in, 71; lacks direct humanitarian and political optimism, 67; law and freedom, 70; law and morality, 69; linked to WW's experience of French Revolution, 76; misuse of language (tool of dehumanization), 73; mock justice/private law lead to monstrous crime, 68, 72; modernity of, 69; natural rights/natural law, 69, 72; overemphasis on reason dangerous, 72; perversion and manipulation of language, 72, 73; poetic quality, 70; rejects Godwin's anarchist philosophy, 67; Rivers denies spiritual bond between men, 75; Romance vocabulary, 74; scepticism in, 70; suggests inner before sociopolitical reform, 70; traditional values replaced by abstract theories, 76; universal brotherhood, 75; unnatural tone through frequent use of "monster", 76; "WW's Paris, Blois, Orleans", 68
The Borderers, "Prefatory Essay" to, 76–77; moral scepticism, 77

Index

British Constitution, 50, 53
The British Critic, 144; reviews *Lyrical Ballads*, 125
Brooke, Henry, *Gustavus Vasa*, 90
Brotherhood/fraternity, 57, 58, 59, 104, 109, 112, 116, 118, 119, 132, 143, 159; active sense of, in lower classes, 48, 58; based on feeling in WW, 62; between man and Nature, 131; definitions, 17–18; extended to animals, 125–26, 128; international, 160; local, 17, 29, 65, 130, 133; of man, 27, 29, 75, 92–93, 155; murder crime against, 74; origin of, in WW, 114; synonyms of, 17; unity of life, 158; universal, 75, 78, 86, 97, 173. See also Preface to *Lyrical Ballads*
"The Brothers", 112, 117–19, 132; brotherhood, active exertion, 119; brotherhood beyond death, 118; brotherhood, vocabulary of, 119; community, 118; lower-class sensitivity and literacy, 119; simple language, equality, and plain setting, 118; village parson integrated in community, 118
Bürger, G. A., 108
Burke, E., 38, 76, 85, 155; *Reflections on the Revolution in France*, 38, 76
Burns, Robert, 91, 149
Byron (Lord), 19, 21, 142

Calvert, Raisley, 53
Cambridge, 27
Censorship, 64, 94, 109
"A Character", 96
Children: WW's love of, 103, 128. See also Children's rights
Children's rights, 60, 117, 126
Chronological method: advantages of, 14, 15, 174
Chronology and dating, 14–16, 147
Citizens army (democracy's), 115
Civil liberties, 105, 163
Clarkson, Thomas: against slave-trade, 120
Class characteristics questioned, 91, 119, 129, 131, 164
Coleridge, Sara, 95
Coleridge, S. T., 66, 78, 96, 120, 123, 144, 150; disillusion over events in France, 145; first visit to Dove Cottage, 125; revolutionary lecturer and poet, 56, 64; *The Ancient Mariner*, 129; *Biographia Literaria*, 20 (liberty in Chaucer, Dante, Milton, Pindar), 91n., 118n.; *Conciones ad Populum*, 56; *The Plot Discovered*, 56; "Satyrane's Letters" and equality, 107n.; *The Watchman*, 64
Collins, William, 149
Colonization, 48
Combination Acts (1799–1800), 13, 109
Commercial and Agricultural Magazine despises smallholders, 134n.

Common man, 25, 42, 71, 81, 111, 129; sensitivity of, 92, 129; WW's ideal political representative, 42
Community, 17, 19, 29, 61, 83, 98, 99, 114, 118, 132, 138
"The Complaint of a Forsaken Indian Woman", 97, 98, 115
Conservative ballad tracts and WW's radicalism, 91n.
"Conversations with Klopstock": WW does not confuse political democracy, equality with vulgarization of literature, 110–11; WW teacher, moralist, aesthete, 110
"The Convict", 66, 67; brotherhood, 66; overt didacticism, 66; poetic regression, 66; republican, humanitarian sentiment, 66; prison conditions, 66; private and public violence, 66
Cowper, William, 149; *The Task*, 17n.
Critics and criticism, 15; biographical, 15; close reading, 15; Freudian, 19; Marxist, 19, 23, 30n., 48n.; New Criticism, 21; socio-cultural, 15

Declaration of the Rights of Man. See *Droits de l'homme*
Democracy, 35, 40, 56, 135, 152; definitions of, 16; direct, by referendum, 39; extended meaning of, 16; and "gift of tongues", 169; popular, 65
Democratic linguistic theory, 16, 22, 107
Democratic subject matter, 16, 25, 98, 99, 107, 115, 122, 126, 127, 131, 139, 151
Democratic tone (poetry), 107, 127
Descriptive Sketches, 13, 27–34, 45, 48, 91, 116, 133, 144, 160; "absolute" liberty and equality of primeval man, 30–31; blames monarchy and aristocracy for loss of liberty, 32; direct references to political theory, 29, 30; freedom of religion, 32; liberty conducive to artistic, intellectual, and martial qualities, 31; liberty, positive effect on Nature, 31, 32, 33; local brotherhood/community, 29; national liberty, 29, 31; and natural rights, 30; personal liberty, 29; political liberty, 29, 32; political liberty and quality of life, 33; slavery, 29; war of liberty, 28, 33
Didactic literature, 13, 66
Dove Cottage, 125
Droits de l'homme, 38, 155, 165
Dyer, John, 149
Dyonysius (tyrant), 166

Early texts, 15, 21, 82, 174
Economic depression (1795), 77
Economic equality and natural law, 39
Economic injustice: emotionally and socially crippling, 117

Economic security: closest human ties impaired by its lack, 102; human dignity and happiness (family affections), 102, 133. *See also* "The Last of the Flock" *and* Fox, Charles
Edinburgh Review, 66n., 144
Education, 106, 151; for democracy, 64, 121, 152, 165, 185; Nature's, 113, 121; political, 40; WW stresses freedom, 152
1800 (general summary), 124, 179–81
Elegies on Matthew (MS. 18A): community, 114; democratic personality of teacher, 114
Eliot, T. S., 23
Emancipation: of Catholics, 32; of Jews, 126
Enclosure of common land, 14, 47n., 96, 97n., 100, 133
Encyclopædia Britannica (1797), 17
Encyclopédie, ou Dictionnaire raisonné (1757), 17n.
English-speaking world and WW, 100
Equality, 35, 55–56, 57, 90, 92, 107, 118, 121, 134, 156; and American and French Revolution, 17; basic/fundamental, 69, 145, 164; economic, and redistribution of excessive wealth, 134; economic inequality, 37; and justice, 17, 37, 162; before the law, 44, 63, 65; and natural law, 69; political, 67; racial, 61, 126; social, 67; universal, of primeval man, 46; between young and old, 131. *See also under* Liberty, equality, fraternity *and* Preface to *Lyrical Ballads*
Erskine, Thomas, 80n.
"Essay on Morals": democratic tone, philosophy understood by common man, 111
"An Evening Walk", 26–27, 28, 48; American Revolution, 27; social protest, 26
The Excursion, 116n., 117n., 145
"Expostulation and Reply", 103, 104
"Expostulation and Reply" and "The Tables Turned": advocate brotherhood, 104; against abstract moral philosophy, 104

"The Farmer of Tilsbury Vale", 96
Fawcett, Joseph, *The Art of War*, 56–57, 63n.
"The Female Vagrant". See *Adventures on Salisbury Plain*
Fleming, John, 123
"The Fountain": free dialogue between young and old, 114; freedom and happiness, 114
Fox, Charles James, 89, 118n., 144; advocates brotherhood and equality, 133; WW's letter to, 133–34
Fraternity. *See under* Brotherhood *and* Liberty, equality, fraternity

Free economy, 85
Free will, 112
Freedom. *See* Liberty
French Revolution, 13, 14, 18, 27, 38, 55, 105; primary aim of, 43
"From the Greek": equality, 25; political liberty, 25

General truth, 69, 146
General Will, 19, 42
Generality: extended to social and political order, 143; in WW, 106, 140 (18th-c. characteristic), 161; in language, 141
Germany: "England hope of world" for liberal faction, 108; more political liberty for English Jacobins in, 95; German universities known for Jacobinism and infidelity, 108
Girondins, 34, 72, 172
Glorious Revolution, 161
Godwin, William, 95, 111; impact on WW, 59n.; *Caleb Williams*, 59n., 63n.; *An Enquiry Concerning Political Justice*, 44; *Political Justice*, 2nd ed. (1796), 68
Golden age, 45, 55–56, 133
Goldsmith, Oliver, 149
"Goody Blake and Harry Gill", 96; equality of justice, appeal to equality and brotherhood, 98; socio-economic injustice, 97
Government legitimacy, 40, 41, 170
Grasmere, 118, 143
Grégoire (Bishop), 36
Grey (Viscount), 23
Guilt and Sorrow. See early versions: *Salisbury Plain* and *Adventures on Salisbury Plain*
Gustavus Vasa, 90n.

Habeas Corpus Act, 49, 109
Hamburg, 110
Hardy, Thomas, 53
Harmodius and Aristogiton, 25
Harrington, James, 18, 41
"Hart-Leap Well": class characteristics questioned, 129; extends brotherhood to animal kingdom, 128, 129; parallel with Coleridge's *Ancient Mariner*, 129
Hawkshead, 25, 151
Hazlitt, William, 13, 95; points to egalitarian implications of *Lyrical Ballads*, 20, 144; *The Spirit of the Age*, 20, 44n., 144
"Her Eyes are Wild", 97
Holcroft, T., 56n., 95
Home at Grasmere, 147
Homelessness, 128
"How Sweet to Walk along the Woody Steep", 44
Howard, John, *State of the Prisons*, 66n.
Human dignity, 86, 130
Human rights, 52, 93

Index

Humanitarianism, 25, 26, 29n., 66, 95n., 110, 122; and Romanticism, 66, 109n.
Hutchinson family, 120

"I Love Upon a Stormy Night", 102n.
Iago, 71
"The Idiot Boy", 63, 122, 143; letter to John Wilson points out democratic implications of, 98; and universal brotherhood of man, 98–99
"The Idle Shepherd-Boys": children's freedom not unduly restricted, 126
"Imitation of Juvenal—Satire VIII", 64–65, 66; anti-monarchy and anti-nobility, 64; indictment of slave trade, 65; inequality before law, 65; liberty impaired by informers, 65; local brotherhood (Burghers of Calais), 65; monarch elected by people, 65; poetic quality impaired by socio-political directness, 64; Poland's loss of national liberty, 65; pseudo-equality practised by king, 65; tyranny of landlords, 64
"In Part from Moschus—Lament for Bion": democratic sentiment, 27
"In the School of — is a Tablet [etc.]", 112n.
Inchbald, E. (Mrs.), 68; *Nature and Art* (1796), 56, 67–68
Industrialization, 14, 96, 133
Inequality. See under Equality
Injustice. See under Justice
"Inscription, for the House (an Outhouse) on the Island at Grasmere", 126
"Inscription for a Seat by the Pathway Side Ascending to Windy Brow": feelings of brotherhood, 48
"Inscription for a Seat by the Road-Side [etc.]", 81; homelessness, 82
Ireland: attempted invasion of, 110; Irish rebellion (1798), 90

Jacobin (English) intellectuals disenchanted with the French (1798), 90
Jacobins, 34, 169
Jeffrey, Francis, 135, 144
Johnson, Joseph (radical publisher), 19, 34
Justice, 112; private. See *The Borderers*
Justice and law, 48, 58, 63, 167. See also "Goody Blake and Harry Gill"

Kames (Lord), 140
Keats, John, 160
Klopstock, Friedrich Gottlieb: WW's and Coleridge's visit, 108; *Der Messias*, 110

Landlords: tyranny of, 47n., 60, 61, 64
Langhorne, John, *The Country Justice*, 62n.; *Fables of Flora*, 127n.

"Language of men", 157; subverts hierarchical order of Augustans, 22. See also Preface to *Lyrical Ballads*
Language and vocabulary, 15, 47, 57, 59, 61, 76, 94, 99, 101, 107, 119, 129, 160, 164, 169, 172; alliteration in key passages, 84, 101, 133; common speech, 99; frequent use of "justice" in *The Borderers*, 68; generality in WW's, 141; Germanic and Romance words juxtaposed, 113, 139; imagery of isolation, 80; images of liberty, 132, 152, 153, 154; indirect socio-political criticism improves poetry, 123, 124; linguistic sensitivity in early WW, 74; manipulation and perversion of, tool of dehumanization, 72, 177; newfangled socio-political vocabulary not used in poetry, 142; political rhetoric, 36, 37, 38, 42, 43; Romance vocabulary, 74, 161; vocabulary studies, 15, 147, 151. See further Preface to *Lyrical Ballads* and Appendix
"The Last of the Flock", 97, 100–02, 143; alliteration in key passage, 101; economic security and human dignity, 100–02; indictment of poor-law bureaucracy, 101; overt social criticism, 100
Law, 31; Nature, reason and, 113n.; people consulted in law-making process, 165; public and private, 68
Law. See also Natural rights/Natural law
Leavis, F. R., 23
Legal system and injustice, 35
"A Letter to the Bishop of Llandaff", 15, 22, 34–44, 50, 51, 70, 116, 134, 142, 161, 162, 165, 170; acknowledges misuse of newly gained political liberty, 40; against tyranny, 36; (new) American democracy, 42; condones execution of Louis XVI, 38; democracy (pure, by referendum, representative), 39, 40, 41; direct political theory (liberty, equality, democracy), brotherhood embedded in, 35–44; economic equality, 43 (and redistribution of excessive wealth, 39); economic inequality (and injustice, 37; and suffrage, 42); education for democracy, 40; end justifies means, 36, 40; equality, 38, 39; franchise, 37; inequality before law, 44 (due to upbringing and habit, 41); "inevitable inequality" inherent in government, 43; judges isolated from common man, 35; legitimacy of government, 40, 41; liberty, 38, 39; liberty and equality inherent in man, 39; liberty and philosophy "eyes of human race", 43; monarchy and aristocracy attacked, 39, 42; natural rights/natural law, 38, 39; original power of people, 39; political rhetoric, 36, 43; republican form of government, 41; revolution "not season of true liberty", 40; Rous-

"Letter to Bishop of Llandaff" (*contd.*) seau's General Will, 42; sides with progressives against traditionalists, 39; supports revolutionary violence, 40; universal nature of man, 39; universal suffrage, 41; WW's ideal political representative, 42; WW more radical than Thomas Paine, 44; language used to separate monarchy, aristocracy from rest of humanity, 36, 37

Letters: WW's social and political thought revealed in his, 28, 34, 49, 50, 66, 130. *See also* Letters to Mathews

Letters to Mathews, 48–54, 116, 142, 162; WW aware of intricacy of political issues, 48; attack on monarchy and aristocracy, 50; freedom of inquiry, 52; freedom of press, 52; growth toward political caution, 50, 53; morality in politics, 53; opposition to British Constitution, 50; "The Philanthropist", 48; plan work on an "opposition paper", 52; pluralism, 53; sympathy with liberty of Poland and Portugal, 52; advocates of liberty: Turgot, Milton, Sidney, Machiavelli, Beccaria, 52; "temple of liberty", 42; uncompromising demand for equality, 50; WW advocates political liberty, 49; calls himself a "democrat", 49; WW's concern with truth, 52; favours "dispassionate advocates of liberty and discussion", 52; for reform, concedes revolution as last resort, 51; WW rejoices over release of political prisoners (Hardy, Thelwall, Tooke), 53

Liberal tradition, western, 16

Liberty, 35, 55–56, 57, 64, 65, 90, 112, 113, 121, 128, 132, 149n., 156, 159; "absolute", of primeval man, 30; is "beneficence" and "doing good", 116; chronological development of, in WW, 146–47; definition, 16–17; WW's own first detailed definition of, 116; "emigration prudent thing for literary men and friends of freedom" in 1798, 95; endangered by *lettres de cachet*, 167n.; franchise, 37; free elections, 13; free will, 112; freedom of inquiry, 48, 52; freedom of press, 13, 52, 64, 81, 108, 109; freedom of religion, 32, 149n.; freedom of speech, 152; "genuine freedom", 147; man's innate love of, 166–67; of mind, 116, 146; mountain liberty, 86, 151, 153; national, 29, 52, 89, 90 (Poland, 56, 65); and Nature, 32, 33; personal, 25, 29, 83, 86, 87, 168 (and independence, 130); political, 25, 29, 42, 48, 49, 109, 117, 166 (of the U.S. and Old Commonwealth, 100); rational, 108, 166; romantic poets defenders of, 13; struggle throughout history, 166; Swiss, 31; war of, 27, 31, 33; WW against laissez-faire economics, 149–50. *See also under* Liberty, equality, fraternity

Liberty, equality, fraternity: based on experience and theory in WW, 156; definitions of, 16–18; development of concepts in WW, 14, 162. *See also under* respective key words and *Prelude*

"Lines Left upon a Seat in a Yew-Tree", 26, 79, 81; separation from brotherhood, imagery of isolation, 80; true knowledge leads to love, 80

"Lines Written as a School Exercise at Hawkshead": freedom of inquiry, 25; personal liberty, 25

"Lines Written at a Small Distance from my House" ["To my Sister"]: universal brotherhood and love, 97

"Lines Written in Early Spring", 103; link between Nature and man, 103

"Lines, Written [etc.] . . . Rydale", 127n.

Literary and socio-political developments: correlation between, 13

Literature and society, 23, 56, 81, 133–34 (WW keen to influence "people of consequence in the state", 144)

Locke, John, 42

London, 27

Longman and Rees (publishers), 133

Lonsdale (Lord), 64

Losh, James, 80n., 95

Louis XVI, 27, 33, 36

"Low and rustic life", 130

Lower-class literacy, 63–64, 119

Lyrical Ballads, 42, 81 ff., 94 ff., 102, 111, 164; 1st ed. sold out June 1800, 143; Hazlitt acknowledges their socio-political radicalism, 95; most poems in *L.B.* centre on man, 96; and *The Prelude*, 151; reception of, 144; WW did not see their political significance, 133

Lysons (Dr.), 79

Machiavelli, Niccolò, 52

Mackintosh, Sir James, *Vindiciæ Gallicæ*, 38

"The Mad Mother", 97, 98

Magna Carta, 155

Malthus, T. R., *Essay on the Principle of Population* (1798), 85

Marathon, Battle of, 29

Marx, Karl, 175

Mathews, William, 34

Mathias, T. J., 90; *Pursuits of Literature*, 81

"Matthew": liberty and restraint, 112

"Matthew" cycle poems, 111, 113, 115, 131

Matthew, Elegies on. *See* Elegies on Matthew

Metaphysical mode, 22

"Michael", 130–35, 143, 154; bond between man and Nature, 131; coloured by WW's Grasmere experience, 130; democratic subject matter, 131; equality between young and old, 131; forebodes negative changes in countryside, 133; and freedom of the land, 132; images of liberty, 132; local brotherhood intact, 132, 133; natural rights extended, 133; radically democratic in questioning class characteristics, 131
Mill, J. S., 23
Milton, John, 18, 48n., 52, 149; *Paradise Lost*, 71; *Tenure of Kings and Magistrates*, 38n.
Monarchy: isolated from common man, 163. See also "A Letter to the Bishop of Llandaff"
Moral relativism, 154–55
Moral responsibility, 86
Morality, 22, 69, 112, 116, 121, 179; and politics, 53, 122, 167, 170; private, 76; WW's healthy moral sense, 104
Mother love: importance of, 120, 150
Myers, John (WW's cousin), 53

Napoleon Bonaparte, 109
"A Narrow Girdle of Rough Stones and Crags", 129
National Convention (French), 36
National self-determination, 184–85. *See also* Liberty, national
Natural rights/Natural law, 30, 31, 38, 39, 69, 72, 79, 156, 161, 163, 165, 167
Nature: interrelatedness between man and, 97; moral force of, 106, 155; restoring impact of, 81, 104, 105
Nelson (Viscount), 107, 108
Nether Stowey, 78
Newspaper Act (1798), 108
"Noble savage", disbelief in, 112n.
Norfolk (Duke of), 89n.
"Nuns Fret Not at Their Convent's Narrow Room", 147
"Nutting": WW's early "fraternal love", 114

"The Oak and the Broom", 27; equality of mankind before levelling fate, 127; and political change, 128
"October, 1803" ("One might believe"), 108n.
"The Old Cumberland Beggar", 82–87, 99, 105, 164; alliteration in key passage, 84; bond of brotherhood between villagers, 84, 86; community intact, 83; defence of, 85–86; democratic note of, 87; human dignity, 83–84; mountain liberty, 86; Nature's law and brotherhood, 84; personal liberty, 83, 86; universal equality and brotherhood, 86

"Old Man Travelling", 81, 82
Orleans, 107
Orwell, George, *Animal Farm*, 136
Owen, Robert, 110n.

Paine, Thomas, 38, 41, 54, 86; *Rights of Man*, 34, 41n., 108 (sales figures, 90)
Paley, William, 111
The Pedlar, 122
Permanence, 105, 106, 141, 142, 146, 177, 178, 183; of liberty, equality, fraternity, 142; in "Prospectus to *The Recluse*", 146
"Peter Bell", 103n.
"The Pet-Lamb": brotherhood extended to animal kingdom, 125–26
"The Philanthropist", 48, 52–53
Pitt, William, 32, 56, 86n., 108, 109
Pluralism, political, 53
"Poems on the Naming of Places", 125
Poetic quality: impaired by socio-political directness, 64
"A Poet's Epitaph": against upper-class professions, 115; challenges abstract politics, 115; message of democratic simplicity, 115
Poland: partition, 56, 65
Political theory, 29, 155
Pollard, Jane, 29n., 148
Poole, Thomas: and brotherhood, 96; known for "democratick sentiments", 78
"Poor Susan", 96n., 99
Poor-laws, 14, 62, 101, 119
Poverty, 57, 165
Preface to *Lyrical Ballads*, 15, 92, 106, 108, 109, 130, 135–42; analyses of "What is a Poet?", 136; what is poetry?, 137; brotherhood and equality, 22, 135–42, 180; close reading of, 137; correspondence between vocabulary studies of poetry and, 135; democratization of genres, 137, 139, 141; Germanic-Romance words juxtaposed (*see also* "Three Years She Grew in Sun and Shower"), 139; its language brings out basic equality of men, 136; "language" defined, 141n.; meaning of "flesh and blood", 138; permanence, 141; vocabulary study, 181; WW and science, 138
"Prefatory Essay" to *The Borderers*. See *The Borderers*, "Prefatory Essay"
The Prelude, 120, 123, 145, 147, 148–73; biographical evidence in, 14; general summary of, 181–83
The Prelude (1798–99), 111, 118, 120–23; announces democratic subject matter of WW's poetry, 122; contains hardly any thoughts on liberty, 120; democratic spirit, 121; egalitarian tone, 122; equality, 121; explains WW's habit of seeing brotherhood everywhere, 122; key to ori-

The Prelude (1798–99) (contd.)
  gin of liberty, equality, fraternity in WW, 120
The Prelude (1805): arch of liberty at Arras, 172; attacks artificial inequality of monarchy, 163; British justice and liberty undermined in 1793, 172; championship of equality, 165; class "characteristics" reversed, 164; common man, 151; common man fit for political office, 169; compared to *Descriptive Sketches*, 160; critics on radical politics of, 158; democratic stance, 161; deplores political extremism, 163; difference between WW and Keats, 160; "equity and reason", 156; favourite words, 151; "genuine Liberty", 147; "hunger-bitten Girl", 165; influence of Beaupuy, 163; influence of Dorothy W. and Coleridge on WW's democratic subject matter, extended brotherhood, unity of life, 156–57; international brotherhood, 160; Jacobins' rule over "Liberty, life, and death", 169; jubilant language depicts new era of liberty and brotherhood, 159; justice and equality, 162; *liberty, equality, fraternity: origin and development in WW,* 148–58 (critics' views, 148–50; origin in childhood, 148; WW's own views, 150; mother love, 150; democratic educational policy of Hawkshead School, 152; democratic spirit of adults, 152; influence of student days, 149, 152, of Milton, Thomson, Dyer, Beattie, Collins, Goldsmith, Burns, Cowper, 149; moral rectitude in adults, 154, 155; influence of Beaupuy and French Revolution, 155, 156; impact of Nature, 155; reading matter, 149n., 153, 155n.); liberty in manner of socialist realism, 161; life of individual linked to socio-political life, 151; link with *Descriptive Sketches* (liberty, equality, fraternity), 158; man capable of "clear truth" and "liberty", 165; man's struggle for liberty in history, 166; "natural rights and civil", 163; "natural right", 156; "noble nature" of man, 156; passages on 1790 focus on brotherhood, those on 1791–92 on liberty, 159; people consulted in law-making process, 165; poetic and political democracy fused, 164; political maturity, 162; "Plains of Liberty" (1792), 168; political liberty, 166; points way to political stability, 169; political theory, 155; political wisdom, 166, 167, 171; "popular Government and Equality", 171; "rational liberty", 166; revolution not season of true liberty, 171; slave-trade debate, 171; socialist and Jacobinical, 159n.; state legitimacy and liberty, 170; theory of natural leader, 170; "tyrannic Power", 156; "universal reason" rational basis for liberty, equality, fraternity, 161; "Vaudracour" story attacks class privilege and prejudice, mock justice, 167, makes liberty concrete, 168; vocabulary of liberty, 152, 153, 154; WW develops democratic faith in simple men, 172; — lashes out against theories of inequality, 173; — optimistic despite revolutionary upheavals, 172; — Republican dedicated to common man, 161–62; — student of Government, law, Constitution, 171; — theme "the very heart of man" and fundamental equality, 173; — tones down September massacres, 168

Press-gang, 58, 104
Previous research, 18–20
"Primary passions" of man, 104, 143
Prison conditions and reform, 66, 110
Privacy of correspondence impaired, 49
"Prospectus to *The Recluse*" (MS. 1), 94, 142, 145–47; date of, 147; fundamental equality, 145; generality, 146; proposes democratic subject matter, 146; stresses liberty of mind, 145
Purpose of WW's poetry, 140

de Quincey, 144

Rational benevolence (Godwin), 87
Readership: WW's classless, 140
Realism: WW's sense of, 153, 154
Reality: neglected in WW criticism, 21
Reason, 90
The Recluse, 145
Restlessness: anathema to WW, 84
"The Reverie of Poor Susan", 96
Reynolds, Joshua, 140
Rights. See Human rights *and* Natural rights
"Rob Roy's Grave": natural rights, 31
Romanticism and social reality, 22–23
Rousseau, J. J., 19, 28, 30, 41, 42
The Ruined Cottage (MS. B), 91–94, 96, 102, 131, 164; anti-war sentiments implicitly pro-brotherhood, 94; "bond of brotherhood", 93; brotherhood of man, 92; class characteristics questioned, 91; creative imagination in common man, 92; democratic stance, 91; democratic subject matter, 93; liberty, equality, fraternity, 91; social injustice, 94; unobtrusively radical, 92; unemployment, 93; war, 93, 94
"Ruth": free will, 112
Rydal Mount, 118

St. Albyn (Mrs.), 79
Salisbury Plain (MS. 1), 44–48, 55, 99, 133, 144; absence of brotherhood in time of war, 47; basic needs unfulfilled, 46;

brotherhood practised by lower classes, 48; colonization, 48; equality general in primeval man, 46; freedom of inquiry, 48; individualization of characters, 46; inequality, 46; lack of brotherhood, 46; political liberty, 48, 55; slavery, 55; tradition of golden age reversed, 45; universal equality *v.* inequality, 46; vocabulary indicates dehumanization, 47
Samson, J., 55
Savoy, 32
Schiller, Friedrich, *Die Räuber*, 67n.; *Wilhelm Tell*, 29n.
Seditious Meetings and Treasonable Practices Bill (1795), 13, 62n., 64
September massacres, 168
1791–94 (general summary), 54, 174–76
1795–97 (general summary), 87–88, 176–77
1798–99 (general summary), 123–24, 177–79
Shelley, P. B., 18, 19, 21
Shuter, William, 95
Sidney, Algernon, 18, 52
"Simon Lee", 97, 99, 122; local brotherhood, 100; personal liberty and independence, 100
Slave trade and slavery, 14, 29, 65, 75, 78, 86, 171
Smith, Charlotte (Mrs.), 56
Social injustice, 61, 63, 94, 102
Social pride: WW critical of, 127, 128
Social responsibility, 121
Socio-economic policies of 18th c., 85
Sockburn-on-Tees, 118, 120
"Song for the Wandering Jew": racial equality, 126
Southey, R.: and *Lyrical Ballads*, 95, 102; revolutionary poet, 64, 66, 67n., 95; *Joan of Arc*, 64, 95
Sturm und Drang, 107
Subversion and invasion fears (1797), 79
Sweden: liberation from Denmark, 90
Switzerland, 29

"The Tables Turned", 103, 104. *See also* under "Expostulation and Reply"
Tell, Wilhelm, 29
Thelwall, John, 29, 49n., 53, 79, 89, 95, 107, 117n.; harassed by Government in 1796, 67; for universal brotherhood, 78; his *Tribune* suppressed in 1796, 64; *Rights of Nature* (1796) demands social equality, 67
"There is a Law Severe of Penury" (MS. 18A), 117, 146; child labour consequence of economic inequality, 117; excessive labour impairs child's free and normal development, 117
"There is an Active Principle Alive in All Things" (MS. 18A): demands acts of brotherhood, 116; WW's liberty defined, 116

Thomson, James, 149
"The Thorn", 97, 99
"Three Years She Grew in Sun and Shower", 116, 151; liberty and discipline balanced in, 113; Nature's education, 113
Timelessness and modernity, WW's, 23, 43–44, 69, 70, 77, 93, 114, 121–22, 126, 163, 171, 176, 183–85; 20th-century WW, 70, 163, 176, 184
"Tintern Abbey", 100, 103, 104–06, 121, 143; act of brotherhood, 105; awareness of human condition ("still, sad music of humanity"), 106; "implicit protest of existing social order", 105; liberty, equality, fraternity, 106; moral import, 106; Nature (public significance, 106; restoring impact, 104–05)
"To a Sexton": brotherhood beyond death, 112
"To Joanna", 130
"To my Sister", 96
Tooke, John Horne, 53
Tory Government, 110
Trade unions, 13, 109
Turgot, A. R. G., 52
"The Two Thieves": social tolerance, 130
Tyranny, 36, 69, 128, 166, 171
Tyson, Ann, 151

Unemployment, 93, 178
Uniformitarianism, 86, 106, 141n., 161
United States. *See* America
Unity of life, 84, 122, 128
Unobtrusive revolutionary poetry, 127

"The Vale of Esthwaite", 25

Wakefield, Gilbert, 90n.
War/Anti-war, 61, 81, 82, 93, 105
Washington, George, 89n., 109
"The Waterfall and the Eglantine", 128
Watson (Bishop). *See* under "A Letter to the Bishop of Llandaff"
"We are Seven", 97, 99
Weimar Republic, 163
"A Whirl-blast from Behind the Hill", 96, 97
Whitehead, A. N., 23, 184
Wieland, C. M., 108; *Oberon*, 110
Wilberforce, William, 75
Williams, Helen Maria, 25
Wilson, John, 98
Wilson, Woodrow, 23
Wollstonecraft, Mary, *Vindication of the Rights of Woman*, 34
Wordsworth, Christopher, 143
Wordsworth, Dorothy, 29n., 49, 95, 98, 106, 120, 143, 145, 148; depicts economic inequality, 132n.; labels liberty and equality as "new-fangled", 32n.; letter on fine

Wordsworth, Dorothy (*contd.*)
  qualities of lower-class neighbours, 130; *Journals of Dorothy Wordsworth*, 98n., 125, 130n., 132n.
Wordsworth, John, 125
Wordsworth, Richard, 49, 50, 144
Wordsworth, William, change from political to "inner liberty", 23–24, 146; chronological development, 51, 53–54, 55, 57, 63, 70, 77, 81, 87, 134, 142, 146, 180, 183; committed *v.* unpolitical reputation, 20–24; democrat, but no popularizer in negative sense, 111; development from revolutionary to conservative politics, 14; his financial worries conducive to his social understanding, 78, 143; interested in social and political affairs, 18; political awareness, 28, 32; radicalism, literary and socio-political, 18; his reading, 28, 80n.; reputation in non-English-speaking world, 21; seminal role in forming liberal democracies, 19, 23; social and political commitment, 18; two voices: private and public, 34, 36; "wise passiveness" not anti-intellectual, 97; and Coleridge and Southey, 56n., 64, 66; difference between Coleridge and, 84
  1791–94: in France 1791–92, 27, 28; in 1793 end justifies means for WW, 36, 43; "freedom fighter" in 1793, 40; adheres to principles of French Revolution despite revolutionary excesses, 34; since *Salisbury Plain* (1793) WW's love for humanity individualized in best poetry, 87; overtly propagandistic prose, implicit political radicalism in poetry (1793–94), 54; growing political caution, 53–54; gradual change from advocacy of political violence to peaceful evolution, 51
  1795–97: vast poetic improvement, 60, 87; against literary Gothicism, 64; no longer overtly concerned with international issues, 55; in *The Borderers* (1796–97) WW treats first time in his opus a member of nobility sympathetically, 77; meets radical farmer Thomas Poole, 78; Thelwall, a "leftist extremist", guest of Coleridge and, 78; intimate contact with Coleridge results in great poetic creativity, 78; denounced as spy (1797), 79, 80; from 1797 WW's concepts of brotherhood and equality independent of temporary political commotions, 81; experiences economic hardship, 78
  1798–99: creative impulse linked to liberty and equality, 90; loses lease of Alfoxden for probably political reasons, 79, 107; and Coleridge "hopping the draft", 90n.; Wordsworths arrive in Germany Sept. 1798, 107; return to England spring 1799, 117; trip to Germany, besides learning German, probably political reasons, 95; stay in Germany results in WW moving further away from political radicalism, 108; in his poetry WW does not react openly to public events, 108; poet of *caritas* (1798), 109; and Coleridge on walking tour in Lake District (Nov. 1799), 120
  1800: democratic stance continues although poetry not as directly concerned with human relationships, 125; the Wordsworths practise brotherhood, 125n.; in letter to C. J. Fox WW hopes "Brothers" and "Michael" bring about political change, 133; (1798–1800) liberty, equality, fraternity embedded in poetry, 110; (1800/1801) WW concerned with direct impact of politics on individual, 134
Work house, 83
Wrangham, Francis, 55n., 78
"Written in Germany on One of the Coldest Days of the Century": vocabulary of brotherhood, 115
"Written with a Pencil upon a Stone in the Wall [etc.]": democratic sentiment, 126
"Written with a Slate Pencil upon a Stone, the Largest of a Heap [etc.]": attacks social pride, 127

Yeats, W. B., 163
Young, Arthur, *Travels in France*, 45

OHIO UNIVERSITY LIBRARY

Please return this book as soon as you
have finished with it. In order...
fine...

PR 5892 .P64 W37x

Wuscher, Hermann J.

Liberty, equality and
 fraternity in Wordsworth,